RETHINKING
RURAL

D1739191

RETHINKING
RURAL

Global Community and Economic
Development in the Small Town West

DON E. ALBRECHT

Washington State University Press
Pullman, Washington

Washington State University Press
PO Box 645910
Pullman, Washington 99164-5910
Phone: 800-354-7360
Fax: 509-335-8568
Email: wsupress@wsu.edu
Website: wsupress.wsu.edu

© 2014 by the Board of Regents of Washington State University
All rights reserved
First printing 2014

Printed and bound in the United States of America on pH neutral, acid-free paper.
Reproduction or transmission of material contained in this publication in excess
of that permitted by copyright law is prohibited without permission in writing
from the publisher.

Library of Congress Cataloging-in-Publication Data

Albrecht, Don E.
  Rethinking rural : global community and economic development in the small
town West / Don E. Albrecht.
     pages cm
  Includes bibliographical references and index.
  ISBN 978-0-87422-319-4 (alk. paper)
1. Rural development—West (U.S.) 2. Economic development—West (U.S.)
3. Rural population—West (U.S.) 4. Sociology, Rural—West (U.S.) I. Title.
  HN79.A17A43 2014
  307.1'4120978—dc23

                                                                2014004599

Fine Quality Books from the Pacific Northwest

Contents

Section One

The Development of the Rural West

M y job as director of the Western Rural Development Center is to improve the quality of life of residents of the rural West. In pursuit of this goal, I have visited rural communities from New Mexico to Alaska and from Hawaii to Montana. I have interacted with federal, state, and local policy makers, agency employees, business people, scholars, conservationists, minority representatives, and other rural residents. I have listened, looked, and learned. This book is the result of these efforts.

It is abundantly clear that rural America is entering a totally new era. After passing though eras sociologists have labeled "Small Town in Isolation" (roughly the years from early settlement to 1950) and "Small Town in Mass Society" (about 1950 to 1980), rural America is entering a new era that I call "Small Town in Global Society." The implications of this new era are immense, especially for the rural West. Traditional primary sources of employment (agriculture, the natural resources industries, and manufacturing) continue to decline. Once-prosperous communities are now struggling. Major geopolitical changes and technological breakthroughs have reduced the relevance of location and increased the importance of amenity resources. These changes have opened the door for increased employment in the service sector and "creative class" industries. Communities that have struggled economically and demographically for decades are now attempting to cope with explosive growth. The composition of the population of the rural West is changing and communities have become much more ethnically, racially, politically, and socially diverse.

The obstacles faced and the opportunities available to rural communities are very different in the global society era than in previous eras. Communities cleaving to "business as usual" are likely to suffer from the pitfalls inherent in the new era, while failing to reap the potential benefits. Communities can deal with these changes directly and have some control over their outcomes, or they can be spectators as outside forces determine their fates. Economic development programs of the past involved the development of traditional natural resources or drawing

1

new businesses to the community. However, employment in the natural resources industries has been declining for decades, and fewer businesses are seeking to relocate within the United States. Advancing technology also means that fewer jobs are created. One objective of this book is to outline approaches that are likely to be successful in the new global world.

Human communities remain totally dependent on the biophysical environment. Yet, the relationship between natural resources and community development has significantly altered. Natural resources on which communities once depended have decreased in importance from an economic development perspective. Changing cultural values and federal and state laws now create obstacles to the traditional uses of these resources. Many communities face ecological damage and resource shortages resulting from the manner in which resources were used in the past. On the other hand, the increased importance of amenity resources—factors that comprise an aesthetically pleasing environment such as climate, landscape, and proximity to recreation—impacts decisions about how such resources should be used. New ways of using resources, such as renewable energy, represent opportunities for many rural communities. Major conflicts over resource use abound, and appropriate and efficient means of dealing with these conflicts are imperative.

A second objective of this book is to help community leaders, policy makers, and those who work with them understand current circumstances involving natural resources and thus assist them in making more informed decisions. A fundamental assumption guiding this book is that development should meet the needs of the present generation without compromising the needs of future generations. Further, development should provide opportunities for employment and the enjoyment of nature for all members of the community. The geographical focus of this book is limited to the rural West because the opportunities and obstacles here vary greatly from the rest of the country.

Section One of this book provides an overview of the previous eras that have led us to the current global society era. Section Two describes the most significant ecological and socioeconomic issues confronting rural communities and outlines options for dealing with these issues. Section Two also includes a discussion of the major federal land management agencies that play a vital role in community development in the West.

CHAPTER ONE

Introduction

N o community is an island. Communities have always been affected by events occurring outside their boundaries. This is especially true of the communities of the rural West. Circumstances such as technological development and changes in the economy resulted in some communities having significant advantages over other communities. Later changes drastically altered the slope of the playing field. Consequently, once-disadvantaged localities exploded demographically and economically, while once-prosperous communities struggled. Each externally imposed change brings with it a whole new set of ecological and socioeconomic issues and concerns (D. Albrecht 2007; Flora and Flora 2008; Power and Barrett 2001; Wilkinson 1992).

Small Town in Isolation

During the westward expansion of the United States, settlers were attracted to areas where available resources allowed them to earn a livelihood. In time, communities emerged (D. Albrecht 2004). By the late 1800s, thousands of communities were scattered across the country, with most remaining small and rural as the years passed. These rural communities were similar to one another in two respects. First, they were primarily dependent on agriculture, forestry, fisheries, mining, or other resource-based industries. Areas with the greatest concentration of traditional resources were in greatest demand as these areas could support the largest populations, and life could be lived more abundantly. Second, these communities were largely self-sufficient in that they were able to meet most of their own food and shelter needs. Self-sufficiency was essential because transportation and communication with the outside world was slow and undependable. Before the middle decades of the twentieth century, rural America could be described as "Small Town in Isolation."

Much of the West did not do well in the isolation era because the traditional resources that were in demand were in short supply or difficult to access. The towering mountains, near-waterless deserts, and deep canyons of many parts of the West created obstacles to transportation and communication. Hence, western populations are sparse and widely scattered. Policy priorities during this period included infrastructure such as roads and railroads to reduce isolation, and developments, such as irrigation projects, to increase the availability of critical traditional resources and enhance the potential of the land to support larger populations at higher standards of living. Throughout the isolation era, the natural environment was largely defined as existing to serve the needs of humans. Ecological constraints were seen as obstacles to progress. Science and technology were considered the outcome of human effort and genius, and were expected to provide the solutions to human problems, especially problems generated by scarce resources. American culture was dominated by a strong anthropocentric tradition in which humans were viewed as separate, apart from, and above the rest of nature (Catton 1980). This worldview has been labeled as "The Human Exceptionalism Paradigm" (HEP) (Catton and Dunlap 1978; 1980). Greater detail on the isolation era is provided in Chapter 2.

Small Town in Mass Society

In the 1950s, Vidich and Bensman (1958) wrote the influential book, *Small Town in Mass Society*, describing how the emergence of "mass society" had ended the era of "Small Town in Isolation." Better communication reduced isolation as residents of both rural and metropolitan areas watched the same television shows, listened to the same radio programs, and read the same newspapers and magazines. Enhanced transportation meant that residents of most rural areas could reach a major urban center in minutes and hours rather than days (Bealer et al. 1965; Bender 1975). Numerous scholars noted how these changes combined to make rural populations less distinct, with norms, values, attitudes, and behaviors becoming increasingly similar to those of urban residents. Regional differences also diminished during this period (Friedland 2002; Wirth 1938).

The emergence of "mass society" had substantial economic implications. Improved agricultural technology meant that individual producers could operate larger farms. As a result, the size of the average farm increased while the number of farms declined (D. Albrecht and Murdock 1990; Dorner 1983; Paarlberg 1980). From around 1940 to 1970, millions of people migrated to the city to seek employment in what Calvin Beale (1993) described as the largest peacetime movement of people in U.S. history. Similarly, technological improvements led to reduced employment in the other natural resources industries. Plummeting rural populations and improved transportation to urban areas meant disaster for many businesses in small towns (Rogers 1982). On the other hand, improved transportation made it possible for the booming manufacturing sector to move to rural areas and employ displaced farm and resource workers, while avoiding unionization and reducing labor costs (Fuguitt et al. 1989). The increased availability of manufacturing jobs in rural areas slowed the pace of rural to urban migration. Eventually manufacturing employment far exceeded both agricultural and resource employment, even in rural areas. This trend has continued into the global society era. According to the U.S. Census Bureau's 2009 Current Population Survey, only 7.5 percent of the nonmetropolitan (nonmetro) labor force was employed in agriculture and other natural resource industries.

The transition from "Small Town in Isolation" to "Small Town in Mass Society" impacted communities in very different ways. Communities near metropolitan areas and major transportation routes were much more successful in attracting manufacturing employment than more isolated communities. Communities that remained heavily dependent on agriculture and other natural resource industries and were unable to attract manufacturing saw economic and demographic declines. In hundreds of communities, populations were reduced by half or more (Johansen and Fuguitt 1984; Fuguitt et al. 1989). During this transition, some communities thrived while others struggled to survive.

Policy priorities during the mass society era were similar to those of "Small Town in Isolation." Efforts to reduce isolation and improve infrastructure enabled more communities to compete for and attract industry. Projects were encouraged to increase the availability of traditional natural resources. In many communities, traditional resources were still in short supply, and isolation and sparse populations made it difficult to compete for industry. As a result, the West in general, and the intermountain West in particular, remained by far the most sparsely populated region in the country. While the Human Exceptionalism Paradigm remained supreme during the mass society era, there were a growing number of voices arguing for the conservation or preservation of resources and expressing concern over the harmful consequences of human action on the environment. Further discussion of the mass society era is provided in Chapter 3.

Small Town in Global Society

Rural America is currently in the midst of another major transformation. Communities in rural America are being forced to transform from "Small Town in Mass Society" to "Small Town in Global Society." For the rural West, the transition to the global society era has been especially momentous.

The emergence of the global society era is a direct consequence of increased globalization. Simply defined, globalization is the internationalization of markets. Globalization occurs whenever a market expands to include producers and consumers in more than one nation (Rudel 2002). The increased importance of globalization is a result of two major international developments during the 1990s. The first was a major change in the manner by which nations related to one another. For forty-five years following World War II, the world was dominated by the Cold War and divided into a Communist camp, a Western camp, and a group of neutral developing nations over which the other two camps fought. Divisions, walls, and curtains between nations dominated world relations (Kennedy and Hitchcock 2000). Trade between nations and communication between individuals across nations was greatly curtailed.

All of this changed with the collapse of the Soviet Union and Communism in Eastern Europe beginning in 1989, and the end of the Cold War. Interaction and integration subsequently spiked, with the result being a much more global world (Barca et al. 2012). Trade between nations, based more than ever on market rules and free trade, has grown (Wolf 2004).

While the end of the Cold War opened the door to globalization, a second set of developments paved the path to global society. These developments include the proliferation of personal computers, the internet, and other forms of information and communication technology. This technology began to have worldwide impact in the 1970s and 1980s, and the 1990s brought rapid advancements in how information could be stored, accessed, and transferred. Further, this technology has become so inexpensive that it is available to most companies and many individuals. With Cold War walls removed, new communication and information technology have made interactions much more rapid and complete, and removed previously existing geographic constraints.

Distinguishing Features of the Global Society Era

Two factors that distinguish the global society era from the mass society era are likely to be significant for communities in rural America and especially the rural West: increased global competition and decreased relevance of location.

Global Competition

While there has always been international trade, historically, most of what was produced in a nation was also consumed in that nation. In fact, commodities were often largely consumed in the same area of the country in which they were produced. Transportation and shelf life were limiting factors. Even products that could be transported were often restricted by tariffs and other restraints on international trade. Thus, many commodities had guaranteed and protected markets in their local areas or home countries.

Removal of many trade barriers following the Cold War completely altered global trade as improved transportation allowed products to be moved more quickly and cheaply than ever before. Relatively inexpensive energy led to the centralization of many industries by multinational corporations, with each region specializing in a small number of products that they produced best for the global marketplace. Simultaneously, rapid improvements in communication technology allowed people to be more aware of available products and to compare and make informed decisions relative to cost and quality of products worldwide. More products than ever before are competing in a global marketplace. If wheat can be produced more cheaply in Argentina or Australia or Russia than it can in Kansas or the Palouse region of Washington State, American wheat farmers will face more serious competition. Buyers all over the world, including those in Kansas City, St. Louis, or Chicago, are going to purchase wheat where it can be obtained at the best market price. Producers are now less protected by trade barriers that prevent competition with producers in other nations, and they are less protected by time and distance. These circumstances also lead to greater volatility for producers at the local level. For most consumers, the consequence of increased competition is better products at lower prices.

Globalization has resulted in higher levels of global competition where stakes are more likely to be "winner takes all." Thus, increased international competition will likely result in circumstances where some areas win and others lose. Areas with comparative advantages over other areas in the world and that are attempting to provide the same product or service will benefit as their potential market increases. Conversely, areas that are comparatively disadvantaged are likely to suffer. Global competition is especially relevant for nonmetro communities that are heavily dependent on a single industry or product. The consequences could be disastrous for a community dependent on a product, service, or industry that loses in the global marketplace, while communities that win are likely to grow and prosper. Regardless, communities that become enmeshed in the global marketplace are increasingly vulnerable to the vagaries of this global marketplace, especially if they are producing undifferentiated commodities.

Decreased Relevance of Location

Throughout U.S. history, most better-paying jobs were located in metro communities that, by definition, had the advantage of being near markets and customers. Thus, rural communities have consistently been disadvantaged economically. In rural areas, average incomes have been lower, poverty levels have been higher, and underemployment and unemployment have been more entrenched (D. Albrecht et al. 2000; Beaulieu 2002; Tigges and Tootle 1990). Consequently, throughout our nation's history, there has been a near-steady migration stream from nonmetro to metro areas as individuals and families seek improved economic opportunities (Johnson 1989).

Now, thanks to computers, the internet, and improved information and communication technology, many high-quality jobs created by globalization have a greater degree of geographic flexibility than in the past. Many individuals, families, and firms can establish their homes and businesses where they wish and still be connected to the necessary markets and consumers. A 1995 cover story in *The Economist* was titled "The Death of Distance." As Thomas Friedman (2007) put it, "the world is flat." Opportunities to earn a living or develop new businesses where one chooses are now available that simply did not exist in previous eras. In particular, rural areas now have a greater potential to attract what Richard Florida (2002) describes as "creative class" jobs. These jobs draw on complex bodies of knowledge and require unique skills to solve specific problems. Individuals holding these jobs often have significant geographic freedom. Without question, nonmetro communities have the potential of capturing a relatively high proportion of these high-quality jobs. This can only occur, however, if nonmetro communities are connected to this global world.

Consequences for Small Towns in the Global Society Era

Increased global competition and reduced relevance of location are likely to have several significant consequences for small towns. Among the most significant are the increased importance of amenities and economic restructuring.

Increased Importance of Amenities

Historically, initial settlement and subsequent development of communities in rural areas was strongly related to the presence or absence of traditional natural resources such as minerals, timber, and most critically, soil, water, and climate conducive to agricultural production (D. Albrecht and Murdock 1990; England and Brown 2003). Where land was too dry or mountainous for agriculture, or where other resources were lacking, settlement was limited. The presence or absence of amenity resources mattered little.

Globalization patterns that resulted in reduced relevance of location have changed the relationship between resources and development. The significance of traditional natural resources in community development has been somewhat diminished, while the importance of amenity resources has increased (Goe et al. 2003; Nelson 1997; Power 1996). Amenity resources are defined as the combination of factors that comprise an aesthetically pleasing environment. Generally, a community with high quality amenity resources may have a favorable climate with sufficient sunshine and without extreme heat or cold, a varied and appealing landscape, and perhaps the availability of water resources such as rivers, lakes, or ocean front (McGranahan 1999). Obviously, communities have different combinations of these aesthetic factors and some are more important to some individuals than to others. Additionally, there are steps that communities can take to enhance their aesthetic qualities. Regardless, in a global society, there are numerous individuals with mobile or creative class jobs that may choose to live in rural areas. Most of these individuals, however, will likely choose to live in select areas with high quality amenity resources (D. Albrecht 2004; Hunter et al. 2005; Nelson 1999; Nelson and Beyers 1998; Rudzitis 1999).

With the reduced importance of traditional resources and the increased relevance of amenity resources, it follows that policy priorities should emphasize the enhancement of amenities and less priority should be given to increasing the availability of traditional resources. Long established institutions and norms do not change easily, however, and the clash between those wishing to enhance amenities versus those wishing to develop and increase the availability of traditional resources will be of utmost importance in the future of numerous communities (Power 1996). Fundamentally, the tenets of the HEP are increasingly challenged by a new worldview which Catton and Dunlap (1980) label as the "New Environmental Paradigm" (NEP). Basic tenets of the NEP include:

1. While humans have exceptional characteristics, they remain one among many species that are interdependently involved in global ecosystems.
2. Purposive human actions have many unintended consequences.
3. Humans live in and are dependent upon a finite biophysical environment which imposes potent physical and biological constraints on human societies.
4. Although the inventiveness of humans and the powers derived therefrom may seem for a while to expand limits, ecological laws cannot be repealed.
5. Humans are one species among many in global ecosystem communities, and all members of these communities have the right to live and prosper. As stated by Aldo Leopold, "A thing is right when it tends to preserve the integrity, stability, and beauty of the biotic community. It is wrong when it tends otherwise" (Leopold 1949).

Economic Restructuring

Along with globalization came a significant economic structure transformation. Rural areas of the United States were once heavily dependent on agriculture and other natural-resource-based industries. Then came the mechanization of agriculture. This transformation resulted in a substantial decline in agricultural employment that has slowed only because the number of farmers is now so small. Today there are concerns that much U.S. animal agriculture is moving to foreign countries, another consequence of globalization. Similar employment declines impacted forestry, mining, and other resource-based industries. Manufacturing eventually replaced natural resource industries as the primary source of rural employment.

The late 1970s marked the beginning of a second major economic structure transformation as the number and proportion of manufacturing jobs in the United States started a decline (Bluestone and Harrison 1982; 2000; Sassen 1990) that has since increased in scope and magnitude (Morris and Western 1999). Some manufacturing jobs were lost as machines replaced human labor in the production process. In many factories, a large unskilled labor force is being replaced by a smaller and highly skilled labor force. Other manufacturing jobs have been outsourced to foreign countries by multinational corporations taking advantage of lower wages (Morris and Western 1999). Numerous rural communities are affected as agriculture and natural resource industries continue to decline, or when manufacturing firms that once provided living-wage jobs for community residents close or employ fewer workers (Falk et al. 2003). At the national level, losses of jobs in natural resources and manufacturing have been more than offset by significant increases in service sector employment (D. Albrecht 2004). The service sector provides intangibles rather than the physical products that result from agriculture, natural resources industries, and manufacturing (the goods-producing industries). Generally, services are intended to make life more comfortable or fulfilling, and include entertainment, education, and health care. As more people are released from other work so they can provide services, and as individuals can afford and have the time for these services, quality of life tends to improve.

Economic restructuring is important because natural resource jobs are fundamentally different from industrial jobs, which in turn are fundamentally different from service jobs. Different industries have different wage structures and work schedules; they require different levels and types of education, training, and skills; they differ in the relationships that exist between owners and workers; and they vary in the proportion of the workforce that is either male or female. These and other factors are likely to have major implications for individuals, relationships within families, the strength of community institutions, political outlooks, and other aspects of life (D. Albrecht 1998).

A significant difference between manufacturing and service employment is that most manufacturing jobs of the past were middle-income while service jobs are much more diverse. The goods-producing industries historically provided solid, middle-income jobs for workers with relatively low levels of education and training. In contrast, some service jobs are high quality jobs that generally require advanced education or training to obtain (Sassen 1990). Many of these are creative class jobs, and often have a great deal of geographic flexibility. However, many service jobs could be described as low-pay, low-skill, temporary, and seasonal (D. Albrecht 2004; Kassab and Luloff 1993). Service sector incomes vary greatly by level of education. As the availability of jobs in the goods-producing industries decline, many workers are forced to take employment in the low-pay service sector. The likely outcomes of replacing largely middle-income manufacturing and resource jobs with more diverse service jobs include higher levels of poverty and greater inequality.

The Implications of the Global Society Era for the Rural West

The implications of the emergence of the global society era for rural America will continue to be immense. Successful community development must vary from approaches that worked during previous eras. Because the West is profoundly different from the rest of the country, the consequences for rural communities will continue to be unique. Ecological differences between the West and the rest of the country made the settlement and development of the West different from the processes that occurred in the rest of the United States. These differences will provide both limitations to and focus for possible policy directives and other means of dealing with emerging issues and concerns.

The fundamental ecological difference between the West and the rest of the country lies in the amount of traditional resources as compared to amenity resources. Simply put, traditional natural resources are relatively scarce in much of the west, while amenity resources abound. Certainly the West does not have a monopoly on amenities and there is breathtaking natural beauty in many parts of the country and throughout the world. Likewise, parts of the West have extensive natural resources, while areas in other regions lack a traditional resource base. However, there is no question that for the region, this general statement is true: the West lacks traditional resources and abounds in amenity resources.

Individuals who have travelled around the west are often awestruck by the grandeur of the mountains and the desert red-rock cliffs. However, mountains and cliffs do not readily transform into prime farmland or other traditional resources that allowed people to earn a living during previous eras. The problems of trying to farm land that is steeply pitched are compounded by a lack of water. Precipitation levels are much lower in many parts of the west than in the rest of the country. Because of the lack of prime farmland, water, or other resources, much of the west

Western amenities have become a major asset in the global society era. *Don E. Albrecht*

struggled economically and demographically during the isolation and mass society eras.

In the global society era scenery and amenities have become prized resources. In fact, because so little development occurred in the past, the amenity values of western lands are greatly enhanced. Nature and solitude are now both highly valued resources. What was once considered harsh and foreboding because it lacked traditional natural resources is now viewed as awe-inspiring and breathtaking. Consequently, many western communities that endured continual and significant struggles during previous eras are now attempting to cope with boom-town growth because of their abundance of amenity resources.

However, traditional resources, especially water, are still in short supply in the West and these resource limitations provide constraints to growth and development. Growth often detracts from the aesthetic qualities of the land, straining fragile habitats and contributing to biodiversity loss. While amenity-related growth helps solve longstanding problems associated with economic and demographic stagnation and decline, this growth contributes to a variety of complex new problems. Further, not all areas of the West would be considered highly aesthetic.

Many communities in these areas have the two-fold problem of fewer jobs in the goods-producing industries and a lack of amenities to attract service sector or creative class employment.

Issues resulting from change in the west are shaped by the fact that so much of the land in the western states is publicly owned. Throughout the nineteenth century, as the United States obtained new lands by conquest or purchase, these lands would initially fall under the ownership and management of the federal government. The policy of the federal government was to get this land into private ownership. Federal legislation, such as the Homestead Act of 1862, made it possible for individuals and families to become landowners. Opportunity for land ownership attracted millions of immigrants from Europe and resulted in the creation of farms and communities throughout the country. Under federal land disposal policies, the vast majority of land east of the Rocky Mountains became privately owned by the end of the nineteenth century.

Few people had interest in claiming ownership to much of the land in the West because it was perceived to be of little economic value. As the twentieth century began, a majority of western land remained in federal ownership. There was also growing public sentiment that the federal government needed to take a more active role in the management of federal land to avoid exploitation and deterioration and to preserve and protect a few areas with truly exceptional amenity values. Thus, federal land management agencies were created to manage federal land. Now, more than 670 million acres, or 29.6 percent of the land area in the United States, is federally managed.

East of the Rocky Mountains, the role of the federal government in land management is limited, with less than 5 percent of the land under federal control. In the thirteen western states, where more than one-half (55.4 percent) of western land is under federal ownership and management, the story is very different. Federal land is effectively off limits for homes, farms, and businesses, and as a result, much of it is attractive to tourists and amenity-seeking residents. Large parcels of federal land, however, have been historically used for timber, mining, livestock grazing, and recreation, activities that now face serious challenges.

Wayne County, Utah—A Microcosm

My childhood home has a history that mirrors many communities in the west. A look at Wayne County, Utah, will provide a snapshot of the issues and concerns faced by many rural communities in the west. Wayne County was settled by Mormon pioneers in the 1880s. While nearby valleys had been settled during the 1850s, pioneers were reluctant to attempt to live in Wayne County for another three decades. Surrounded by mountains, the Fremont River Valley (often called Rabbit Valley) in Wayne County is over 7,000 feet in elevation, so the growing season is very short. Frost in early June and late August is fairly common, and frost in July is infrequent, but possible. The short growing season is compounded by a lack of precipitation. Rainfall in the valley averages only about seven inches; crops cannot be grown without irrigation.

Wayne County is spectacular. The upper end of the valley is ringed by mountains reaching over 11,000 feet in elevation, offering ample opportunities for camping, hiking, fishing, and hunting. Following the valley toward the southeast, the elevation drops sharply into a desert featuring the sheer, red-rock cliffs of Capital Reef and Canyonlands National Parks. To early settlers, however, this dramatic scenery was largely irrelevant as it did little to provide an economic livelihood. Because of the initial lack of interest in the mountain and desert land, 97 percent of the land in the county is publicly owned (87 percent by the federal government and 10 percent by the State of Utah).

Early farmers and their descendants for over a century scratched out a meager living by planting crops that could mature in a short growing season and then praying the frost would hold off. They built dams to catch the spring snow melt from the mountains and dug canals to irrigate fields. Livestock grazing on lands unsuitable for crop production, including federal land, was a major source of income for local families. With marginal agriculture as the primary industry, the county remained thinly populated and geographically isolated. Wayne County did not fare well in the isolation era.

Circumstances became even bleaker for Wayne County residents during the middle decades of the twentieth century, the mass society era. Machines began replacing human labor, which resulted in fewer and larger farms. Wayne County was too isolated and its population too small to attract any of the expanding manufacturing sector and so as agricultural employment declined, the population plummeted. By 1970, the population of Wayne County was just over one-half of what it had been in 1940. Wayne County did especially poorly in the mass society era.

But then things began to change. Tourists by the thousands began coming to visit Capitol Reef and Canyonlands National Parks and to camp, fish, hunt, and hike in surrounding mountains (Krannich et al. 2006). Tourist dollars created numerous though generally low-paying jobs in emerging restaurant and motel industries and other retail sectors. Trophy homes began appearing in the valley, some as second homes and others for retirees or persons with geographically flexible jobs. As in many communities in the rural west, however, inconsistent internet and cell phone connections were a limitation to amenity and creative class employment growth. Land prices in some locations began rising precipitously, quickly pricing out many long-time local residents. Increased demand for water and other resources placed a burden on agricultural and other traditional uses of these resources. Interactions between the new and long-time residents became strained as locals tended to support policy decisions that enhanced agriculture, timber harvesting, mining, or other traditional resource-based occupations that employed them and their families for generations. The new residents generally preferred the preservation of resources to maintain the amenities that attracted them to the area. With vastly greater economic opportunities, but with growing contention and an economic divide that mirrors national trends, things are very different for Wayne County in the global society era. Similar stories abound throughout the west and the rest of the country (Green et al. 1996; Power and Barrett 2001).

CHAPTER TWO

The Rural West in the Isolation Era

In the spring of 1804, Lewis and Clark began their epic exploration of the American West. As commissioned by President Thomas Jefferson, the purpose of the expedition was to explore the possibility of a water transport route between the Missouri and Columbia River, make scientific observations, gather knowledge of the people living west of the Missouri River, and to evaluate the agricultural and commercial potential of the western lands.

Throughout the summer of 1804, Lewis and Clark and their associates struggled up the Missouri River, finally stopping for winter at a Mandan Indian settlement near present day Washburn, North Dakota. In the spring of 1805, the journey began anew, still following the Missouri. This time they were joined by a French trapper named Toussaint Charbonneau, his young Shoshone wife, Sacagawea, and their infant son, Jean Baptiste.

When the expedition entered modern day Montana, it became clear that the West was very different from anything these explorers had encountered in the East. Most obvious was the lack of water. The further west they travelled, the more arid the land became. The land was harsh and rugged, and featured deep canyons and towering mountains. It was evident that much of the West was ill-suited for agriculture, at least as traditionally practiced in the East.

In their final reports, Lewis and Clark described hundreds of strange animals that were previously unknown to scientists in the East. Their stories of soaring mountains and varied Native American tribes captivated public attention. However, in many ways their findings were a disappointment to Jefferson. There was no easy passage to the Pacific, much of the land was too dry or rugged for traditional agriculture, and other potential commercial uses were not readily apparent.

Like Jefferson, later federal administrators sought to find useful lands or resources in the West and other exploration parties were commissioned to find areas with the potential for settlement. Like Lewis and Clark, these later nineteenth-century explorers found little of value in much of the West. After making a scientific survey of the Colorado River basin in 1859, John N. Macomb stated, "I cannot conceive of a more worthless and impracticable region than that area we now find ourselves in." Lt. Joseph C. Ives, a government engineer, after surveying the southwest, maintained, "The region last explored is, of course, altogether valueless. Ours has been the first, and will undoubtedly be the last party of whites to visit the locality" (Fradkin 1995: 181). Even the Central Valley of California received an unenthusiastic review. After the California Gold Rush began in 1849, the U.S. government sent Lt. George Derby to survey agricultural potential in the valley. Where the San Joaquin and Merced rivers converged, he wrote: "Exceedingly barren, and singularly destitute of resources, except a narrow strip on the borders of the stream; it was without timber and grass, and can never, in my estimation, be brought into requisition for agricultural purposes." As he moved south, his concerns were amplified. Near present day Bakersfield, Derby observed, "The most miserable country that I have ever beheld. The soil was not only of the most wretched description, dry, powdery and decomposed, but everywhere burrowed by gophers, and a small animal resembling a common house rat" (Worster 1985: 9).

From the days of early exploration, ecology has shaped western economic development and demographic patterns. This was especially true during the isolation era when most people were directly dependent on traditional natural resources for their economic survival. According to the U.S. Environmental Protection Agency, most of the eleven western states that are part of the contiguous United States can be categorized into five major ecological regions, with great variation within each region. The eastern parts of Montana, Wyoming, Colorado, and New Mexico are a part of the Great Plains. The Great Plains region consists of flat to rolling prairie land and was historically covered with grass and very few trees. Much of the Great Plains has been converted to farm land, including some of the most productive farm land in the world. Lower levels of precipitation in the western states of the Great Plains limit agriculture as compared to the Corn Belt further east. Less rain meant later settlement and has always resulted in reduced agricultural production. The second ecological region, Marine West Coast Forests, extends along the Pacific Coast from Alaska to Northern California and consists of areas that receive substantial rainfall and are covered by temperate rainforests. Some of the most productive forest land in the world is found in this region. Further south is a third region called Mediterranean California, consisting of areas with dry summers and mild, somewhat wet winters, and some fabulously rich soils. These three regions (Great Plains, Marine West Coast Forests, and Mediterranean California) were at least somewhat attractive to settlers for their supplies of traditional resources for agriculture and other natural resource industries.

To get from the Great Plains to the coastal regions settlers could not avoid passing through two other much less inviting ecological regions: the Forested Mountains and Deserts. The forested mountains include the highlands of the Sierra Nevada and Rocky Mountains. The mountains are rugged and steep, largely forest-covered with intermittent grassy meadows, and with significant precipitation, much of it in the form of winter snow. Finding a passable route through the mountains was a high priority of early explorers and settlers. Most of the land between the Sierra Nevada, Cascade, and Rocky Mountains are deserts characterized by low precipitation and sparse plant cover. There are four deserts in the western United States. The Great Basin Desert is centered over the State of Nevada, but extends into parts of California, Oregon, Idaho, and Utah. It is covered with sagebrush, is high in elevation, and relatively cold. The Sonoran Desert of Arizona and extreme southern California is low and

Saguaro cactus in the Sonoran Desert. *Don E. Albrecht*

hot. The Mojave Desert, located between the Sonoran and Great Basin Deserts, is the hottest and driest of the American deserts and is characterized by Joshua trees. Finally, the Chihuahuan Desert covers large portions of Mexico, but also extends into New Mexico, Arizona, and Texas.

Settlement

As the isolation era unfolded, the same obstacles observed and encountered by Lewis and Clark and other early explorers dramatically impacted the settlement and subsequent development of the American West. As nineteenth-century settlers moved westward in search of areas where available resources would allow them to earn an economic livelihood, lands between the Great Plains and West Coast were largely ignored. It was a large space to be crossed as quickly as possible to reach more propitious areas.

Vivid accounts from early settlers about western deserts and mountains abound. A representative description was provided by William Manly, who was among thousands of Americans who crossed the continent in 1849 seeking gold in California. Like all migrants travelling to the West Coast, Manly was required to pass through mountains and deserts to reach his destination—something he and others considered a temporary price to pay for the rewards that awaited them. While passing through Death Valley, Manly remembered the "bounteous stock of bread and beans on my father's table, to say nothing about all the other good things, and here was I, the oldest son, away out in the center of the Great American Desert, with an empty stomach and a dry and parched throat, and clothes fast wearing out from constant wear." After reaching the West Coast, Manly wrote, "We were out of the dreadful sands and shadows of Death Valley, its exhausting phantoms, its salty columns, bitter lakes, and wild, dreary, sunken desolation. We had crossed the North American Continent, from a land of plenty, over great barren hills and plains, to another mild and beautiful region, where, though still in winter months, we were basking in the warmth and luxuriance of early summer. We thought not of the gold we had come to win. We were dead almost, and now we lived" (Worster 1985: 66).

Coping with Resource Limitations

Throughout the isolation era, individuals, companies, and federal, state, local, and territorial governments made efforts to reduce western isolation. Roads and railroads crossed the country; the telegraph greatly improved communication. Historian Bernard DeVoto (2000) argued that development of the West had to wait for industrialization to provide such products as barbed wire and repeating rifles. Despite these advances, much of the rural West remained far more isolated than rural areas in other parts of the country. Distances were great and the costs of infrastructure were often prohibitive. The major problem in much of the west, however, remained the lack of traditional natural resources. Where the land was too dry or mountainous, and where timber, minerals, or other resources were absent, development was stymied.

Water and Agriculture

Productive farms and vibrant farm communities sprang up on the West Coast and the Great Plains from the middle of the nineteenth century onward. After 1840 thousands of settlers crossed the continent to farm the productive and fertile Willamette Valley (Robbins 1997). Some land developers and even some scientists argued that nature would change with civilization and that rain would respond to earnest efforts and follow the plow. Charles Dana Wilber, an amateur scientist and founder of the town of Wilber, Nebraska, stated, "God speed the plow. By this wonderful provision, which is only man's mastery over nature, the clouds are dispensing copious rains. The plow is the instrument which separates civilization from savagery; and converts a desert into a farm or garden. To be more concise, rain follows the plow." During the 1870s and early 1880s, unusually heavy rainfall made these claims sound plausible and thousands of families moved to the semi-arid plains and other regions in the west, and set to using farming techniques that had worked in the humid East. Then the ever variable western weather again turned dry with disastrous results (deBuys 2001).

It was soon apparent that since nature could not provide critical resources, widespread development would require altering nature. Such attitudes were consistent with a fundamental assumption of the Human Exceptionalism Paradigm, which was accepted virtually without question by most Americans during the isolation era. Many felt it was their Christian duty to "conquer the wilderness," by establishing farms, homes, and communities (Udall 1963). Wilderness and the wild animals in it were obstacles to progress (Nie 2003). As Reverend Thomas Starr King of California stated in 1862, "The earth is not yet finished. It was not made for nettles, nor for the manzanita and chaparral. It was made for grain, for orchards, for the vine, for the comfort and luxuries of thrifty homes. It was made for these through the educated, organized, and moral labor of man" (Worster 1985, 97). John Widtsoe, a church and civic leader in Utah, maintained, "The destiny of man is to possess the whole earth; and the destiny of the earth is to be subject to man" (Powell 2008, 59). The prevalent world view was that an uncontrolled resource was a wasted resource.

In the humid East, conquering wilderness had meant clearing the forest, plowing sod, and removing rocks. Most of the country east of the 98th meridian had been settled by individuals and families who would lay claim to a piece of land and then carve their home and farm from the wilderness. Western obstacles were different. Successful farming in much of the West required much more water than was naturally available. Perhaps the most fundamental difference between the West and the rest of the country is precipitation. In nonwestern cities, precipitation levels are high, with New Orleans averaging 61.9 inches per year; Atlanta, 50.9; New York, 47.3; Boston, 41.5; Houston, 46.1; and Chicago, 35.8. In comparison, precipitation levels in western cities are much lower, with Las Vegas averaging 4.1 inches per year; Phoenix, 7.7; Albuquerque, 8.8; San Diego, 9.9; Los Angeles, 12.0; Boise, 12.2; Cheyenne, 14.4; Denver, 15.4; and Salt Lake City, 16.5.

Successful farming would thus require irrigation—capturing water at the time and place where it is abundant, and then moving it to where it is needed. The primary problem facing western farmers is that effective irrigation projects are simply too large, too complex, and too expensive to be undertaken by an individual or family, and in many cases even a community or state. Irrigation development requires massive amounts of labor and technical expertise.

While some societies have practiced irrigation for thousands of years (Wittfogel 1957), including several Native American tribes in the West, few early settlers arrived with such knowledge or expertise. Most Americans had spent their lives in the eastern United States or areas of Europe that received sufficient rainfall for farming, and did not depend on irrigation. Not only was there a lack of knowledge, but the legal, organizational, and administrative structure to support irrigation did not exist. Societies of the past in arid and semi-arid regions, such as Egypt and Mesopotamia, that had successfully developed major irrigation systems tended to be ruled by leaders with absolute authority who could use this authority to obtain essential resources and organize labor (Wittfogel 1957; Worster 1985). The West would require a legal structure, capital, technical expertise, and organized labor to prosper. Despite myths to the contrary, the West would not be won by "rugged individuals" alone.

Imagining the potential of irrigation, John W. Noble, Secretary of the Interior from 1889 to 1893, stated,

> I have no fear that America will grow too big. A hundred years hence these United States will be an empire, and such as the world never before saw, and such as will exist nowhere else upon the globe. In my opinion the richest portion of it, and a section fully as populous as the East, will be in the region beyond the Mississippi. All through that region, much of which is now arid and not populated, will be a population as dense as the Aztecs ever had in their palmiest days in Mexico and Central America. Irrigation is the magic wand which is to bring about these great changes. (Barrows 1894)

Throughout the later decades of the nineteenth century, residents of the West worked to develop successful irrigation projects. In some areas, streams were dammed and diverted and the water was used to irrigate small, nearby acreages. Attempts to divert larger rivers and move water greater distances were largely unsuccessful. Small dams and crude canals would be built, but were often destroyed under the torrents resulting from the melting of mountain snow each spring, or from flash floods from sudden summer downpours. Private irrigation companies using eastern money took on irrigation projects, and where the topography was right, successful agricultural based economies emerged. Many companies, however, went bankrupt. A number of state efforts to develop large scale irrigation systems also failed. The irrigation projects envisioned were simply too massive given the assets available to private irrigation companies and state governments.

The most successful nineteenth-century irrigation systems were developed by Mormons (members of the Church of Jesus Christ of Latter-day Saints) in Utah and surrounding areas of the Intermountain West. After being driven from their homes in Ohio, Missouri, and Illinois, Mormons began arriving in Utah in 1847, intentionally seeking out places that were less desirable to others so that they would be left alone. Mormons established scores of communities in arid and semi-arid valleys. Their economy was based on irrigated agriculture. Their efforts were successful primarily because they pooled resources and worked collectively, constructing dams to store water from the spring snow melt and canals to move the stored water to the farmers' fields (Arrington 2005).

The Bureau of Reclamation

Visionaries examined Mormon irrigation works and dreamed of the potential of even more large-scale irrigation systems in other parts of the West. Leaders maintained that successful large-scale irrigation projects would require the resources of the federal government, and western congressional delegations began pushing for federal involvement (CAST 1988). The obstacles to obtaining federal support were numerous. Eastern congressmen were unconvinced that it was in the best interest of their constituents to spend taxpayer money on projects that would result in irrigated farms in the West that would then compete with farmers in the eastern states. After years of concerted effort the Bureau of Reclamation (originally called the United States Reclamation Service) was established in the Department of the Interior on June 17, 1902. The goal of the new agency was to make federal resources and technical expertise available for major western irrigation projects (Pisani 2002).

During the bureau's early years, only a few projects were completed, and significant problems arose. Nonwestern congressional representatives, while allowing the creation of the agency, were hesitant to spend large sums of money on western water projects. Adding to their reluctance was the fact that several early projects encountered major problems. Farmers lacking both experience and assistance flooded and waterlogged their lands, and allowed silt to clog their irrigation systems. Often projects were undertaken with only a sketchy understanding of the area's climate, growing season, soil productivity, and market conditions (Powell 2008). Some projects failed to meet expectations for the amount of water that could be delivered and the number of acres that could be irrigated. In other cases, project costs exceeded expectations and irrigation farmers were often delinquent in repaying borrowed funds.

The successful completion of some projects, however, meant that additional land became available for cultivation, more families were able to make a living, and communities grew. The town of Powell, Wyoming, for example, sprang up in 1909 when the Buffalo Bill Dam and a canal transporting water thirty miles from the dam to a previously arid region were completed, making the area hospitable to farming for the first time. Other small-scale developments resulted in the emergence of other viable communities.

The most significant of early reclamation projects was the Salt River Project in Arizona. Begun in 1905 and completed in 1911, a 280-foot-high dam was constructed on the Salt River about sixty miles east of Phoenix. Named in honor of Theodore Roosevelt, it was the highest dam in the world at the time. It was also the first truly multipurpose project as it provided consistent irrigation water for thousands of acres of farmland, a steady municipal water supply that made the expansion of the Phoenix metropolitan area possible, flood control, and hydroelectric power generation. Using irrigation water from the Salt River Project, Maricopa County, Arizona, became one of the most productive agricultural counties in the nation until expanding urbanization paved over vast amounts of farmland.

Another important early project was in the Klamath Basin of southern Oregon and northern California. At one time, the Klamath Basin was an extensive series of valleys with shallow lakes and swamps comprising about 185,000 acres of natural wetlands and providing one of the most prolific waterfowl areas of North America. The Klamath Irrigation Project built a system of dams and canals that provided irrigation water for a large number of acres. In the process, much of the marshland and many shallow lakes were drained. Widespread irrigation greatly increased agricultural production, but fewer than 75,000 acres of natural wetlands remain (Anderson and Huggins 2008; Robbins 1997).

From the late 1920s onward, several truly massive projects were completed by the Bureau of Reclamation. Three of these, the Hoover Dam, the Central Valley Project, and the Grand Coulee Dam, are briefly described here.

Hoover Dam

From the beginning, irrigation developers had eyed the Colorado River, by far the most significant southwest river. However, the wild and seemingly uncontrollable Colorado presented numerous obstacles. The river begins at the continental divide at an elevation of 14,000 feet and then plummets through mountain canyons before emerging into the arid and semi-arid Colorado Plateau. The river has made a path through the Colorado Plateau by carving deep and rugged canyons such as Glen Canyon, Marble Canyon, and Grand Canyon. Often a mile or more below surrounding land, the water was unreachable to those who desired to use it. Violent floods from spring melts wiped out most nineteenth-century attempts to build dams and harness water for irrigation or municipal uses (Fradkin 1995; Hundley 2001; Powell 2008; Reisner 1993).

Around the turn of the twentieth century, efforts were initiated to utilize Colorado River water to irrigate farms in the Imperial Valley of California, located just north of the Mexican border and west of Arizona. A canal was built to carry diverted Colorado River water to the valley. It was quickly apparent that with adequate moisture, Imperial Valley soils were extremely productive. However, during the 1905 spring runoff, the canal system was overwhelmed, destroying homes and crops, flooding most of the valley, and creating the Salton Sea. Each subsequent spring, valley residents were concerned that the river would again overflow its banks and wipe out results of their hard work (Hundley 2001). Thus, from the valley perspective, an upriver dam to control spring flooding and store runoff water to be used to irrigate crops during later portions of the year was desperately needed. Valley residents also desired a more adequate canal that, unlike their earlier canal, would be entirely within the boundaries of the United States.

In 1922, a proposal was made by Arthur Powell Davis to build a dam on the Colorado River at Boulder Canyon along the Arizona–Nevada border. Davis, nephew of early Colorado River explorer John Wesley Powell, was director of the Bureau of Reclamation. His proposal included a high dam for flood control and to store water for irrigation and municipal purposes, hydroelectric generation plants, and an improved canal to transport Colorado River water to the Imperial Valley.

The Davis proposal immediately raised concern among the other states in the Colorado River basin about the apportionment of basin water. These worries were amplified that same year, when a Supreme Court decision in *Wyoming v. Colorado* reaffirmed prior appropriation water rights. Under the riparian system of water laws as they existed in England and the eastern United States, location next to a stream meant everything as owners of that land have the right to use water in the stream. Such a system was problematic in the arid west where streams are rare. Under prior appropriation, the key was putting the water to beneficial use, even if that use was distant from the stream. Simply put, prior appropriation means first in time is first in right. In other words, if the State of California used Colorado River water first, then California would always have first rights to Colorado River water (Hundley 2009; Pisani 2002).

As a result, other basin states refused to support the Davis bill until their rights to some of the water in the Colorado River were assured. Negotiations were successful and in November of 1922 delegates of the seven Colorado River basin states agreed to a pact that divided Colorado

River water between an upper basin and a lower basin. Under the pact, Colorado River water is evenly divided between four upper basin states (Wyoming, Colorado, Utah, and New Mexico) and three lower basin states (Arizona, Nevada, and California). Each basin has rights to 7.5 million acre-feet per year. An acre-foot of water is the amount of water it would take to cover an acre of land to a depth of one foot—or about 325,851 gallons. Problems have existed ever since because the original measurements were made during relatively wet years and in most years the Colorado River does not carry the requisite 15 million acre-feet (Hundley 2001; 2009; Powell 2008; Powell 2010). Thus, between 1906 and 1929, average flow for the Colorado River was 17.8 million acre-feet; then for the next eighty years from 1930, average flow has been only 12.4 million acre-feet. Yearly flows vary even more widely, ranging from 25.4 million acre-feet in 1984 to 5.4 million acre-feet in 1977.

After additional negotiations determined how much water each state within each basin would get, Congress gave final approval of the Hoover Dam project in 1928. Construction began shortly thereafter, and the 726-foot-high dam was completed in 1935. During the construction period, the nearby desert outpost of Las Vegas began transforming into one of the world's more unique cities. The dam was named after President Herbert Hoover and the resulting reservoir was named Lake Mead in honor of Elwood Mead, who succeeded Arthur Powell Davis as Reclamation chief. With completion of the "All-American" canal, irrigation water was carried consistently to farmland in the Imperial Valley. In 2007, 376,535 acres of farmland in Imperial County were irrigated, and the value of agricultural production from the county was about $1.3 billion, nearly as much production from this one county as from the entire state of Utah. In addition, an aqueduct carries extensive amounts of Colorado River water to Los Angeles and other Southern California cities. Another project (the Central Arizona Project) delivers Colorado River water to Phoenix, Tucson, and other Arizona cities. Finally, large amounts of electricity are produced. Until completion of the Grand Coulee Dam a few years later, the Hoover Dam produced more hydroelectric power than any other facility in the world.

Problems resulting from inadequate water have been troubling ever since the Colorado River Pact was signed in 1922. In fact, three upper-basin states (Colorado, New Mexico, and Utah) now take some of their water from the Colorado River Basin before it ever reaches the downstream dams. In Colorado, the Bureau of Reclamation's Colorado–Big Thompson diversion project uses a package of dams, reservoirs, and pumps to transfer water from the Colorado River drainage on the west side of the mountains, which receives most of the precipitation, through a thirteen-mile tunnel drilled through the mountain to the east side, where population density is greater along the Colorado Front Range (Powell 2008). Similarly, water is taken from the San Juan River (a major Colorado River tributary) and transferred to the Rio Grande River Basin, where the majority of New Mexico's population lives (Wilkinson 1992). Finally, the Central Utah Project takes water from Colorado River tributaries and transfers this water through the mountains to the heavily populated Wasatch Front.

The Central Valley Project

The Central Valley of California lies between the Sierra Nevada on the east and the Coast Range on the west. The valley is about 450 miles long and forty to seventy miles wide. The northern portion of the valley is drained by the Sacramento River while the southern portion is drained by the San Joaquin River. These two rivers then converge and meander through a large delta before emptying into San Francisco Bay. Most of the water in the two rivers results from Sierra Nevada drainage. Despite reports by Lt. Derby to the contrary, Central Valley's broad alluvial plains provide phenomenally rich soil and an ideal temperature for producing a wide range of agricultural products. All that was lacking from turning the Central Valley into an agricultural paradise was sufficient water. Precipitation is light (average annual precipitation in Fresno, California, for example, is only 11.2 inches), and—owing to the Mediterranean climate—generally falls in winter after the harvest is complete. The water picture is more complicated because precipitation levels are greater in the north and consequently the Sacramento River portion of the valley has only one-third of the land but two-thirds of the water, while the San Joaquin portion of the valley has two-thirds of the land but only one-third of the water.

Californians had long dreamed of a massive hydraulic system that would bring irrigation water to fertile land throughout the entire valley. As part of Franklin D. Roosevelt's New Deal legislation, money was approved to begin construction on such a system. Additional funding and projects were provided by the State of California. When completed several decades later, the Central Valley Project included twenty major dams and more than five hundred miles of canals through four major

Irrigation results in highly productive Central Valley agriculture. *istockphoto.com*

canal systems. Major dams include the Shasta and Keswick Dams on the Sacramento River and Friant Dam on the San Joaquin River. A great deal of water from the northern portion of the valley is transported to the southern portion. Some water is even transported to Southern California cities (Hundley 2001).

Largely because of the Central Valley Project, the State of California had more than eight million acres of farmland under irrigation in 2007, and this highly productive farmland has transformed California into the nation's leading agricultural state. California irrigated agriculture produces vast amounts of everything from almonds to lettuce to grapes and strawberries. In 2007, market value of agricultural products in California was $33.9 billion, far greater than the next highest states of Texas ($21.0 billion) and Iowa ($20.4 billion). Additionally, the majority of agricultural production in California is crops ($22.9 billion or 68 percent), while the majority of agricultural production in Texas (68.6 percent) is from livestock and animal production. In Iowa agricultural production is nearly evenly split between crops and animals or livestock. Gross farm sales from several Central Valley counties, including Fresno County ($3.7 billion), Tulare County ($3.2 billion), and Kern County ($3.2 billion) are higher than any other county in the entire United States. Farm sales from Fresno County alone exceed farm sales of eight of the twelve other western states. Fresno County production is based on nearly one million acres of irrigated cropland. Other Central Valley counties with farm sales exceeding $1 billion in 2007 include Kings ($1.4 billion), Merced ($2.3 billion), San Joaquin ($1.6 billion), and Stanislaus ($1.8 billion). In each case, production is heavily dependent on irrigation water made available from the Central Valley Project.

The Grand Coulee Dam

In 1933 President Roosevelt authorized the Grand Coulee Dam on the Columbia River in Washington State as a Public Works Administration project, which was a part of the New Deal legislation intended to help the country get out of the Great Depression. When completed the dam was nearly a mile long (5,223 feet), 550 feet high, and is still the largest concrete structure in the United States. The resulting reservoir, Lake Roosevelt, stretches for 151 miles in length. Because the Columbia is the largest river in the western United States and has a relatively large elevation drop, there is tremendous potential for hydroelectric generation. Grand Coulee Dam is still the largest producer of hydroelectric power in the United States. Large amounts of cheap power were vital to Pacific Northwest industrial development, and in particular development of the aeronautics industry in Seattle. Grand Coulee Dam and its system of canals provide irrigation water for thousands of acres of fertile yet arid central Washington farmland. In 2007 Grant County had 469,790 acres under irrigation and gross farm sales of $1.2 billion. Nearby Yakima County had 267,566 acres under irrigation from projects built on the Yakima River, a Columbia tributary. In 2007, Yakima County had gross farm sales of $1.2 billion. Outside of California, Weld County, Colorado, was the only county in the nation that had farm sales greater than these two counties in 2007.

Western Rangelands

Even with extensive irrigation development efforts, much of the West has remained beyond the reach of irrigated agriculture, including most of the mountain and desert lands. Vast stretches of land, perhaps as much as 400 million acres, could be classified as rangeland—land that is largely devoid of trees and has not been converted to crop production. Western rangelands include large portions of the Great Plains in the eastern parts of Montana, Wyoming, Colorado, and New Mexico, and much of the arid and semi-arid regions between the Rocky Mountains on the east and the Sierra Nevada or Cascade Mountains on the west. While much of this land is covered by sagebrush or grass, in the more arid desert regions there is very little vegetative cover.

When people first considered living on these rangelands, they faced a major conundrum. In the eastern part of the country and on the West Coast, the major settlement pattern of Americans had been for families to move to and homestead previously unsettled regions. However, settlers were reluctant to homestead western rangelands. A lack of precipitation made crop production risky to impossible, and without water for irrigation, the 160 acres available through the federal homestead laws were inadequate to support a family (Holechek et al. 2000).

Beginning in about 1850 some emigrants began bringing cattle into the West and soon it became widely accepted that livestock grazing was the most productive use of much western rangeland. After the Civil War great numbers of cattle were brought north from Texas (Merrill 2002). Other large herds were driven from California into Nevada and southeast Oregon (Robbins 1997). Ranching grew rapidly as the expansion of the railroad made it easier to transport cattle to urban markets. At the same time, the price of beef soared as demand from the expanding eastern industrial centers increased. Millions of cattle were soon scattered across western ranges, many of them under control of large-scale "cattle barons." Robbins (1997) describes cattle operations in eastern Oregon and Nevada that were running 30,000 head of cattle on the open range. The Swan Land and Cattle Co., financed by Scottish and English investors, had control of a range in Wyoming and Colorado that was one hundred miles long by fifty- to one-hundred-miles wide, with about 125,000 head of cattle (Frink et al. 1956; Merrill 2002). Later, millions of sheep were introduced on the western ranges. Sheep had the advantage of being able to find forage where cattle had already grazed, and could range further from water.

Nineteenth-century ranchers had three major problems in securing a stable living (Merrill 2002). First was establishing ownership of livestock sharing open rangelands. The solution was to brand the cattle. Each rancher had a unique brand registered in the state or territorial offices, and cattle rustling or trying to claim cattle belonging to someone else became a serious offense. This problem was less severe for sheep ranchers as sheep tend to stay together in flocks.

The second problem was more difficult as it involved somehow securing the land on which one's livestock grazed. Most grazing land was, in fact, publically owned. Illegal fences and intimidation were two strategies some ranchers employed to protect their grazing rights. The problem became more complex when homesteaders arrived to settle and farm some western rangelands. In the minds of many ranchers, homesteaders disrupted grazing land and often settled on the best land near rivers and streams. A few "range wars" erupted between ranchers attempting to keep the rangelands open and homesteaders attempting to build homes and farms. Sometimes these conflicts were exacerbated when ranchers began bringing sheep onto land that had previously been grazed exclusively by cattle. Among the best known of the range wars are the Johnson County War in Wyoming, which was portrayed in the classic western movie *Shane,* and the Lincoln County War in New Mexico involving celebrated gunman Billy the Kid.

A third problem faced by western ranchers was how to sustain their livestock through the winter months. Most ranchers did not use irrigation and thus were unable to grow crops for winter feed. Ranchers were protected for several years immediately following the Civil War by above-average precipitation and mild winters. The long-term consequences of the second and third problems were disastrous. With high prices, cooperative weather, and virtually no control over grazing, the number of livestock grazing on western rangelands soon greatly exceeded capacity. Grazing on western rangelands represented an archetypal "Tragedy of the Commons" (Hardin 1968); ranchers realized that if their livestock did not eat the grass, then livestock belonging to someone else would. The result was that the land was soon severely overgrazed. With virtually every living plant eaten, the fortunate weather years came to a crashing close with the bitterly cold winter of 1886-87. Vast numbers of cattle starved to death and many more malnourished and weakened cattle froze in the vicious cold. Without a way to feed their cattle, ranchers took many more emaciated animals to market, causing prices to collapse (Wilkinson 1992).

Following the crash of the late 1880s, the ranching industry was never the same. Recognizing the folly of depending on livestock to find winter grazing, especially in the north, ranchers made efforts to grow feed for winter. More ranching operations came to consist of homesteads, irrigated cropland for the production of winter feed, and nearby public lands where livestock could graze during the summer months. Under this scenario, many of the very large cattle companies that were dependent on outside investment went out of business. With time, a growing proportion of ranches became relatively small, family-type operations, where both privately-owned cropland and publicly-owned grazing land were critical to economic survival.

Many areas in the west may never recover from overgrazing that occurred in the 1800s. Wilkinson (1992) provides the example of Camp Creek in Central Oregon. Early explorers described the valley floor as a meadow with grass that grew up to seven feet tall. After the grass was wiped out by overgrazing in the 1880s, extensive erosion occurred. Now the creek no longer runs through a grassy meadow, but on the hard-packed floor at the bottom of a twenty-five-foot-deep arroyo. Erosion continues and a reservoir built on Camp Creek filled with silt in only twenty-five years.

Most policy makers at the time believed that private ownership was the best solution to rangeland problems (Merrill 2002). Ranchers who were dependent on public land grazing, however, were not so sure that private ownership was the best solution. Farmer–ranchers were concerned about the security of their access to public lands and feared that critical grazing land would someday be claimed by a homesteader and thus no longer available for livestock grazing. Regardless, policy emphasis continued to focus on ways of making homesteading work and getting federal land into private ownership. When it became apparent that the traditional 160-acre homesteads were unworkable, Congress passed additional homestead laws hoping to attract settlers to arid and semi-arid portions of the west. The "Enlarged Homestead Act" of 1909 allowed settlers to claim 320 acres, while the "Stock-Raising Homestead Act" of 1916 allowed 640 acres. Both of these acts led to large numbers of failures and many families found that they still could not make a living on a 640-acre ranch devoted primarily to livestock grazing.

In the 1890s public land policy began to shift. First, forest reserves were set aside for special management. In 1905 the U.S. Forest Service was organized under the direction of Gifford Pinchot within the United States Department of Agriculture (USDA) to manage these reserves. It became apparent that these lands were intended to be under permanent federal management and would never again be open to homesteaders. While the initial focus of the Forest Service was to manage federal timber assets, grasslands and large numbers of livestock also lay within forest boundaries. The Forest Service took their role as land stewards seriously and began concerted efforts to manage and control livestock grazing on

Western rangelands. *istockphoto.com*

their lands. In time, the Forest Service developed a permit system based on their determination of the number of animals that could graze in various locations, and times during the year when grazing should be allowed. Individuals were granted ten-year permits and charged fees on a "per head" basis to graze their livestock on federally owned land. Priority access to grazing permits was given to individuals who had previously had livestock in the area, and permits could be bought and sold in the open market.

While establishment of the Forest Service brought management and control to forest lands, large stretches of land remained in the public domain. For the most part, these were lands that no one wanted. Still open for homesteading in the early years of the twentieth century, these lands suffered from a lack of consistent management and continued overgrazing. Spurred by the Dust Bowl of the 1930s, Congress passed the Taylor Grazing Act in 1934, creating the U.S. Grazing Service. This act largely ended homesteading and provided consistent management for livestock grazing in the public domain. Twelve years later, in 1946, the Grazing Service and General Land Office were merged to create the Bureau of Land Management (BLM). Like the Forest Service, the BLM brought management and control to grazing on public lands.

Western Forests

While much of the West lacked traditional natural resources, the Pacific Northwest offered early migrants vast expanses of resource-rich temperate forests. Along the Pacific Coast from Alaska and British Columbia through Washington, Oregon, and into Northern California, massive trees grew in forests so dense that travel was made difficult by the tangle of underbrush and fallen trees. Some of the trees in the coastal forests were five hundred years old and three hundred feet tall. Lewis and Clark described one with a forty-two-foot circumference (Robbins 1997). Northern California was home to redwood forests featuring the tallest living entities on earth. On the eastern slopes of the Cascade Mountains of Washington, the Blue Mountains of Oregon, and other inland mountain ranges, were vast forests of ponderosa pine. Many of these pines were more than two hundred feet tall, and were surrounded with so little underbrush that a wagon could be drawn through the forest without difficulty (Kelly and Bliss 2009; Langston 1995). Elsewhere in the Rocky Mountains and Sierra Nevada grew forests where timber of commercial value was found, including the giant sequoia.

After a slow start, the forest industry took off in the late nineteenth century with the advent of improved transportation and technology. Mills

Pacific Northwest forests. *istockphoto.com*

were built beside rivers and streams where the current could generate power to operate equipment to cut trees into boards for building. Later, steam power made this equipment even more efficient. Teams of oxen were replaced by "steam donkeys," which could drag fallen trees for a mile or more to a mill, or to the edge of a river where the trees could be floated to a mill. A later improvement to this system was the "high-lead," where suspended cables lifted one end of the tree into the air while the other end dragged on the ground. The invention and continual improvement of gasoline-powered chain saws allowed forest workers to greatly increase the number of trees they could cut. The timber industry grew as railroads expanded and could transport lumber to meet the demands of expanding urban markets in other parts of the country and throughout the world.

Timber industry practices of the isolation era took their toll on the environment. It was a largely opportunistic industry where only the most valuable trees were harvested, and cut-and-run harvesting patterns left millions of acres dramatically altered (Kelly and Bliss 2009). Huge volumes of biomass waste left behind increased the potential for destructive forest fires. As steam donkeys dragged large trees, they tore up soil and destroyed younger trees, removing protective plant cover and contributing to erosion. As a result, rainfall drove silt into rivers and streams, changing conditions for fish and other aquatic life. Little effort was made to replant, and eroded soil was not conducive to the growth of new trees.

Like the range industry, the forest industry faced a "Tragedy of the Commons." Much land remained in public ownership because individuals realized that they could not make a long-term living on 160 acres of forest land. Loggers realized that if they didn't cut the trees, then someone else would. In time, some large lumber companies were able to amass large holdings of private forest land. Railroads were given wide expanses of land to encourage railroad construction. Much of this land was later sold to private timber companies. For example, in 1900 Weyerhaeuser bought 900,000 acres of timberland from the railroads for six dollars per acre. By 1903, the company owned 1.3 million acres of forest land in the Pacific Northwest (LeMonds 2001). Then the Forest Reserve Act of 1891 and the eventual creation of the Forest Service in 1905 provided for guidance and control of forest resources. It was generally believed that government control of timber harvests could provide for a continuous supply of timber resources, with stable communities as an added benefit.

Western Minerals and Energy

The scarcity of prime farmland in the West led to efforts to find and develop other traditional natural resources that would enable individuals to make a living and communities to prosper. Historically, at the top of the list were valuable minerals. The quest for western minerals was given a major boost on January 24, 1848, when gold was discovered at Sutter's Mill along the American River in California. When word of this discovery reached the eastern United States it led to the California Gold Rush of 1849, and thousands of people crossed the continent seeking wealth. Soon after, gold was discovered at Pike's Peak in Colorado and silver at Comstock Lode in Nevada (Stiller 2000). Other strikes followed in scattered western locations unearthing gold, silver, copper, lead, zinc, and other minerals. Wilkinson (1992) estimated that in the 1860s at least 25 percent of the residents of Nevada, Idaho, and Montana were working miners. The economic impact of mining was far greater than this number would indicate as many others were indirectly involved in the industry as assayers, providing transportation, and supplying mining towns with clothing, food, housing, entertainment, and other services.

Mining activities in the United States have been governed by the General Mining Act since the passage of the law in 1872. The law stated that individuals had the right to prospect for minerals on federal land, and then gave those who discovered minerals the right to stake mining claims to extract "gold, silver—or other valuable deposits." Through this process, land could eventually become privately owned. Throughout the isolation era, federal, state, and local laws as well as cultural values were supportive of the mining industry.

The mining industry has been critical to the development of the American West. The value of minerals removed numbers in the billions of dollars, and huge fortunes have been amassed. Some have grown rich providing services to miners. Leland Stanford, for example, made a fortune from his gold-rush-era general store in California and later used this wealth to invest in other endeavors and eventually to found Stanford University. The mines at Butte, Montana, produced more wealth than any other mines in the world through the 1950s, giving mine officials tremendous clout in Montana politics. A number of western communities had their beginning as mining towns. The mining industry has tended to be a "boom and bust" endeavor. The "boom" occurs with the discovery of minerals as miners and others move to the area seeking jobs and the chance for riches. The "bust" follows as the minerals become exhausted. Communities that later became world-renowned resorts—such as Aspen, Breckenridge, and Telluride, Colorado and Park City, Utah—were originally mining communities. Other communities that lacked amenities of future resorts became "ghost towns" when their resource base was exhausted, and many of these mining ghost towns can still be found throughout the West (Stiller 2000; Wilshire et al. 2008).

Environmental problems are among the most lasting legacies of mineral extraction in the West. By definition, mining is not sustainable. Minerals were created through geologic time and when removed they are simply gone and unavailable for future generations. By its very nature, mining is environmentally disruptive. Minerals are typically underground, and soil and rocks must be removed or tunnels dug to reach them. Further, valuable minerals generally are only a small proportion of the rocks and soil they are found within. The ore removed in copper mining, for example, typically contains less than one percent copper. The valuable ore must be separated from other material, a process which sometimes involves the use of acids and other chemicals including mercury and cyanide. Tailings or overburden (waste) that remain after the minerals have been removed represent a substantial hazard as they are often laced with poisonous acids, chemicals, or heavy metals, all of which tend to be washed or leached into nearby water supplies. Miners and nearby community residents often breathe dusty, contaminated air, and respiratory problems are common. Additional environmental problems from mining operations result from their extensive use of water and energy.

Among the more serious environmental problems resulting from mining is water pollution. After being dislodged from surrounding rocks, heavy metals can accumulate in nearby streams and lakes, where they become concentrated in fish and other aquatic life. High acid levels are another issue. Acid problems in mining begin with high levels of sulfides that naturally accompany valuable minerals such as gold, copper, zinc, and lead. When exposed to water and oxygen, sulfides oxidize and become sulfuric acid. This process occurs naturally, but through mining processes the amount of acids released is hundreds of times greater than what happens in nature (Stiller 2000). As water becomes too acidic near mines, aquatic life is limited or eliminated, and trees and other plants near streams or lake shores are often destroyed. Problems can continue even decades after mines are closed as acids are continually leached into nearby water sources. Once prime trout streams become lifeless, community water supplies become contaminated, and area residents can suffer health problems and high death rates.

Early mining practices had little consideration for the environment. In keeping with the HEP-based "myth of superabundance," miners and others considered the damage to be small relative to the vast amount of land surrounding the mine. The old adage was "the solution to pollution is dilution." Environmentally harmful mining practices were common. For example, nineteenth century California gold miners made extensive use of hydraulic hoses to blast away hillsides to wash large amounts of potentially gold-bearing ore into sluice boxes where gold could be extracted. This caused widespread loss of topsoil and washed massive amounts of sediment and toxins into rivers and streams, soon clogging rivers and filling bays and estuaries (Rohe 1985). The consequences for Sacramento River salmon were disastrous (Wilkinson 1992). Similarly, Montana gold, silver, and copper mines made little effort to prevent heavy metals and acids from washing into nearby streams and lakes (Stiller 2000). Eventually, however, the environmental problems were simply too vast and too toxic to be diluted.

Conclusions

During much of the isolation era, large parts of the West were ignored because they lacked traditional natural resources. Efforts to overcome this lack of resources included the creation of the Bureau of Reclamation and the construction of massive hydraulic systems to move water to arid and semi-arid areas for irrigation. As a result, farms and communities emerged in previously inhospitable areas. Additionally, efforts were made to utilize rangelands, forest, and mineral resources. Isolation era resource-use patterns resulted in some major ecological problems. With the emergence of the mass society era, prominent policy directives continued attempts to increase the availability of traditional natural resources consistent with the Human Exceptionalism Paradigm. Significantly different forces, however, would have major implications for the West as the mass society emerged.

CHAPTER THREE

The Rural West in the Mass Society Era

By the middle decades of the twentieth century, major technological developments brought an end to the isolation era and ushered in the mass society era (Vidich and Bensman 1958). Cars and improved highways, including construction of the Eisenhower Interstate Highway System beginning in the 1950s, meant that most rural residents could reach an urban center relatively quickly. Parts of the rural West, however, remained isolated.

Improved communications were also changing the lives of rural residents. By the 1950s, most rural Americans were watching the same TV shows, listening to the same radio programs, and reading the same newspapers and magazines as urban Americans. Numerous scholars noted how these changes combined to make rural populations less distinct, with norms, values, attitudes, and behaviors becoming increasingly similar to those of urban residents (Bealer et al. 1965; Bender 1975; Friedland 2002; Wirth 1938).

Emergence of the mass society era also meant a major transformation in the way that many rural people earned a living. Employment in the natural resource industries and agriculture declined while employment in the manufacturing sector increased. These changes were especially apparent in agriculture. From 1910 to 1940, the number of farms in the United States exceeded six million, and the farm population surpassed thirty million. Since that time, technology steadily replaced human labor in the production process and made it possible for an individual farm operator to cultivate many times the number of acres managed by his predecessors (D. Albrecht and Murdock 1990; Paarlberg 1980). The major breakthrough in this technological revolution was the all-purpose tractor. Continual improvement of the tractor, and development of other machines, changed the very nature of farm work.

In addition to labor-saving technological developments, other break-throughs—such as chemical fertilizers and pesticides and hybrid seeds—greatly increased productivity. Thus, not only did the number of acres that an individual farmer could operate increase, but productivity per acre and per animal rose as well. Between 1950 and 2000, the amount of milk produced per cow per year increased from 5,314 pounds to 18,201, the amount of corn produced per acre increased from 39 to 153 bushels, and the output per hour of farm work increased twelvefold (Fuglie et al. 2007). In 1900 the average farm worker produced enough to supply food and fiber for seven other people. By 1940 production had increased only slightly and the average farmer was able to produce enough for eleven people. Increases have been dramatic since that time. In 1970 the average farmer produced enough food and fiber for forty-eight people, by 1984 this number had risen to seventy-seven people, and in 2007 the average farmer produced enough for 143 people.

In 2007, the average farm was 418 acres, more than three times larger than the average farm in 1910. The consolidation of farms into larger units led to a rapid decline in farm numbers. By 2007 there were only 2.2 million farms, a two-thirds decline from 1940. Declining numbers of farms resulted in an even more rapid farm population loss. The farm population declined from 30.5 million in 1940, to 23.0 million in 1950, to 15.6 million in 1960, to 9.7 million in 1970, to 6.0 million in 1980, to 3.9 million in 1990, and finally to less than three million in 2000. Because numbers were so small, the Census Bureau quit counting the farm population after 2000. In 1900, more than 40 percent of the U.S. population lived on farms. This number declined to 23.2 percent in 1940 and by 2000 barely one percent of the U.S. population lived on farms.

Even current estimates of farms and the farm population are misleading in that a large majority of today's farms are part-time and hobby operations and produce only a very small share of our total food and fiber. In 2007, about 84 percent of U.S. farms had sales of less than $100,000, and these farms generated less than 7 percent of total farm sales. In contrast, only 2.5 percent of farms had sales exceeding $1 million, but these farms produced 59.1 percent of total farm revenue. The vast majority of household income for the smaller farms comes from nonfarm sources. In fact, only 17 percent of the total household income of all farm families comes from agriculture, with the remaining 83 percent coming from off-farm sources (Fernandez-Cornejo 2007). Most food and fiber in this country is produced by a small number of commercial farms using advanced technology.

Technological developments also led to decreased employment in other natural resource industries such as forestry, fishing, and mining.

Advancing technology also had major implications for other sectors of the economy. At the close of World War II, the U.S. industrial sector experienced major growth as technological developments increased our capacity to produce higher quality products in greater quantities and then to market them worldwide. Employment in the manufacturing sector increased dramatically as large numbers of farmers and other natural resource workers displaced by technology migrated to the city to seek employment. As a result of in-migration, the urban population of the United States more than doubled from 74.7 million residents in 1940 to 149.6 million in 1970. Urban population growth in the West was even more dramatic, increasing from about 8.4 million in 1940 to 28.9 million in 1970. Much of this growth was in the coastal cities of California and the Pacific Northwest as cheap hydroelectric power and manufacturing endeavors continued to blossom in the post-war years. The urban populations in intermountain states mushroomed as well, growing from 1.8 million residents in 1940 to 6.1 million in 1970. The cities of Phoenix and Denver grew especially rapidly.

While urban populations doubled, the population of rural America remained remarkably stable. In 1930, the population of rural areas in the United States was 54.0 million; in 1970 it was 53.6 million. This overall stability, however, belies extensive turbulence as some communities grew, some declined, and some remained stable. Farm and natural resource-dependent communities that were unable to attract industry experienced demographic and economic declines. In many farm-dependent rural communities, the population in 1970 was less than one-half of what it had been in 1940.

Eventually, the manufacturing sector began moving to rural areas to employ displaced farm workers, avoid unionization, and keep labor costs down. Soon manufacturing replaced agriculture and the natural resources industries as the primary employer of Americans, even in rural areas. In many communities, economic development efforts focused on attracting manufacturing firms that wished to build new plants or relocate. Communities that were initially less dependent on agriculture and were more effective in attracting industry tended to flourish. Generally, communities most effective in attracting industry were those near urban areas and those on major transportation routes (Johansen and Fuguitt 1984; Fuguitt et al. 1989). Overall, the isolated rural communities of the Intermountain West tended to do quite poorly during the mass society era with the total number of inhabitants declining from 2.4 million in

1940 to 2.2 million in 1970. In sum, during the transition from the isolation era to the mass society era, some communities thrived while others struggled to survive. The struggle was especially difficult for communities that were more dependent on farms or natural resources and for those that were more isolated.

Resource Issues

Throughout the mass society era, the extent to which communities were dependent on traditional natural resource industries for their employment steadily declined. Despite this decline, primary policy objectives in the rural West continued to focus on programs and developments to increase availability of those traditional natural resources that had historically been in short supply (Baden and Snow 1997). Many western rural communities continued to define themselves as resource communities and believed that exporting resources brought money into the community that then made possible the existence of other services (Power 1996; Power and Barrett 2001). Thus, efforts were made to build new dams to increase the supply of irrigation water for agriculture. Similarly, widespread exploration occurred to find minerals and energy resources, and it seemed that the focus of the Forest Service and Bureau of Land Management (BLM) was to provide a continuous source of timber and grazing land to help economically sustain local communities.

During the mass society era, powerful voices began challenging long established assumptions about traditional, economic based uses of natural resources. Generally, these voices came from outside of the rural West and represented a worldview totally foreign to long held assumptions that conquering or subduing nature was appropriate and that resources existed to be used by humans. The longstanding and largely unchallenged assumptions of the HEP were increasingly questioned and the New Environmental Paradigm (NEP) received growing acknowledgement. This trend was enhanced by a rapidly increasing urban population and a growing proportion of individuals who were not economically dependent on resource-based industries. The first significant challenge to traditional resource uses came from individuals concerned with potential amenity, aesthetic, and recreational uses of resources (Hays 2007). These individuals sought to preserve some especially high-quality areas from timber harvest, mining, or dam construction so that these lands could be used for camping, hunting, fishing, hiking, or photography.

A second challenge came from scientifically based ecological studies that found that some traditional uses of resources were causing detrimental and sometimes irreparable damage to the environment and even to human health (Anderson et al. 2008). A watershed event was publication of Rachel Carson's *Silent Spring* in 1962. Using careful scientific research, Carson noted negative environmental consequences resulting from the use of pesticides. Her insights included an explanation of how poisons become increasingly concentrated in body tissues as one moves up the food chain, causing genetic and reproductive disruption. Subsequent research resulted in an improved understanding of the complexity of nature and knowledge that human actions had unintended and sometimes long-term negative consequences on ecosystems. Arguments followed that attention should be paid to species beyond their economic value to humans. To some, these species represented markers or indicators of the health of the environment, and were an essential component of biodiversity and balance of nature. Others maintained that all species, regardless of their economic value to humans, have the right to exist. This represented a major departure from earlier decades when efforts were made to exterminate plants and animals thought to be harmful to humans or that were viewed as having no economic value. Additionally, some severe resource problems increased awareness of the potential dangers and pitfalls of unrestricted resource use (Baden and Snow 1997).

The culmination of these challenges was passage of several laws that forever ended the unfettered development of resources for traditional uses without significant opposition and compromise. These laws provided evidence of the growing force of the NEP. Among the most important of these were the Wilderness Preservation Act of 1964, the National Wild and Scenic Rivers Act of 1968, the National Environmental Policy Act (NEPA) of 1969, and the Endangered Species Act of 1973. The National Wild and Scenic Rivers Act was intended to preserve free-flowing rivers with outstanding scenic, recreational, geological, fish and wildlife, historic, or cultural value. As of 2004, 156 rivers were protected under the act, which effectively put these rivers off limits for dam construction. NEPA required that environmental consequences of proposed federal actions be carefully analyzed before those actions take place. This analysis includes a consideration of a wide range of species and more complex and longer-term environmental impacts. NEPA also requires a Social Impact Assessment (SIA) to consider socioeconomic, demographic, and cultural impacts of proposed actions on individuals and communities. The Endangered

Species Act, administered by the U.S. Fish and Wildlife Service, requires agencies to investigate whether species might be endangered or threatened as a consequence of economic growth or development or other human actions. Further, the general public can petition the agency to list a species as endangered. After a species has been declared as endangered, action must be taken to protect that species from extinction. In the end, with new laws in place and new NEP-based cultural views about resources more widely accepted, attempts to utilize resources in traditional ways became a very different process.

Water and Agriculture

The shortage of water continued to be the issue of greatest concern throughout much of the West during the mass society era. Proposals for water storage and irrigation development were legion and, consistent with the HEP, it seemed that attempts were made to wring every drop of water from western streams and put each drop to some "useful" purpose. The so-called "iron-triangle" emerged to obtain federal funds to construct dams and canals for massive water-moving projects. The three corners of the triangle included local farmers, ranchers, and community leaders who would benefit from federally subsidized water; the Bureau of Reclamation, an organization of engineers and professional dam builders whose continued employment depended on building dams; and western congressional delegates who determined that the best path to reelection was to get approval for irrigation projects that would then benefit their constituents. With the HEP-consistent goal of conquering the wilderness and the benefits of putting water to productive use self-evident to nearly everyone in the West, the system was poised to march forward.

Water has always been a contentious issue in the West. They say that in the West, whiskey is for drinking and water is for fighting. I have also been told that there are two things that western men will fight over: water and women, in that order. Typically, arguments, disagreements, and court battles were over where dams should be built and how water should be distributed, rather than whether or not a project should be built at all. Several western water battles even reached the Supreme Court, where decisions determined who owned the water and how much of the water different entities would get. Despite these internal contentions, overall goals of controlling, storing, and harnessing water for "useful" purposes had historically received virtually unanimous support in the western United States.

Yet even during the isolation era, a few faint voices expressed opposition to some projects, usually because of amenity or environmental concerns. Most prominent of early projects that generated opposition was a proposed dam on the Tuolumne River in the Sierra Nevadas of California. The river flowed from the Sierra Nevadas through Hetch Hetchy Valley and eventually into the Central Valley. Perpendicular granite walls rising 2,500 feet from the river in the valley floor made Hetch Hetchy Valley one of the most visibly breathtaking places in the world. Hetch Hetchy Valley was similar to nearby Yosemite Valley and since 1890 both had been a part of Yosemite National Park.

Early in the twentieth century, the burgeoning city of San Francisco proposed building a dam on the Tuolumne River at Hetch Hetchy to store water from spring runoffs, and constructing an aqueduct from the dam to transport water to the city for municipal purposes. Their proposal gained momentum after the devastating 1906 earthquake caused numerous fires that destroyed much of the city. It was argued that if more water had been available, some of the fires could have been controlled. A group of preservationists led by John Muir expressed strong opposition to the dam because they felt the beauty of Hetch Hetchy Valley would be compromised. Muir enlisted the aid of his newly formed Sierra Club and recommended that another river be used instead. After extensive debate and lawsuits Muir and the preservationists lost and President Woodrow Wilson signed a bill authorizing the dam in 1913. Construction began shortly thereafter, and much of the Hetch Hetchy Valley is now under water. This controversy was instrumental in leading to creation of the National Park Service in 1916. Previously several national parks had been established, but these parks had no agency to manage them and no consistent plan to guide management decisions. The Hetch Hetchy controversy made this shortcoming apparent and creation of the National Park Service was an attempt to remedy the situation.

The few faint voices of opposition that were heard during the isolation era grew to a loud chorus during the mass society era as an NEP-based world view gained force. Each significant proposed water project faced scrutiny and often major opposition. Rather than drawing all water from western streams for irrigation purposes, a growing number of people argued that aesthetics and habitat for aquatic life were also relevant and valuable uses of water. As a result, many proposed projects were dropped and many others turned out vastly different from what was originally proposed.

The increased strength of the movement opposing continual water development became apparent on several proposed projects on the Colorado River Basin. In the 1950s, the Bureau of Reclamation proposed construction of a number of dams on the Colorado River and its major tributaries above Hoover Dam, maintaining that additional dams were essential to store water during wet years so that a consistent flow to the lower basin could be maintained during dry years. One proposed dam was on the Green River in Echo Canyon, just below the confluence of the Green and Yampa Rivers near the Utah-Colorado border. This dam would inundate Dinosaur National Monument, which was known for its unparalleled collection of fossils, as well as scenic canyons of the Green and Yampa Rivers (Powell 2008). Immediate and strong opposition was expressed by the Sierra Club and other environmental organizations. Under direction of David Brower, executive director of the Sierra Club, a major campaign was developed that included paid advertisements, a film, and a book, all depicting a national monument of great scenic, scientific, and cultural value being covered with water. With letters to Congress running about ninety to one in opposition to the dam, the bureau was forced to back off plans for the Echo Canyon Dam (Schulte 2002).

In a subsequent political compromise, environmental groups agreed to a revised plan (Powell 2008). The Colorado River Pact of 1956 was passed by Congress and included Glen Canyon Dam (completed in 1964), which formed Lake Powell on the Colorado River near the Utah-Arizona border; Flaming Gorge Dam (completed in 1964) on the Green River upstream from Echo Canyon and near the Utah-Wyoming border; Navajo Dam (completed in 1963) on the San Juan River in New Mexico; and three dams on the Gunnison River in Colorado. David Brower rafted through Glen Canyon after the pact had been finalized but before construction was completed on Glen Canyon Dam. He then stated that he had been unaware of the beauty and natural wonders of Glen Canyon and that his concession to construction of the Glen Canyon Dam was the biggest mistake of his career. He remarked, "Glen Canyon died, and I was partly responsible for its needless death. Neither you nor I, nor anyone else, knew it well enough to insist that at all costs it should endure. When we began to find out, it was too late" (Brower 1966).

Each of these projects had significant socioeconomic and ecological consequences. For example, the isolated rural Utah county of Daggett, home of the Flaming Gorge Dam, had a 1960 population that was three times greater than their 1950 population as a result of the influx of construction workers. The population declined considerably following completion of the dam when construction workers moved away. A totally new community, Page, Arizona, was built at the construction site of the Glen Canyon Dam on land that had previously been part of the Navajo Reservation.

Ecologically, the consequences were profound. The Colorado River flowing through the Grand Canyon became a completely different river following construction of the Glen Canyon Dam. Prior to the dam, the river had carried vast amounts of silt through the canyon and spring flows far exceeded flows later in the year. After the dam was built, most of the silt settled out in Lake Powell, the river became much clearer, and the amount of water in the river became much more even from one part of the year to another. The lack of silt to build up the sandbars of the river greatly altered the ecology of the canyon. Water temperature changed. Before the dam, river temperatures varied from near freezing in the winter to about 80 degrees Fahrenheit in the summer. After dam completion, water was released from a depth of 230 feet at a nearly constant temperature of 46 degrees. These changes had dramatic effects on the species of fish that could thrive and the plants that could grow along the banks of the river. The humpback chub is now protected by the Endangered Species Act and the Colorado pikeminnow, a fish that grows to more than three feet long and lives for up to fifty years, is now listed as endangered in the Colorado River overall and is no longer found in the Grand Canyon. In contrast, non-native rainbow trout thrive in the clear, cold waters of the Colorado River in Grand Canyon (Powell 2008). Another ecological concern is the decline of the Colorado River Delta where the river reaches the sea. At one time, silt-laden waters of the Colorado River created a massive marshland of nearly two million acres teaming with life. With completion of numerous dams and removal of vast amounts of water for irrigation and municipal uses, there are now times when the Colorado River water no longer reaches the ocean. Consequently, the delta has largely vanished (Fradkin 1995; Powell 2008).

Another major proposed project during the mass society era was the Central Arizona Project. This project was intended to move water through canals and aqueducts for 336 miles from the lower Colorado River to growing desert cities of Phoenix and Tucson for municipal, industrial, and agricultural purposes. Moving large amounts of water uphill for great distances requires huge amounts of energy. Initial Bureau of Reclamation proposals included two dams on the Colorado River within Grand Canyon

National Park. The purpose of these dams was to provide a consistent supply of water and hydroelectric plants to generate energy to pump the water. Brower and the Sierra Club again unleashed a dramatic ad campaign in 1966. This campaign included full page ads in the *New York Times* and the *San Francisco Chronicle* under the headline, "Should we also flood the Sistine Chapel so tourists can get nearer the ceiling?" Brower implied that the dams were going to fill the Grand Canyon like an enormous bathtub, and that the view from the North Rim to the South Rim would consist of a flat expanse of water. The Central Arizona Project was eventually passed in 1968, but there were no dams in Grand Canyon National Park as a part of the project. This time the political compromise involved using coal from the Navajo Reservation to generate energy. A coal-fired plant was built on the reservation, and a coal-slurry pipeline was built to transport coal from the mine on the reservation for 273 miles to a coal-fired power plant in Laughlin, Nevada, near where the water would be pumped. While there were no dams constructed within Grand Canyon National Park, there has been a noticeable decline in visibility resulting from the haze emanating from the coal-fired power plant.

A significant battle also unfolded over the fate of the Stanislaus River in California. The Stanislaus River rises from the Sierra Nevadas north of Yosemite and eventually joins the San Joaquin River west of Modesto. The public expressed little concern when the New Melones Dam on the Stanislaus River was proposed as part of the original Central Valley Project. The proposal called for construction of the nation's fourth highest dam that would flood a beautiful stretch of canyon that had become some of the West's most heavily used white-water rapids. By the time construction got under way in the 1960s, public sentiments had changed dramatically. Even when the dam was completed, the public sought to prevent closing the gates on the dam to begin backing up water. At one point, a young man chained himself to bedrock near the rising water announcing, "The life of the nine-million-year-old Stanislaus Canyon is far more significant than my short tenure on this planet" (Hundley 2001). Eventually, however, the opposition was overcome and the reservoir filled to capacity.

Western Rangelands

Throughout the isolation era, grazing livestock was considered the most productive use of western rangeland that would otherwise be considered "useless." By the mass society era, many ranching operations had emerged consisting of both private land for the homestead, with irrigation water available to produce winter feed, and open public range lands (Hussa 2009). The nature of range management began to change as major opposition to livestock grazing on public lands emerged. Scientific research showed evidence that livestock grazing was a primary factor in the spread of invasive plants and the changing fire ecology of western ranges. A key event was in 1974 when a federal court ordered the Bureau of Land Management to comply with the National Environmental Policy Act. Consequently, the BLM was required to provide detailed statements on environmental impacts of livestock grazing on public lands. Providing these statements was costly and time consuming and their findings were often challenged. The major concerns of the opposition involved desire for enhanced amenities and recreational opportunities and apprehension that grazing was having a negative impact on biodiversity (Merrill 2002).

Western Forests

A majority of western forests are on federally owned land, most of it managed by three agencies, the U.S. Forest Service, National Park Service, and Bureau of Land Management. Thus, what occurs in western forests is largely a function of federal laws and policies. Despite a vast range of potential benefits that are available from our forests (ranging from solitude and bird watching to livestock grazing and mining), from the time of Gifford Pinchot, federal policy has largely emphasized wood production. Policies and programs were developed to produce the greatest number of board feet for the least cost (Hays 2007). With perhaps the exception of large mammals that were popular with hunters, little concern was exhibited for any forest species except commercially valuable trees. Circumstances changed as the forestry industry was forced to consider a wider range of ecological concerns and the interests of a broader population. Mass society-era laws such as the Wilderness Act, NEPA, and the Endangered Species Act would strongly impact western forests as HEP-based practices were strongly challenged by the NEP.

Two examples of forced changes in forest policy relate to fire and clearcutting. A third example, protection of the northern spotted owl under the Endangered Species Act, is discussed in Chapter Seven. Throughout the twentieth century, forest fires had been suppressed largely because of concerns that commercially valuable trees that could have been used for homes, fences, and furniture would be destroyed. Smokey Bear and his slogan, "Only you can prevent forest fires," has been among the most successful public relations campaigns ever. By the mass society era, researchers were gaining a better understanding of the integral role that fire plays in the natural ecology of a forest, and recognized that the health and survival of many species depend on periodic wildfires. By the time these factors were understood, however, in many places conditions were ripe for large, catastrophic fires. Best known of these fires occurred in Yellowstone National Park and surrounding areas during the summer of 1988 (D. Smith 2013). Years of suppression combined with especially dry conditions resulted in a massive fire that burned for several months. Despite efforts of thousands of firefighters and modern technology, only the arrival of cool and moist weather in the late autumn brought the fires to an end. In total, nearly 800,000 acres were burned. Now in some places and under certain conditions fires are allowed and sometimes even encouraged to burn.

A second issue in the forests where policies were forced to change was with respect to clearcutting. For decades, under HEP assumptions when emphasis was clearly on wood production, foresters sought the most efficient way of getting trees to the mill, with clearcutting the harvesting method of choice. Then during the mass society era, it became increasingly apparent that clearcutting resulted in detrimental effects on many other forest species, which led to growing public opposition (Hays 2007). Growing evidence revealed that under some circumstances, clearcutting tends to increase soil erosion, which then impacts many aquatic species. Clearcutting tends to make a varied forest environment much less diverse, with negative consequences for biodiversity. Dramatic events also increased awareness of problems associated with clearcutting. In 1965, following extreme clearcutting, the banks of the South Fork of the Salmon River in Idaho gave way. The result was that hundreds of thousands of tons of silt filled the river. The consequence has been that the river has never again been able to support salmon from that point upstream (Barker 1997; Wilkinson 1992). Concern with biodiversity loss increased as human appreciation of nongame species grew. Finally, the role of aesthetics came into play. Many people preferred looking at trees and found clear cuts to be visually unappealing. The laws passed during the mass society era gave ammunition to those opposed to clearcutting. Environmental impact statements required by NEPA necessitated consideration of a broad range of species and outcomes prior to approval of a clearcut. Under such growing pressure, obtaining endorsement for a clear cut became increasingly difficult despite the resulting increased wood production costs.

Western Minerals and Energy

Awareness of environmental and human health consequences of mining increased during the mass society era, which resulted in pressure on the mining industry to reduce pollution and toxic waste and to pay for damages previously inflicted. As a consequence, the profitability of mining was reduced and a number of operations were closed. At the same time, technological developments and geopolitical changes were providing opportunities for development of western energy resources. The first of these was the uranium boom of the 1950s; the second was the energy boom of the 1970s. Economic and political benefits resulting from energy development represented a major departure from the expanding limitations on development that were occurring during the mass society era.

The Uranium Boom of the 1950s

As a result of the Manhattan Project during World War II, the United States military developed the nuclear bomb. Essential fuel for this bomb is uranium. During the war, uranium was imported from the Congo region of Africa as there were no known economically viable sources in the United States. Following the war, demand for uranium increased because of the need for Cold War bombs, and for other potential uses of nuclear energy such as power plants to produce electricity. Substantial efforts were then made to find domestic sources of this critical resource. Attention quickly focused on the Colorado Plateau in the four corners area where Utah, Colorado, Arizona, and New Mexico meet. In July of 1952, Charlie Steen discovered a significant uranium reserve near Moab, Utah, that he called Mi Vida (My Life). The reserve eventually produced an estimated $61 million in high-grade uranium, and Steen became a multimillionaire. Discoveries of high-grade uranium were made in other parts of the Colorado Plateau and soon hundreds of prospectors were combing the region. Several uranium milling plants were built and a significant workforce was employed in mines and mills. Communities such as Moab, Utah, and Grand Junction, Colorado, experienced boom-like growth throughout the 1950s. In 1960 the Atomic Energy Commission (the only legal buyer of uranium and uranium products) announced it had sufficient supplies. Prices plummeted and uranium boom towns experienced their "bust." Even Charlie Steen had to declare bankruptcy.

Like many other mining endeavors, serious environmental problems confront the uranium industry. Tailings from the Mi Vida mine were stored in a pond near the Colorado River and it soon became apparent that radioactive tailings were leaching into the river and having disastrous effects on fish populations. These tailings are now being transferred to a safer location at the cost of millions of taxpayer dollars. The small southeastern Utah town of Monticello hosted a uranium processing mill owned by the U.S. government during the uranium boom years. The facility left behind two million tons of tailings and enough contamination to warrant a $250 million EPA Superfund project during the 1990s. Even though contamination has been removed, the town still suffers from excessively high cancer rates and respiratory problems (Malin 2008).

In the early years of the twenty-first century, demand for uranium is again increasing as nuclear power is seen as a way to reduce U.S. dependence on foreign oil and decrease the production of climate-changing greenhouse gasses. Concern, however, remains high regarding potential human health and environmental problems. With the growing strength of NEP values, future developments will be required to go through a much more careful planning process, including detailed plans for avoiding the most serious potential problems.

The Energy Boom of the 1970s

From the time of early settlement, people were aware of the existence of fossil fuels in some areas of the West, and these resources (especially oil) were sometimes commercially developed. During the 1970s, however, energy development became an even more crucial part of the western rural economy. The OPEC oil embargo of the early 1970s not only caused a significant and rapid increase in energy costs, but also made it apparent how dependent the United States was on foreign energy producers. Dependency means vulnerability. Immediate efforts ensued to make the United States more energy independent with immense consequences for the rural West. Early efforts to attain energy independence were based on increased use of our most abundant fossil fuel—coal. In the initial rush of the 1970s, eleven coal-fired power plants were constructed. Plans were discontinued for a twelfth plant, the Kaiparowits in southern Utah, because of public concern that it would produce enough pollution to reduce visibility in several national parks. The role of coal and other energy resources for economic development in the West are described in Chapter Six.

Conclusions

During the mass society era, much of the West was disadvantaged by a relative lack of traditional natural resources. As the nation made the transition from dependence on the natural resource industries to dependence on manufacturing, the West remained disadvantaged because of relative isolation. These problems were confounded as new laws and cultural values placed substantial barriers to development efforts to increase the availability of traditional natural resources. Energy development was perhaps the major exception. Thus circumstances were increasingly bleak for much of the rural West as growing obstacles were instigated, preventing the use of already scarce resources. This, however, was about to change as the global society era emerged.

Section Two

The Rural West in the Global Society Era

During the 1970s, rural America and the rural West in particular saw momentous changes as the country began a transition that would end the mass society era and usher in the global society era (Ferguson et al. 2010). As described in Chapter One, the events culminating in the global society era were significant improvements in information and communication technology, the impacts of which were strengthened by the end of the Cold War. Globalization reduced relevance of location and brought major economic restructuring processes. Values and attitudes that emerged during the mass society era that recognize the ecological complexity of the world and of the impact of human actions on the environment were strengthened in the new era. The Human Exceptionalism Paradigm (HEP) has faced considerable challenge from the New Environmental Paradigm (NEP).

How do individuals, families, and communities of the rural West confront issues and problems as well as enjoy opportunities inherent in the global society era? To better understand these issues and to seek approaches to effectively address them, I participated in thirteen rural development strategic roundtable planning session during 2009, one in each of the states comprising the western region (Alaska, Arizona, California, Colorado, Hawaii, Idaho, Montana, Nevada, New Mexico, Oregon, Utah, Washington, and Wyoming). Made possible by generous funding from the Farm Foundation, the goal of these roundtable discussions was to understand both the positive features of the rural West and the major problems, issues, and concerns faced by rural residents and communities. Whether I was in Maui, Hawaii; Anchorage, Alaska; Cheyenne, Wyoming; or Davis, California, the extent of agreement from one state to another was profound. Based on the results of these roundtable sessions, chapters comprising Section Two seek to portray the major issues and concerns that emerged and then discuss approaches for addressing them. Briefly stated, the three major issues and concerns facing the rural West in the global society era are:

1. *Determining appropriate natural resource uses.* From the time of initial settlement, many rural communities have been economically dependent on the development and utilization of natural resources. Much has changed in recent years. Population growth and an improved standard of living have increased demand for some of these resources. Some resources were used unsustainably and supplies are now limited. In some cases, legal and cultural changes have limited access of rural residents to resources in a manner that allows them to maintain an economic livelihood. In many cases, the best potential use of resources in the global era is to preserve amenities. Fortunately, in many instances there is a sustainable balance that can be achieved through open dialogue and thoughtful community development planning. Chapter Four paves the way for a discussion on western resource issues by describing federal land ownership, which provides both opportunities and constraints for western communities. Chapters Five, Six, and Seven describe natural resource concerns. Chapter Five focuses on water, a resource that is absolutely vital yet has always been limited in the West. Chapter Six explores prominent energy issues. Finally, Chapter Seven discusses other resource issues, including biodiversity, rangeland, forests, and mineral resources.

2. *Coping with limited economic opportunities through place-based rural development.* In recent decades there has been a steady decline in employment in agriculture, natural resource industries, and manufacturing—the traditional primary employers of rural workers. As a consequence, traditional approaches to improve economic opportunities in rural areas are much less successful than in the past. When most nonmetro jobs were in agriculture and the natural resource industries, community development efforts tended to focus on enhancing the supply of or demand for natural resources. With growth of manufacturing, the most common rural development path was to seek to entice some industrial firm to build or relocate to the community. In today's global world, opportunities for resource development are limited, the traditional "buffalo hunt" for industrial firms is more costly, the odds of success are greatly reduced, and overall this approach is much less effective as a rural development strategy. At the same time, there are development opportunities that simply did not exist in the past. With

computers, the internet, and cell phones, it is now possible for individuals and firms to be connected to the global world while enjoying the benefits of rural living.

A major obstacle to economic development in many rural communities involves infrastructure that is often significantly inferior to that available in urban communities. Thus, it is imperative that infrastructure improvements occur, especially improved telecommunication technology. Economic development in the global world is dependent on being connected through broadband and widespread cell phone availability. Much of the West is inadequately served, and obstacles for achieving better service are daunting. Yet it must be done if rural communities are to survive and thrive. Chapter Eight describes these issues in greater detail and makes suggestions for communities to address place-based economic development. Chapter Nine discusses place-based economic development in the West's most vulnerable communities.

3. *Enhancing human capacity through people-based rural development.* With declines in traditional sources of rural employment, it is increasingly apparent that the education, skills, and training of many rural workers do not translate easily into the education, skills, and training needed for high-quality employment in a global world. Programs and policies must be implemented to enhance the workforce skills of rural residents. Additionally, there is a great need to improve leadership capacity in many rural communities. Without strong leadership, communities lack direction and therefore inadequately deal with many questions and concerns that confront them. It is also important to note that wide inequality exists in the rural West, and that the need to increase human capacity among some segments of the population is especially great. Chapter Ten describes in more detail the need to increase human capacity in the rural West, and outlines policies and programs to accomplish this goal. Chapter Eleven discusses people-based economic development among the most vulnerable residents of the West. Finally, some concluding thoughts are provided in Chapter Twelve.

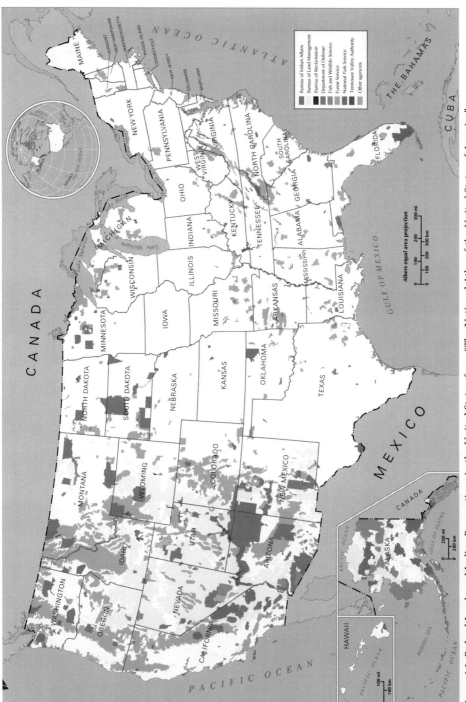

Figure 4.1 Federal Lands and Indian Reservations in the United States, from "The National Atlas of the United States of America"
U.S. Department of the Interior, U.S. Geological Survey

CHAPTER FOUR

Federal Lands

Federal land in the West is ubiquitous. Over 90 percent of the land in the State of Nevada is federally owned, as is two-thirds of Utah, Alaska, and Idaho, and more than one-half of Arizona, Oregon, and Wyoming. In California, the nation's most populous state, 46.9 percent of the land is federally owned. In total, nearly one million square miles (55.4 percent) of the West is owned and managed by the federal government. In comparison, in the thirty-seven nonwestern states, less than 5 percent of the land is federally owned. Federal land is the attraction that draws millions of tourists each year. Historically, it has provided grazing for thousands of cattle and sheep. Vast amounts of timber have been harvested and minerals extracted from federal land. Federal lands are the major source of collected snowfall which melts to become the rivers and canals that irrigate the West and provide drinking water for its inhabitants. The presence of huge expanses of federal land and decisions affecting how this land is used has immense implications, and in the global society era, these decisions are fraught with controversy (Kemmis 2001).

Emergence of Federal Land

At the close of the American Revolution, the original boundaries of the United States included all land east of the Mississippi River, south of the Great Lakes, and north of the 31st parallel (the present northern boundary of Florida). The lands west of present boundaries of the original thirteen states were claimed by Massachusetts, Connecticut, New York, Virginia, North Carolina, South Carolina, and Georgia. The six states which did not have western claims demanded that other states cede their claims to the federal government. These sessions gave 236.8 million acres to the public domain of the United States. As the young country grew through purchases (such as the Louisiana Purchase from France) or conquest (such as the Mexican-American War of 1848), newly acquired land became a part of the public domain and was managed by the federal government.

61

For the first century of our nation's existence, federal ownership was perceived as merely temporary and prevailing U.S. policy was to get land into hands of private settlers for the purpose of developing the country. Best known of the federal land disposal policies was the Homestead Act of 1862. After laying claim to 160 acres and paying a small registration fee, an individual could gain clear ownership of this land after five years by living on the land and making improvements. Through homestead laws and other land disposal policies, more than 285 million acres of land were claimed by individuals and families and resulted in farms and communities being established throughout the country. Through such policies, the majority of land east of the Rocky Mountains was in private ownership by the end of the nineteenth century. However, vast tracts of western land, primarily the mountains and deserts, remained unclaimed by individuals as this land was perceived to be of little economic value, and it was virtually impossible to make a living on the 160 acres available to homesteaders.

In the latter decades of the nineteenth century, the federal government became more involved in management of federal lands, and in some cases it became apparent that federal management was becoming more than just temporary. In 1872, Congress made its first important reservation of public land by creating Yellowstone National Park. Some two million acres of federal land were withdrawn from settlement and sale and dedicated as a public park "for the pleasure and recreation of the people." Within a few decades, other areas such as Sequoia and Yosemite were preserved as national parks.

By the late nineteenth century, there was also a growing awareness of the need for conservation resulting from concerns that federal lands were being exploited. Prior to this time, there was little apprehension about exploitation of resources in general or public lands in particular. American views of land and nature were tempered by what Stewart Udall (1963) called "The Myth of Superabundance." This myth was based on assumptions that the supply of resources was infinite and thus wise management was superfluous. This worldview was a consequence of early Americans finding themselves on a vast continent with seemingly endless resources. Trees could be cut down, minerals extracted, and topsoil eroded, but there were always more of these resources just over the next hill. Then, the 1890 census declared that the frontier was closed. Suddenly, what once seemed to be an endless supply of resources now seemed limited and calls for more effective management of federal lands grew more persistent. By the late 1800s, federal lands were being exploited by indiscriminate harvesting of timber, widespread and unrestrained grazing of cattle and sheep, and uncontrolled removal of minerals, all for private use and gain. In effect, federal lands were being treated as a vast "Tragedy of the Commons." Public concerns led to creation of four major agencies to manage federal land.

United States Forest Service

By the closing decades of the nineteenth century, there was growing public concern that existing logging patterns would result in American timber supplies eventually becoming depleted. This concern was fueled by the shocking speed at which Great Lakes forests had become exhausted. Logging companies would move to old-growth forests, which were often on publically owned land, remove the best trees, and then move elsewhere, leaving the land scarred and eroded and the ground covered with stumps, culls, and dead limbs that provided prime conditions for devastating fires (Hays 2009). As a consequence, an 1891 act gave the president the right to set aside land covered with timber as public reservations as a way of protecting these lands from indiscriminate harvest. While authorizing establishment of forest reserves, the act made no provision for their management and use. The 1897 Organic Administration Act stated that forest reserves were to be administered to improve and protect their water flow and to assist in furnishing a continuous supply of timber for the use of the citizens of the United States. Still, no agency or management approach was established. A strong critic of the way forest reserves were being managed was Gifford Pinchot. Largely as a result of his persistent efforts, and with the support of President Theodore Roosevelt, the United States Forest Service was created in 1905, with Gifford Pinchot as first director. Working together, Pinchot and Roosevelt were able to have 194.5 million acres set aside as Forest Service land by the time Roosevelt left office.

In addition to getting extensive amounts of land placed under management of the Forest Service, Pinchot and Roosevelt were instrumental in establishing the Forest Service's philosophy and mode of operation. Both Pinchot and Roosevelt were conservationists—they believed that land and its resources should be used, but used wisely. They felt that the way to avoid exploitation and deterioration of land was through involved federal management. They fought and succeeded in having the Forest

Service housed in the Department of Agriculture. Pinchot saw forestry as a practical agricultural science. He stated "Forestry is tree farming…to grow trees as a crop is Forestry. Trees may be grown as a crop just as corn may be grown as a crop" (Robinson 1975: 9). Thus, trees were to be grown on Forest Service land with the goal that those trees would someday provide timber for homes, schools, and farm buildings. It was also expected that timber would be grown sustainably so that trees would continue to be available for generations to come. "Sustained yield" has always been an important segment of Forest Service philosophy.

During the early years, the Forest Service placed heavy emphasis on wood production and livestock grazing and the primary goal was clearly resource development (Davis 2001). Through the years, however, other factors played an increasingly important role on the Forest Service agenda, often as a result of public pressure. The 1960 "Multiple Use Sustained Yield Act" institutionalized the policy that National Forests were to be administered for outdoor recreation, grazing, timber, watershed, and wildlife and fish purposes (Hays 2009; Nie 2008). When faced with choices about which use should be emphasized, the Forest Service would seek to provide "the greatest good for the greatest number." In ensuing decades, the Forest Service proceeded to develop management plans for their land. Individuals were able to obtain a permit to have a predetermined number of livestock graze on Forest Service land, and through a bidding process, individuals and companies could obtain rights to harvest timber. Minerals could be extracted from Forest Service lands by following provisions established by the 1872 Mineral Act. For the past century, numerous families have earned some or all of their income by harvesting timber or extracting minerals from Forest Service land, by having their cattle or sheep eat Forest Service forage, or by operating a motel or restaurant near the boundary of Forest Service land which catered to persons fishing, hunting, camping, or in other ways enjoying Forest Service amenities.

At the present time, the Forest Service operates 192.5 million acres of land, slightly less than when Roosevelt left office. (Some land that was part of the original Forest Service is now under private ownership or is managed by another federal agency.) About 85 percent of this land is in the thirteen western states (see Figure 4.1). Substantial amounts of land have been obtained through the years from the private sector; often cutover timberland that private owners no longer wanted. The states with the most Forest Service land include Alaska (22.0 million acres), California (20.7 million acres), Idaho (20.5 million acres), Montana (16.9 million acres), Oregon (15.7 million acres), and Colorado (14.5 million acres). Traditionally, travelling through Forest Service land, one was likely to see timber being harvested, cattle grazing, mining activities, and people hunting, fishing, camping, and hiking. Some major ski resorts are even found on Forest Service land.

The Forest Service now faces issues that differ widely from the concerns of previous eras (Nie 2008). Most significantly, through their early decades, Forest Service professionals were largely concerned with only a few commercially valuable species of trees, and perhaps some large mammals that were prized by hunters (Davis 2001). Today, a greater emphasis is placed on "ecological forestry" where managers are required to consider the consequences of their actions for thousands of species that inhabit the forests, including those with no apparent economic value (Hays 2009). Virtually every proposal for extractive uses of forest products is now challenged on ecological grounds. Consequently, the amount of timber harvested on national forest lands declined by 84 percent between 1986 and 2001. Thus, by 2001, timberlands under federal ownership accounted for only 2 percent of U.S. timber harvest (W. Smith et al. 2004). A high proportion of U.S. timber now comes from private lands in the South. In like manner, livestock grazing on Forest Service land is under pressure and in decline as a result of concerns that these activities have negative implications for the environment and biodiversity. For example, in 1998, conservation organizations and the Gila National Forest signed a legal agreement that excluded 15,000 cattle from 230 miles of rivers and streams across Arizona and New Mexico (Shepherd 2007). Reductions in logging and grazing often have significant consequences for western rural communities that were economically dependent on natural resource based industries utilizing Forest Service land (LeMonds 2001).

In addition, millions of acres of Forest Service land have been set aside as congressionally designated wilderness areas. The Wilderness Act of 1964 provided Congress and the president the right to designate some federal land as wilderness. The Wilderness Act defines wilderness as land "where the earth and its community of life are untrammeled by man, where man himself is a visitor who does not remain...generally appears to have been affected primarily by the forces of nature, with the imprint of man's work substantially unnoticeable...has outstanding opportunities for solitude or a primitive and unconfined type of recreation." Wilderness land is generally administered by the federal agency that managed the land prior to its designation as wilderness.

Thus some wilderness is managed by each of the four major federal land management agencies.

As of 2008, there were 704 wilderness areas in the United States comprising 107.5 million acres. About 53.3 percent (57.4 million acres) of wilderness land is in Alaska. About 35.5 million acres of Forest Service land is designated wilderness. Thus, one-third of the land in the wilderness system is managed by the Forest Service, and 18 percent of all Forest Service land is designated as wilderness. The Forest Service manages 419 wilderness areas. The majority (84 percent) of Forest Service wilderness land is in the contiguous forty-eight states, with the remaining 16 percent in Alaska. Initially, most wilderness on Forest Service land consisted of high alpine areas comprised primarily of rock and ice. While often extremely beautiful, these areas generally had limited value for timber, grazing, or other economically productive uses. Recently, areas with commercially valuable trees or other potentially valuable resources have been designated as wilderness, often with considerable controversy (Hays 2007). In many ways, wilderness has become more valuable as potential wilderness lands become scarcer and civilization becomes more abundant.

National Park Service

During the summer of 1870, an expedition led by Henry Washburn and Nathaniel Langford and escorted by U.S. Army Lt. Gustavus C. Doane, was nearing completion of an exploration of the Yellowstone area in what is now the northwestern corner of Wyoming. According to longstanding Park Service lore, the company was camped at Madison Junction where the Firehole and Gibbon Rivers join to form the Madison River. While sitting around a campfire one evening, the group was discussing the spectacular sights they had seen and agreed to recommend to congress that the area be preserved as a public park. Less than two years later, U.S. Congress designated more than two million acres as Yellowstone National Park, the world's first national park.

It is now evident that the motives of the Washburn and Langford group weren't purely altruistic. In fact, the Northern Pacific Railroad had employed Langford and funded part of the expedition. The railroad felt that the Yellowstone area had the possibility of becoming a popular tourist destination and they could then profit from transporting tourists in and out of Yellowstone. For this to happen, however, it was essential that the

Yellowstone, the world's first national park. *Don E. Albrecht*

area remain open and not fall into private hands. Thus, capitalists and the profit motive did play a role in the creation of the first national park.

Regardless of motives, the United States had created a national park, something completely unknown to the world at that time. In time, other national parks, such as Yosemite and Sequoia, were created. At times the parks were protected by the military, and at other times they were largely left unprotected. With no plan or consistent policy, some parks permitted livestock grazing, some allowed mining, and others the harvesting of timber. It was forty-four years after the creation of Yellowstone that the National Park Service was finally created in 1916. The Park Service was created after the Hetch Hetchy controversy (Chapter Three) made the lack of direction apparent. In many ways, the Park Service was created as a reaction to the Forest Service and from the very beginning the purposes and direction of national parks were very different from Gifford Pinchot's Forest Service. The Park Service's emphasis was on preservation rather than conservation. The philosophical basis for National Parks came from the views of transcendentalists such as Ralph Waldo Emerson and Henry David Thoreau who believed that some untrammeled wilderness should be set aside where individuals could escape from civilization and even become closer to God. There was no attempt for multiple use, sustained yield, or greatest good for the greatest number. The goal of the Park Service was to preserve nature and history unimpaired for the enjoyment of future generations. The Park Service was the culmination of the dreams of John Muir and other preservationists who desired that especially high quality areas be preserved to be enjoyed as nature had created them.

Once established, the National Park Service was housed in the Department of the Interior. By 2008, the National Park Service managed about seventy-nine million acres, 91.2 percent of which are in the thirteen western states (see Figure 4.1). About fifty-five million acres of NPS land is in Alaska. The best known of the entities managed by the National Park Service are the fifty-eight national parks, which include the large and spectacular parks such as Yellowstone, Grand Canyon, and Yosemite. Thirty-nine of these parks are in the thirteen western states. There are numerous other entities under park service management—391 units in all—including seventy-four national monuments (such as Rainbow Bridge in Utah and Canyon de Chelley in Arizona), twenty-four national battlefields and military parks (such as Gettysburg and Shiloh), twenty national preserves (such as Mojave in California and Bering Land Bridge in Alaska), ten national seashores (such as Canaveral in Florida and Padre Island in Texas), and eighteen national recreation areas (such as Lake Mead in Nevada and Arizona and Glen Canyon in Arizona and Utah). The NPS manages the White House and National Mall in Washington, DC, Ellis Island and the Statue of Liberty in New York, and numerous other natural and historic sites.

In addition, the National Park Service manages fifty-six wilderness areas and over 43.5 million acres of wilderness land. About 76 percent of National Park Service wilderness is in Alaska where the NPS manages eight very large wilderness areas, which combined have almost 33 million acres. The Wrangell-Saint Elias Wilderness, with over nine million acres, larger than the State of Maryland, is the nation's largest wilderness area.

The National Park Service is confronted with numerous troubling issues in the global society. While their goal is to preserve nature and history unimpaired, they are attempting to do so in a flawed world that makes accomplishing this goal virtually impossible. Nature does not recognize the artificial boundaries of national parks. Animals move freely in and out of parks, and events occurring outside of Park Service boundaries have profound effects on plants and animals living within the park. Perhaps only in the very large national parks of Alaska where an entire ecosystem is within a single park is the goal of preserving the environment unimpaired possible.

Further, allowing people to enjoy the parks while leaving them unimpaired are goals that are in direct opposition to one another. Roads, trails, and lodges that allow people to enjoy the park can disrupt biotic communities within the park. Numerous controversies have arisen over whether emphasis should be placed on preservation of resources or allowing people to enjoy these resources. Historically, the NPS prioritized its public use obligation over preservation as a way to build a supportive constituency. Thus, the Park Service had a cozy relationship with the railroad industry, made a concerted effort to eliminate wolves, suppressed fire, and introduced exotic fish and game species (Nie 2008). Recently, the emphasis has changed. An example is the controversy over snowmobile use in Yellowstone National Park. The Clinton administration decided to ban snowmobiles and stated that when there is a conflict between conserving resources and providing for the enjoyment of the resource, conservation is to be the primary concern. The Bush administration then allowed snowmobiles back into Yellowstone, arguing that the primary beneficiaries of the parks should be the visitors and businesses that serve them.

Bureau of Land Management

By the early decades of the twentieth century, millions of acres of public domain remained largely unmanaged. By this time the U.S. Forest Service had been created and was managing millions of acres of land that had at least some forest cover. The National Park Service had been created to manage some of the truly spectacular areas. For decades, individuals and families had been given opportunities to homestead public land. Yet millions of acres remained in the public domain unclaimed by individuals and other federal agencies. It seemed that this was land that nobody wanted. In some respects, the public domain was under the direction of the General Land Office which had been created in 1812, primarily to oversee the Homestead Acts and the sale of public land to the general public. The role of the General Land Office in actual management of public domain land was minimal. Again, because of concern for abuse of and subsequent deterioration of these public lands, the U.S. Grazing Service was created in 1934 by the Taylor Grazing Act for the purpose of managing the public domain as described in Chapter Two. Twelve years later, in 1946, the Bureau of Land Management was created through the merger of the General Land Office and the U.S. Grazing Service. At this time, the option of homesteading public land was largely eliminated.

The Bureau of Land Management is housed in the Department of the Interior and now has management responsibility for over 260 million acres, more than any other federal agency. More than 40 percent of federally owned land in the United States is managed by the BLM and more than 99 percent of BLM land is in the thirteen western states (see Figure 4.1). The states with the largest amounts of BLM land include Alaska (86 million acres), Nevada (47.9 million acres), Utah (22.9 million acres), Wyoming (18.4 million acres), Oregon (16.1 million acres), and California (15.1 million acres). More than two-thirds of all land in Nevada is managed by the BLM.

Obviously to have remained unclaimed for so long, most BLM lands were thought to lack traditional natural resources that would have put them in high demand during the isolation era. These lands are generally characterized by grassland, high mountain forests, arctic tundra, and desert. Later and more careful examination, however, has found some BLM lands with exceptional qualities. Extensive amounts of minerals and energy resources have been found on BLM land, and some lands are used for timber, grazing, hunting, camping, and fishing. There are significant archaeological, paleontological, and historical sites on BLM land. BLM lands represent some unique ecosystems, critical biodiversity, and provide homes for species found nowhere else. Some national monuments are managed by the BLM such as Grand Staircase Escalante National Monument in southern Utah created by President Bill Clinton in 1996. There are also 190 wilderness areas on BLM land covering about 7.8 million acres, all of it in the contiguous forty-eight states. Just over 7 percent of the nation's wilderness is on BLM land. The BLM also has responsibility for about 700 million acres of subsurface mineral estate, including minerals on tribal lands. In 2007, revenue from BLM mineral leasing activities generated an estimated $4.5 billion, about one-half of which was returned to the state where the minerals were mined.

As with other federal agencies, significant issues confront the BLM in the global society era. The primary reason for the creation of the BLM was to manage grazing on public lands. Like the Forest Service, the BLM is now charged with maintaining the ecological integrity and biodiversity of their lands and serious challenges are being made relative to continued livestock grazing (Holechek 2001). The Federal Land Policy Management

Act of 1976 states that BLM lands are to be managed for "Multiple Use Sustained Yield." Now extensive controversy surrounds agency land use decisions. Arguments on one side of the livestock grazing controversy maintain that removal of livestock is essential to retain ecosystem integrity and biodiversity. On the other side, individuals, families, and communities are economically dependent on livestock grazing on public lands and it is argued that livestock grazing is an important management tool to address invasive species and other issues.

U.S. Fish and Wildlife Service

During the last few decades of the nineteenth century, two federal programs were created to help stem declines of the nation's fish and wildlife resources. The U.S. Commission on Fish and Fisheries in the Department of Commerce was created by Congress in 1871 to find solutions to declining populations of food fishes. Then in 1885, the Division of Economic Ornithology and Mammalogy in USDA was created by Congress to help stop declining bird and mammal populations. This division was later named the Bureau of Biological Survey. In 1939, these two agencies were combined and moved to the Department of the Interior and were named the Fish and Wildlife Service.

Through the years, several important decisions were made to define and strengthen the role of the Fish and Wildlife Service. In 1903, President Theodore Roosevelt created the first Federal Bird Reservation on Pelican Island, Florida, in an attempt to protect the habitat of species of birds whose populations were in serious decline largely because the feathers were being widely used in women's hats. The Bureau of Biological Survey was given management responsibility for this reservation. Other reservations followed, and in 1942 these reservations were designated as "National Wildlife Refuges." The 1937 Pittman-Robertson Act provided funding for improvement of wildlife habitat, wildlife management research, and distribution of information. In 1973, the Endangered Species Act was passed and the Fish and Wildlife Service was given responsibility for administering this act. In 1980 the Alaska National Interest Lands Conservation Act dramatically increased the size of the National Wildlife Refuge System by adding over 53 million acres of land to the system. Finally, the National Wildlife Refuge System Improvement Act of 1997 provided mandates for management of National Wildlife Refuge land. This act establishes a hierarchal priority for use in each refuge (Nie 2008).

Top priority is protection of the species or habitat for which the refuge was created. The second priority is resource conservation, followed by wildlife-dependent recreation such as hunting and fishing. All of these uses come before other recreational uses or other economic activities.

By the early twenty-first century, the National Wildlife Refuge System included 548 refuges with involvement in all 50 states. Over 96 million acres of land are included within the system, with 88.8 percent of the land located in the 13 western states. Over 80 percent of the land managed by the U.S. Fish and Wildlife Service is in Alaska (see Figure 4.1). There is tremendous diversity from one refuge to another. Some refuges are extremely small (only a few acres) while others are very large. For example, the Arctic National Wildlife Refuge in Alaska is 19.2 million acres and the Yukon Delta National Wildlife Refuge, also in Alaska, is 19 million acres. These two units combined are larger than the State of Georgia. Some of the refuges are extensively managed. The San Luis National Wildlife Refuge in California is intensively managed through an intricate canal system to produce optimum wetland systems. In contrast, nearly 21 million acres of Wildlife Refuge System land are a part of the Wilderness Preservation System, and are managed in a manner where the human footprint is extremely limited. Most of the National Wildlife Refuge System Wilderness is in Alaska.

Like other federal land management agencies, the U.S. Fish and Wildlife Service deal with significant and controversial issues. The question of whether or not to pump oil from the Arctic National Wildlife Refuge has been a significant issue in national political campaigns. Without question, the Endangered Species Act is among the most powerful and controversial legislations that impact rural development in the West. Decisions made by the U.S. Fish and Wildlife Service relative to the northern spotted owl, delta smelt, and other species have had major implications for many rural western communities.

Conclusions

There is no doubt that public land decisions will be very controversial during the global society era (Kemmis 2001). Some reasons why were outlined by Nie (2008). He mentioned that in many cases the costs or benefits of decisions are not evenly distributed. For example, with the Endangered Species Act, costs of saving a species fall very heavily on the few that are economically dependent on the effected resource. In addition, checkerboard patterns where private and state-owned lands are dispersed within federal land create a management nightmare. Often the particular issue being fought over is only a surrogate for much larger issues, and both sides tend to use science in ways that confuse both the courts and general public. Finally, reduced federal spending has put severe restraints on all land management agencies as they endeavor to meet management objectives. In the chapters that follow, the significant role of these federal land management agencies on community development in the rural West will be apparent.

CHAPTER FIVE

Western Water

D r. Ismail Serageldin, former vice president of the World Bank, famously stated in 1995, "If the wars of this century were fought over oil, the wars of the next century will be fought over water." Water is a resource that is absolutely essential for life; yet in the modern world demand for water is growing while water resources remain constant. In addition, escalating levels of pollution make the water supplies available for human use ever more inadequate (Pearce 2006). Water concerns are especially troubling in the West where a lack of water has impacted human settlement from the beginning. It is no wonder that resource issues in general, and water issues in particular, emerged as a major concern during the rural development roundtables.

Western Water and Agriculture

Throughout the isolation era, agriculture was the biggest employer of American workers, but the lack of water placed severe limitations on farming in the West. Consequently, Herculean efforts and vast sums of money were spent to increase the availability of scarce water supplies for agriculture (Schulte 2002). At one level results seem rather impressive. By the global society era, hundreds of dams had been constructed to store water, thousands of miles of canals built to carry this water to farmers' fields, and millions of acres of farmland were under irrigation (Clark 2009).

Yet at another level, agriculture's toehold in the West seems rather precarious. One day while driving across the Arizona desert, I crossed a canal. This canal was carrying water from some distant source to farmers' fields and perhaps to other municipal and industrial uses. The canal was obviously not intended to provide life along its path, but simply to transport this life-giving water as efficiently as possible to its intended destination. Much of the canal was cement-lined to avoid water loss to seepage, and also to prevent plants from growing along the banks, which might then extract some of the precious liquid. Thus, there were no green

Canal across the Arizona desert. *Don E. Albrecht*

plants along the banks of the canal. There were no fish or ducks or other animals splashing in the cool water. There were no fisherman standing on the bank, nor were there any families camped by the water's edge. Other than me, no one was taking pictures of the scenery. In fact, the canal was nothing more than a line of blue water surrounded by the reds and browns of the desert.

After driving a few more miles, I reached the agricultural fields that were the destination of some of the canal's water. The transition from desert to irrigated farmland was profound. The irrigated fields were luxuriant and the corn was tall and green. Yet, mere feet from the fields, where the irrigation water did not reach, there was barely a living plant anywhere and the desert stretched to the far horizon. The absolute dependence of crop production agriculture in the arid West on irrigation water was striking. Take away the life-giving irrigation water for even a few weeks and the corn would wilt in the blistering desert sun; remove the water for a season and the land would quickly be reclaimed by the desert. From the luxuriant cornfields in the Arizona desert, one can drive for hours and see no other signs of viable agriculture and little evidence of human habitation.

Highway 93, known as the Great Basin Highway, enters Nevada from Arizona at the Hoover Dam. The highway then goes north to Las Vegas and merges with northbound Interstate 15 for the next twenty miles. From this point, Highway 93 separates from I-15 and traverses much of the length of the Great Basin from south to north. The Great Basin is a vast desert area where none of the rivers have an outlet to the sea. The few meager Great Basin streams, many of which are seasonal, meander through the desert until they either simply expire or empty into a lake. Many of these lakes are dry for much of the year and others are salty. Driving north, mile after mile of vast, sagebrush-covered valleys surrounded by rugged mountains are all that is visible. The vast majority of the Great Basin is federally managed, and large portions are under the control of the Bureau of Land Management. On rare occasions along the highway are headquarters of a ranch where there is a home, some outbuildings, and often a small amount of irrigated farm land where winter feed is grown for the cattle. Most of the cattle spend much of the year grazing on surrounding federal land. Such ranches are rare because there are few places with sufficient water.

About every two hours or so is a community large enough to provide an opportunity to fill a car with gas, find a place to eat, and even get a motel room. The first such community, Caliente, had a population of 1,130 in 2010 and is about 130 miles from the I-15 turnoff. The next significant community, 135 miles later, is Ely, population 4,255. Wells (population 1,292) is 139 miles beyond Ely. Beyond Wells is another 70 miles of Great Basin Desert. Finally, after 470 miles and encountering three communities with populations over 1,000 people, is the State of Idaho. Very little changes for the next twenty-five miles or so, and then suddenly travelers reach a region where there are miles of productive farms and vibrant communities. Forty-seven miles from the Nevada/Idaho border is Twin Falls, Idaho, with a population of over 40,000. Why the sudden transition? The answer of course is water. Just beyond the Idaho border is the Snake River Valley where significant amounts of irrigation water are removed from the Snake River to transform parts of southern Idaho into some of the most productive agricultural regions in the country. Snake River Valley farms are especially famous for their potatoes. The transition is abrupt. After 500 miles of few towns and a very low population density, a land of productive farms and vibrant communities appear as soon as water is available. Even then, farms and communities are dependent on major dams and canals to make the water usable. The city of Twin Falls did not exist until the early years of the twentieth century when a Bureau of Reclamation project made Snake River water available to irrigate previously parched land (Pisani 2002).

On another occasion I had a window seat on a flight from the East Coast to the Intermountain West. From the plane I watched the green and fertile fields of the Midwest gradually become browner and more arid until the only green was in the round circles of center-pivot irrigated agriculture. As we moved further west, the ground became much more rugged and agricultural production was soon limited to widely scattered green strips along river valleys where the land was flat enough to farm and irrigation water was available. Eventually my view consisted of soaring, snow covered mountains that were followed by a rugged red and brown desert landscape where I could see no evidence of human life. These experiences again made it obvious to me that water supplies are simply insufficient to transform the West into a vast agricultural paradise. Even if more water somehow became miraculously available, much of the land is still too harsh and rugged for agriculture. Many other people have made that same claim. More than a century ago in 1893, John Wesley Powell, who years earlier had explored the Green and Colorado Rivers by raft, stated, "When all the rivers are used, when all the creeks in the ravines, when all the brooks, when all the springs are used, when all the reservoirs along the streams are used, when all the canyon waters are taken up... when all the wells are sunk or dug that can be dug in all this arid region, there is still not sufficient water to irrigate all this arid region." Wallace Stegner (1992) wrote "We can't create water or increase the supply. We can only hold back and redistribute what there is. If rainfall is inadequate, then streams will be inadequate, lakes will be few and sometimes saline, underground water will be slow to renew itself when it has been pumped down, the air will be very dry, and surface evaporation from lakes and reservoirs will be extreme."

Table 5.1 shows that in 2007, there were nearly 25 million acres of land under irrigation in the thirteen western states, which was 44 percent of all irrigated acreage in the United States. Just over eight million acres were irrigated in California, more any other state except Nebraska, which had 8.6 million acres irrigated. Over one million acres were also irrigated in Idaho (3.3 million), Colorado (2.9 million), Montana (2.0 million), Oregon (1.8 million), Washington (1.7 million), Wyoming (1.6 million), and Utah (1.1 million). The value of the crops produced from irrigated farms in the West accounts for billions of dollars.

Table 5.1 Irrigated Agriculture and Agricultural Production in the Western States, 2007

State	Total Land Area (1,000 acres)	Total Land in Farms (Acres)	Percent	Harvested Cropland (Acres)	Percent of Total Land Harvested	Percent of Farm Land Harvested	Irrigated Acres	Percent of Harvested Cropland Irrigated	Total Crop Sales ($1,000)	Total Farm Sales ($1,000)
Alaska	365,482	881,585	0.2	30,772	0.0	3.5	3,730	12.1	24,749	57,019
Arizona	72,688	26,117,899	35.9	832,406	1.1	3.2	876,158	105.3	1,913,014	3,234,552
California	100,207	25,364,695	25.3	7,633,173	7.6	30.1	8,016,159	105.0	22,903,021	33,885,064
Colorado	66,486	31,604,911	47.5	5,888,926	8.9	18.6	2,867,957	48.7	1,981,399	6,061,134
Hawaii	4,106	1,121,329	27.3	103,120	2.5	9.2	58,635	56.9	429,916	513,626
Idaho	52,933	11,497,294	21.7	4,225,786	8.0	36.8	3,299,889	78.1	2,324,789	5,688,765
Montana	93,271	61,388,462	65.8	9,163,867	9.8	14.9	2,013,167	22.0	1,273,721	2,803,062
Nevada	70,264	5,865,392	8.3	504,311	0.7	8.6	691,030	137.0	219,341	513,269
New Mexico	77,766	43,238,049	55.6	1,009,683	1.3	2.3	830,048	82.2	553,140	2,175,080
Oregon	61,599	16,399,647	26.6	3,037,261	4.9	18.5	1,845,194	60.8	2,976,087	4,386,143
Utah	52,697	11,094,700	21.1	964,702	1.8	8.7	1,134,144	117.6	372,396	1,415,678
Washington	42,694	14,972,789	35.1	4,387,169	10.3	29.3	1,735,917	39.6	4,754,898	6,792,856
Wyoming	62,343	30,169,526	48.4	1,536,240	2.5	5.1	1,550,723	100.9	213,808	1,157,535
WEST TOTAL	1,122,536	279,716,278	25.0	39,317,416	3.5	14.1	24,922,751	63.4	39,940,279	68,683,783
(Percent)	49.3	30.3		12.7			44.0		27.7	23.1
REMAINDER OF U.S.	1,152,807	642,379,562	55.7	270,290,185	23.4	42.1	31,676,554	11.7	103,872,834	228,536,698
(Percent)	50.7	69.7		87.3			56.0		72.3	76.9
U.S. TOTAL	2,275,343	922,095,840	40.6	309,607,601	13.6	33.6	56,599,305	18.3	143,813,113	297,220,481

Source: United States Department of Agricultue, Census of Agriculture

Because of the lack of water, the proportion of land devoted to agriculture in general, and harvested cropland in particular, is much lower in the West compared to the rest of the country (see Table 5.1). Nearly 50 percent of the land area in the United States is in the western states. However, the proportion of western land in farmland (25 percent) is much smaller than the remainder of the country (55.7 percent). Primarily because of a lack of water, a larger proportion of western farmland is used for grazing and pasture and a much smaller percent is in harvested cropland. Only 3.5 percent of the total land and 14.1 percent of farmland in the western United States is harvested. In comparison, 23.4 percent of the total land and 42.1 percent of farmland in the rest of the country is in harvested cropland.

It is also apparent from Table 5.1 that in much of the West, crop production is almost totally dependent on irrigation. In five states (Nevada, Utah, Arizona, California, and Wyoming) the number of acres irrigated exceeds the number of acres harvested, indicating that in some places even grazing and pasture land is irrigated. Only in Montana and Colorado, where crops are grown on the Great Plains in eastern parts of the states, and in the Pacific Northwest states of Washington and Oregon, where some portions of the state have more abundant rainfall, is there a significant amount of cropland without irrigation. Overall, 63.4 percent of western harvested cropland is irrigated, compared to only 11.7 percent in the rest of the country.

It is also relevant to note that per acre production of crops is significantly greater on irrigated compared to non-irrigated land. With irrigation, water can be applied in the amount desired and at the time it is most needed. Irrigation also greatly reduces the potential of a complete crop failure as a result of insufficient rainfall or because rain comes at the wrong time. Additionally, with a supportive climate, crops with greater per acre value can be produced with irrigation. Thus, while only 12.7 percent of the nation's harvested cropland is in the western states, because it is extensively irrigated, this land produces 27.7 percent of the market value of crops. Nationwide, only 16 percent of cropland is irrigated, but this cropland produces 50 percent of the crops sold. Widespread irrigation and a supportive climate made California the nation's most productive agricultural state in 2007 with farm sales of $33.9 billion. Other leading western agricultural states were Washington ($6.8 billion), Colorado ($6.1 billion), Idaho ($5.7 billion), and Oregon ($4.4 billion), all states with large amounts of irrigation.

While irrigation is used to produce extremely high value crops in California and a few other places where the climate permits, circumstances are very different in the high elevations of the Intermountain West. Short cool summers and long cold winters are not conducive to producing high-value fruits and vegetables. Thus a majority of irrigated land in these areas is used to produce alfalfa, which is then employed to feed livestock. Many agricultural enterprises in the Intermountain West consist of cattle or sheep that graze on public land during part of the year, and then are fed alfalfa during the winter months. Economic return for each acre-foot of water used on these farms is small compared to a farm producing strawberries or similar high-value crops in California's Central Valley; thus the continued economic viability of this type of agriculture is questionable.

Societal changes are resulting in increased demand for scarce water resources from other sectors, which can often afford to pay more for water. These changes make it very likely that the amount of irrigated farmland in the West will shrink rather than grow in the years to come (CAST 1988). As water is diverted from agriculture to other uses, more green fields will disappear, and more families will have to find other ways of making a living. While the loss of farm production in some areas may not be significant in the overall scheme of feeding the world's population, these farms do contribute to the vitality of rural communities and to the livelihood of families who live on them (see Hussa 2009). Additionally, numerous rural communities throughout the West emerged when irrigation became feasible and to varying degrees these communities remain economically dependent on irrigated agriculture. In the global society era, survival of family farms is heavily dependent on economically viable rural communities that provide off-farm employment opportunities, as 83 percent of farm family income comes from non-farm sources.

It is expected that the world's population will exceed nine billion people by 2050. Highly productive irrigated agriculture in parts of the West may be needed to play a significant role in feeding this growing population, especially if larger amounts of agricultural land are diverted from food production to energy production (Farm Foundation 2008). Within the United States, many people place a high priority on our nation remaining self-sufficient in food production, arguing that food security is homeland security (Family Farm Alliance 2008).

Western Water and Industrial and Municipal Uses

While early efforts to harness scarce water resources were focused on agriculture, demand for water from other sectors has increased significantly in recent decades. One major source of increasing water demand is population growth. The population of the western states has grown rapidly in recent decades, far outpacing growth rates in other parts of the country. As populations skyrocket, an increasing amount of water is needed for drinking, bathing, brushing teeth, flushing toilets, washing clothes and dishes, sprinkling lawns and gardens, for swimming pools and other recreational purposes, and for industry. Per-person consumption of water has increased as growing prosperity allows families to live in larger homes with bigger lots and to be involved in more water consumptive activities. The size of the average new home in the United States has doubled since 1970 while the number of people living in these homes has declined. In 1920, average density in cities, suburbs, and towns in the United States was ten persons per acre. By 1990, average density had dropped to four persons per acre (McKibben 2007). Thus, more people are living in relatively more and larger homes that are located on larger lots. The obvious result is that more water is being consumed for residential purposes. A recent study of Phoenix, Arizona, residents found that water consumption increased as household income, home size, and lot size increased. Attitudes about water conservation were largely irrelevant and not related to water consumption (Harlan et al. 2009).

Meeting water needs of a growing population has been made even more challenging because population growth has been highest in more arid areas. For example, the population of Clark County (Las Vegas), Nevada, in the heart of the Mojave Desert, increased from 463,087 in 1980 to 1,951,269 in 2010, a 321 percent growth in just thirty years. Likewise, the population of Maricopa County (Phoenix), Arizona, in the heart of the Sonoran Desert, grew from 1,509,052 in 1980 to 3,817,117 in 2010, an increase of 153 percent.

For nearly a century, to meet growing urban water needs, cities have been securing water rights of sometimes distant rural areas and then transporting water from these rural areas to the city. In 1913, a 223-mile aqueduct was completed to transport water from Owens Valley to Los Angeles. The loss of this water severely crippled Owens Valley agriculture. When Owens Valley water was shipped to Los Angeles, Owens Lake dried up and resulting dust storms blowing from the lake bed have become a major environmental problem (Hundley 2001; Reisner 1993). Los Angeles and surrounding Southern California cities import significant amounts of water from the Colorado River and from areas in Northern California. Other western cities have followed suit and the process of diverting water from rural areas to meet urban needs has continued unabated. Like Los Angeles, other major cities such as Las Vegas, Phoenix, Salt Lake City, and Denver use their political clout, financial resources, and abundant lawyers to obtain water from outgunned rural areas. As desert cities continue to grow, they send out tentacles further and further away to find water for their continued growth. Thus the Central Arizona Project transports Colorado River water for hundreds of miles to Phoenix and Tucson, where much of it is then used to keep suburban lawns and world class golf courses green and even to support one of the world's tallest fountains, where water is shot more than 500 feet into the desert air. The Central Utah Project transports water from eastern Utah to Salt Lake City and the rapidly growing Wasatch Front. In each case, increasing the amount of water devoted to urban and industrial uses means that there is less water for agriculture or other potential uses (C. Miller 2009).

Western Water for Biodiversity and Amenities

In the mass society era, there have been profound changes in values, attitudes, and laws about how water should be used. At one time, few people questioned the HEP perspective that widespread efforts should be made to ensure that water is put to use in ways that benefit humans. Even "Prior Appropriation," the basis of western water law, assumes that water should be put to some "useful" purpose. Efforts to build dams and canals to store and transport water for agricultural and municipal uses were seldom questioned. Thus, the Grand Coulee Dam on the Columbia River was placed like a giant plug in the river with little concern for its effect on migrating salmon. Similarly, other water development projects were completed with little thought of biodiversity or amenity implications. Circumstances have changed in the global society era, and a much broader range of outcomes are considered before developments are undertaken. Now there is growing pressure to retain some rivers in their natural state, and to preserve wetlands and other habitat for fish and other aquatic species. Additionally, public pressure is exerted to ensure that water-related amenities are retained and to preserve water for recreational uses such as fishing, boating, water skiing, and rafting. As more water is retained for biodiversity and amenity purposes, less water is available for agriculture, industrial, and municipal uses.

Perhaps the conflict between the HEP-based uses of water and NEP-based efforts to protect water for biological habitat is nowhere more apparent than in controversy over the delta smelt in California (Tharp 2009). The delta smelt is a fish about two to three inches long and found only in the delta at the confluence of the San Joaquin and Sacramento Rivers. Smelt were once abundant, but their numbers have declined appreciably in recent years, largely as a result of declining water quality and fluctuating water levels as water is pumped from the delta and transported south for Central Valley agriculture and Southern California municipal uses. As their numbers continued to decline, delta smelt were declared threatened in 1993 by both the California Endangered Species Act and Federal Endangered Species Act, which required that action be taken to preserve smelt habitat. In consequence, water levels must be maintained in the delta even if water available for agriculture and municipal uses are reduced. Controversy is extensive as a large number of acres that are a part of a multibillion-dollar agriculture industry have been forced to become fallow for a largely unremarkable fish with virtually no economic value. The idea that science should guide water-use decisions continues to be challenged and some maintain that reduced pumping from the delta will not positively affect the smelt. Rather, they argue that pollution from urban sources and a dramatic growth in the number of non-native striped bass and large-mouth bass that prey on smelt and young salmon are responsible for their declining numbers (Keppen 2010).

The other side of the argument is the claim that the smelt is an indicator species and its condition reflects overall ecosystem health. At one point, the delta was a magnificent place, teeming with wildlife. Over decades, receding boundaries, drawing water for farms and cities from rivers that flow into the delta, and increasingly high levels of toxins have combined to drastically alter the ecosystem. Thus, the continuing use patterns that endangered the smelt place the entire delta ecosystem in a precarious situation (Zakin 2009).

One region where irrigation water reductions are profoundly felt is on the western side of Central Valley in Fresno and Kings Counties in an area managed by Westlands Water District. Westlands Water District was formed in 1952 with the goal of bringing a reliable supply of irrigation water to area farmers. At that time, most farming in the district consisted of cereal grains such as wheat and barley that could be grown in spring when the ground remained moist from winter rains, supplemented by irrigating with groundwater. In 1961, the federal government and State of California signed a joint-venture agreement to construct the San Luis Unit of the Central Valley Project. The project was completed in 1968 and the district began receiving irrigation water immediately thereafter. Irrigation water that comes to Westlands District is pumped from the Sacramento–San Joaquin Delta and then taken seventy miles through a canal to San Luis Reservoir. Water is then released from the reservoir as needed and delivered to farmers through two major canals. Once water leaves the canals, it is delivered through 1,034 miles of underground pipe directly to more than 600 farmers who then irrigate 610,000 acres of farmland in the district. The results of irrigation in Westlands Water District were dramatic. Farmers now grow more than sixty high-value crops including tomatoes, grapes, almonds, and pistachios. Water is costly and is used with great care with the most efficient irrigation technology available. An area farmer told me that every drop of water is used when and where it is needed with the precision of an eye-dropper. In the typical year, farm sales from the region exceed one billion dollars and thousands of agriculturally-based jobs are provided.

Then in 2009, Westlands District farmers received only ten percent of their allotment of water from the Delta as a consequence of efforts to protect smelt. As a result, 250,000 acres of extremely productive farmland were held out of production, and additional acres were planted into lower value crops that require less water. Estimates are that 20,000 farm jobs were lost, and area communities such as Mendota and Firebaugh had 30 to 40 percent unemployment. No question, the problem is complex.

Another major water use conflict has occurred along the Klamath River in Oregon and California. The Klamath River originates in Oregon, flows through the Cascade Mountains, and eventually empties into the Pacific Ocean in Northern California. Historically, the Klamath River was prime salmon habitat, and at one time vast marshes were found along the river. Throughout the twentieth century, dams were built and water was diverted for irrigated agriculture and other urban or municipal uses. Early in the twenty-first century, Native American tribes, environmentalists, and fisherman began pushing for removal of some dams to protect salmon, whose numbers have declined precipitously with development. In 2001, water for irrigated agriculture was temporarily halted to protect fish populations in the Klamath River.

While efforts are being made to get some dams removed for ecological purposes, other dams have already been removed, and still others are slated for removal (Clark 2009). For example, in the State of Washington, two dams along the Elwha River are being removed with the hope of restoring one of the state's legendary salmon rivers. Beginning in 2008, the 108-foot-tall Elwha Dam (completed in 1913) and the 210-foot-tall Glines Canyon Dam (completed in 1927) were torn down in stages, reopening seventy miles of prime salmon habitat. Such removal projects are costly and complicated. Dams hold vast amounts of water that can't all be turned loose at once, and several decades worth of silt, often laced with contaminants, are uncovered as water levels recede. Controversies such as these are likely to increase as the demand for scarce water resources increase.

Additional Problems Facing Western Water

Several emerging concerns make the water problems facing the West even more challenging. A few of these will be briefly described below.

Decline of the Hydrological System

A significant problem is the diminishing capacity of the western hydrological system. Donald Worster (1993) noted, "Reclamation cannot be indefinitely sustained. As the irrigation system approaches its maximum efficiency, as rivers get moved around with more and more thorough, consummate skills, the system begins to grow increasingly vulnerable, subject to a thousand ills that eventually bring about its decline. Despite all efforts to save the system, it breaks down here, then there, then everywhere." History is full of failing irrigation systems that led to decline of the societies that built them. Human-built structures age, decline, and fail. No one can doubt this after watching the levees in New Orleans collapse during Hurricane Katrina in 2005. In 1976, Bureau of Reclamation's Teton Dam in Idaho collapsed. Eighty billion gallons of water roared downstream, forcing 300,000 people to evacuate, killing eleven people, wiping entire small towns off the map, and causing nearly $1 billion in property damage. In spring 1983 after much heavier than normal precipitation, Lake Powell was filled to capacity and many have argued that Glen Canyon Dam was on the verge of failure. Powell (2008) explains, "High temperatures had begun to melt the late spring snowfall that blanketed the western slopes of the Rocky Mountains, sending half a million gallons each second rushing down the length of the Colorado River into Lake Powell. The reservoir's two giant spillways, designed to convey high water around the dam and discharge it harmlessly below, had begun to crumble. Water entering the spillways was as clear as glass, but, emerging below the dam, the water had turned red. Chunks of concrete—some the size of a Volkswagen—shot out with the red spillway discharge. Evidently, water under high pressure was eroding through the concrete spillway linings and into the rust-colored bedrock below, the same bedrock that held up the massive dam." The dam survived this crisis, but Glen Canyon or other dams in other locations at other times may not. When dams fail the consequences are generally catastrophic.

An additional problem facing the western hydrological system is that erosion and subsequent siltation are steadily filling reservoirs and depleting their capacity. Siltation reduces the capacity of dams to store water or generate electricity. Eventually all reservoirs will fill up with mud and cease to function. Hundley (2001) writes that all reservoirs "will become vast bodies of mud crossed by rivers tumbling over dams transformed into waterfalls." Powell (2008) adds, "Most important, in the long run, what do the dam-builders have in mind when reservoirs fill with silt, as they inevitably must unless the law of gravity is repealed? What do we do when across the West are spread not beautiful blue-water lakes, but a hundred million acre-feet of mud, some of it laced with toxins? Where then will our successors go to get their water?" Replacing old dams will be most difficult in a climate of resistance and when nearly all of the best sites have been taken.

Water Quality

Irrigated agriculture faces persistent problems of salinization, or poisoning of water and soil by salt buildup (CAST 1988; Worster 1985). The severity of this problem is apparent from an examination of history. For example, it is widely believed that irrigated agriculture in ancient Mesopotamia resulted in increased salinization over time, which eventually caused production declines and collapse of a once-great civilization (Steward et al. 1955; Wittfogel 1957). All water, even fresh rainfall, has some level of salt content. When plants take up water they leave salt in the soil. When salt levels in soil become too high it becomes difficult for plants to thrive. Except in arid regions, there is generally enough rainfall to continually wash away excess salt from soils. Irrigation in arid regions can exacerbate soil salinization problems. By increasing the amount of water in an area, the water table often rises, bringing with it dissolved salts that then intrude on the root zone of plants. When this occurs, the only options are to decrease irrigation, which hurts production; to install expensive drainage systems to keep groundwater levels lower; or to increase irrigation levels to wash excess salt into rivers or streams. These later options then increase salinization problems downstream. As a result of irrigation, salt levels in the Colorado River become progressively higher as one moves downstream and are now so high where the river crosses into Mexico that it has become a significant source of international contention. Desalinization plants have been constructed to improve water quality as the river enters Mexico. Throughout the west, many acres of once productive farmland have been lost to salinization, and there are no easy solutions to prevent even more land from being lost.

Irrigated agriculture can lead to severe pollution problems. Runoff from irrigated farms often becomes concentrated with extremely high levels of toxic chemicals from fertilizers and pesticides. The problem becomes most severe in areas where agricultural production is most intense. Contamination of Kesterson National Wildlife Refuge is one of several examples. The Kesterson wetlands were artificially created from drainage from irrigated agriculture in California's Central Valley. By 1983, large amounts of fertilizers and pesticides were draining from farms into these wetlands, resulting in high levels of selenium in the water that killed waterfowl and caused widespread birth deformities among young birds (Hundley 2001).

Water Quantity

Through the years, much discussion has focused on increasing the supply of western water. Approaches considered include transferring water from other places such as the Columbia River Basin or even Alaska. Estimated costs of such projects are prohibitive, and of course, other states are not thrilled about sending their water to California or other arid regions. Desalinization of ocean water is another suggested approach that at present is prohibitively expensive. Groundwater from underground aquifers has been used throughout the West to augment surface water supplies. An aquifer can be compared to a bank account with water in the aquifer analogous to money in the account. Aquifers develop over geologic time and water is removed much faster than it is being

Water quantity is a growing concern in the global society era. *Zack Guido*

recharged. In effect, we are withdrawing money from the bank without making subsequent deposits. Obviously, should this pattern continue, the account will eventually be empty. Las Vegas, Phoenix, Tucson, and other western cities have extensively exploited their groundwater resources, and as a result groundwater levels have declined from 300 to 500 feet (Bartolino and Cunningham 2003). An added problem is that in many cases, groundwater depletion has led to subsidence where the ground falls like a balloon when air is released. In some cases subsidence has exceeded six feet, resulting in damage to roads and buildings. Subsidence problems have been especially troubling in California's Central Valley where groundwater has been pumped to augment surface water used for irrigated agriculture (Reilly et al. 2008).

Perhaps the most ominous problem confronting western water supplies is global climate change (Hundley 2009; Powell 2010). Models generally indicate that climate change will result in less snowpack in western mountains as precipitation that traditionally fell as snow is now falling as rain and immediately running off (Wagner 2007). This means that much of the water comes to farmers and ranchers earlier than in the past, at times when it may not be useful and may even represent a threat. Higher temperatures associated with climate change will also result in increased evaporation. Likely resulting from climate change, the early years of the twenty-first century were very hot and dry in the western states, and snowfall and runoff were well below normal (Jenkins 2009). Three-year average flow in the Colorado River from 2001 to 2003 was only 5.4 million acre feet and, ending in 2009, the ten-year total flow was less than 100 million acre feet. This is far less than the 15 million acre feet per year that the 1922 Colorado River Compact is based upon. As a consequence, by early 2005, Lake Powell was only one-third full (Powell 2008). The end result is that future water needs will be greater than ever but water availability will be reduced (Family Farm Alliance 2007; Wagner 2003; C. Miller 2009).

Invasive Species

Invasive species are compromising rivers, irrigation, and water transport systems and consequently reducing scarce water supplies. Among the more problematic of invasive species is tamarisk or salt cedar, which has spread widely along water courses throughout the Intermountain West and Southwest. Tamarisk was intentionally imported to help solve erosion problems resulting largely from overgrazing along western streams. Without natural competitors and predators, tamarisk spread rapidly and now covers thousands of miles of streambed. Over time tamarisk has eliminated native trees and shrubs that once lined rivers and streams and disrupted habitat of everything from insects to fish and mammals. Invasive tamarisk draws vast amounts of water from streams in an already water scarce environment. Efforts to control tamarisk have proven most difficult. Thousands of hours of hard labor have been spent on attempts to chop, dig, or burn out tamarisk with only limited success. Recently a beetle imported from Kazakhstan, tamarisk leaf beetle, has been released in an attempt to combat spread of the unwanted invasive tree. This beetle fed on tamarisk in their native lands, and while initial results look promising, one always worries about the long-term implications of introducing another non-native species into the environment.

Conclusions

Throughout time, water scarcity has placed severe limitations on human settlement in the West. As the population of the western states increases there is a corresponding boost in water demand. Further, cultural changes have resulted in other water uses, such as amenities, recreation, and biodiversity preservation, receiving greater priority than in the past. As water supplies remain constant and demand grows, the West's future has never seemed so insecure. There are several approaches to assuage potential water problems that should be implemented. First, improved conservation is an absolute necessity. If all water users, from farmers to suburbanites, used water more efficiently, the amount of water available for everyone would increase. Residents of the West need to remember that they live in arid and semi-arid climates and act accordingly. Western water laws as currently constituted actually discourage conservation. For example, if a farmer has right to use four acre-feet of water, but then through implementation of more efficient irrigation techniques only needs two acre-feet, he faces the possibility of losing the right to the other two acre-feet. Based on prior appropriation water law, you have to use it or lose it and use rights are an economically valuable resource.

Some recent water conservation efforts appear promising. Between 2002 and 2007, Las Vegas saw its annual water use decline by eighteen billion gallons even as its population increased by 330,000. Declining water use was made possible by using recycled water for car washes, golf courses, hotels, and other ventures. Success was achieved by cash incentives to cooperating businesses and other consumers. Denver and Fort Collins, Colorado, decreased residential water use by 18 percent through voluntary conservation efforts (Hundley 2009). However, some research casts doubt on the effectiveness of voluntary programs or programs that simply encourage a change of attitudes. Research by Harlan et al. (2009) described earlier found that larger family incomes, larger homes, or larger lot sizes resulted in greater water consumption regardless of conservation attitudes. Thus, as long as we continue to live in larger homes on larger lots, water consumption is unlikely to decline very much.

Second, it is essential that all interested parties find a way to sit around the same table and collaborate. Historically, water laws and decisions about the distribution of water have been made in courts of law where the decisions are often unsatisfactory to everyone. Open dialogue may be a better approach because water scarcity is here to stay and we are all in this together. Collaborative approaches are described later in this book.

Fossil fuel energy production. *istockphoto.com*

CHAPTER SIX

Western Energy

Historically, the primary sources of energy for agriculture, transportation, and other endeavors were the physical efforts of humans and their domesticated animals. Wood and other forms of biomass were the major sources of heat for cooking and to keep homes warm. Limitations imposed by these energy forms obviously suppressed productivity and living standards. Transportation was slow, work was tedious, and productivity minimal. Further, a significant proportion of farm production was used to support work animals, and a substantial amount of time had to be devoted to gathering and chopping wood.

Much changed with emergence of the Industrial Revolution and the growing capacity of humans to harness and utilize fossil fuels as an energy source. Fossil fuels evolved from organisms that lived long ago and over time have become transformed into coal, oil, natural gas, or other products that burn easily and can be converted to energy. The capacity of humans to efficiently use fossil fuels as an energy source has completely transformed life for millions of people and has resulted in rapid economic growth. Fossil fuels power cars, trucks, trains, and planes and have dramatically increased transportation speed and capacity. Fossil fuels are used to operate farm equipment and factories and have greatly increased the work capacity of individuals. Machines have replaced work animals, and it is no longer necessary to devote farm acreage for support of these animals. Fossil fuels heat and cool our homes and provide electricity to keep the lights on and to operate our televisions, radios, and computers, and allow us to do so with the flip of a switch.

Table 6.1 provides data on international energy consumption. This table shows that in 2006, while the United States had only 4.6 percent of the world's population, Americans consumed 21.1 percent of the energy. The average American consumes twenty-one times more energy than the average African or person from India, six times more than the average Chinese, and twice as much as the average European (where in many countries incomes are as high or higher than in the United States). Energy consumption is also strongly related to gross domestic product.

Table 6.1. International Energy Consumption in 2006.

Region	Total Population (Millions)	Percent	Energy Consumption (Quadrillinon BTUs)	Percent	Per Capita Energy Consumption (Mllion BTUS)	BTUs per 2000 U.S. Dollars Using Purchasing Power Parities
North America	438.60	6.7	121.182	25.7	276.2	8,933
United States	298.36	4.6	99.856	21.1	334.6	8,841
Central and South America	456.21	7.0	24.176	5.1	53.3	7,283
Europe	593.64	9.1	86.422	18.3	146.2	6,536
Eurasia	284.60	4.4	45.880	9.7	160.8	20,137
Middle East	190.46	2.9	23.806	5.0	127.2	13,709
Africa	924.51	14.1	14.495	3.1	15.9	6,651
Asia & Oceania	3,649.36	55.8	156.313	33.1	42.8	9,241
World Total	6,537.37	100.0	472.274	100.0	72.4	8,874

Source: Energy Information Administration, U.S. Department of Energy

Generally, countries that consume the most energy have the highest GDPs. Table 6.1 shows, however, that Europeans are more efficient than Americans in that they produce more with less energy.

There are major concerns with our fossil fuel economy, and alternatives must be sought. Among the major problems associated with a fossil fuel economy are:

1. The inevitable depletion of a nonrenewable resource.
2. U.S. dependence on foreign energy.
3. Climate-changing greenhouse gasses.
4. Environmental consequences of fossil fuel extraction and transport.

Resource Depletion

Table 6.2 provides data on energy production and consumption in the United States from 1950 to 2011. Most significantly, this table shows that energy consumption increased greatly during this period. In 2011, Americans were consuming about three times more energy than in 1950. Some of this increase, of course, is a consequence of population growth. Extreme dependence of the United States on fossil fuels is also apparent. In 2011, 82.1 percent of energy consumed in the United States was from fossil fuels, 8.5 percent from nuclear power, and 9.4 percent from renewable energy sources. Also apparent from Table 6.2 is that the United States consumes significantly more energy than it produces and that until the last few years the gap between production and consumption was getting continually larger. This gap is made up by imports.

Table 6.3 provides a more detailed examination of fossil fuel production and consumption in the United States from 1950 to 2011. Coal (24.6 percent) and natural gas (31.1 percent) provided more than one-half of the energy from fossil fuels consumed in the United States in 2011. Coal is primarily used to generate electricity, and over one-half of electricity utilized in the United States is from coal. Natural gas is used widely in the industrial sector, to generate electricity, and for residential heating. From Table 6.3 it is apparent that the United States continues to be able to produce most of the coal and natural gas that is consumed. The country has significant coal deposits, and recent technological breakthroughs, such as hydraulic fracturing (fracking), have allowed production of natural gas from shale deposits. These breakthroughs have greatly increased available gas supplies and natural gas production in the United States (Yergin 2011). On the other hand, almost half (44.3 percent) of the fossil fuel energy

Table 6.2 Energy Production and Consumption by Source in the United States, 1950–2011 (Quadrillion BTU)

Year	Fossil Fuels		Nuclear		Renewable		Total	
	Production	Consumption	Production	Consumption	Production	Consumption	Production	Consumption
1950	32.563	31.632	0.000	0.000	2.978	2.978	35.540	34.616
1955	37.364	37.410	0.000	0.000	2.784	2.784	40.148	40.208
1960	39.869	42.137	0.006	0.006	2.929	2.929	42.804	45.087
1965	47.235	50.577	0.043	0.043	3.398	3.398	50.676	54.017
1970	59.186	63.522	0.239	0.239	4.076	4.076	63.501	67.844
1975	54.733	65.355	1.900	1.900	4.723	4.723	61.357	71.999
1980	59.008	69.826	2.739	2.739	5.485	5.485	67.232	78.122
1985	57.539	66.091	4.076	4.076	6.187	6.187	67.801	76.493
1990	58.560	72.333	6.104	6.104	6.208	6.208	70.872	84.654
1995	57.540	77.258	7.075	7.075	6.705	6.707	71.320	91.174
2000	57.366	84.733	7.862	7.862	6.262	6.260	71.490	98.975
2005	55.056	85.817	8.160	8.160	6.410	6.423	69.628	100.484
2011	60.601	79.779	8.259	8.259	9.236	9.135	78.096	97.301

Source: Energy Information Administration, U.S. Department of Energy

Table 6.3   Fossil Fuel Production and Consumption by Type in the United States, 1950–2011 (Quadrillion BTU)

Year	Coal Production	Coal Consumption	Natural Gas Production	Natural Gas Consumption	Petroleum Production	Petroleum Consumption
1950	14.060	12.347	6.233	5.968	12.270	13.315
1955	12.370	11.167	9.345	8.998	15.650	17.255
1960	10.817	9.838	12.656	12.385	16.396	19.919
1965	13.055	11.581	15.775	15.769	18.404	23.246
1970	14.607	12.265	21.666	21.795	22.913	29.521
1975	14.898	12.663	19.640	19.948	20.103	32.731
1980	18.598	15.423	19.908	20.235	20.503	34.202
1985	19.325	17.478	19.980	17.703	21.233	30.922
1990	22.488	19.173	18.326	19.603	17.746	33.553
1995	22.130	20.089	19.082	22.671	16.329	34.437
2000	22.735	22.580	19.662	23.824	14.969	38.264
2005	23.185	22.797	18.574	22.583	13.297	40.393
2011	22.181	19.643	23.506	24.843	14.914	35.283

Source: Energy Information Administration, U.S. Department of Energy

consumed in the United States in 2011 was from petroleum, most of which is derived from crude oil. The transportation sector uses about 71 percent of the petroleum consumed in this country, keeping approximately 250 million vehicles on the road. To put U.S. oil consumption into perspective, according to the Energy Information Administration, about 378 million gallons of gasoline are consumed each day—and this is not counting diesel, jet fuel, home heating oil, asphalt, plastics, and other uses of oil.

U.S. petroleum production reached a peak in 1970 and was on the decline until recent years (Table 6.3). This increased crude oil production is again a consequence of fracking. Prior to fracking, declining production was rather pronounced. In 2005 only 32.9 percent of petroleum consumed in this country was produced in the United States. As a consequence of recent production increases and consumption declines, by 2011 the United States was able to produce 42.3 percent of petroleum consumed. The gap between production and consumption is still considerable and thus the need for imports remains.

Table 6.4 makes reasons for declining U.S. oil production more apparent. This table shows that overall U.S. oil production increased until

1970 as discovery of new oil fields and improved technology pushed production to a high of 18.1 barrels per well per day. Since that time, per well production has declined significantly as oil resources have become depleted and wells in less productive locations have been brought on line. By 2008, per well production was averaging only 9.4 barrels per day. Again, there have been increases in recent years as a result of fracking.

The decline of U.S. oil production was initially offset by increased production from Alaska. In the 1960s, what proved to be the largest oil field in North America was discovered at Prudhoe Bay on the North Slope of Alaska. This oilfield originally had an estimated twenty-five billion barrels of oil. In 1975, construction began on an 800-mile pipeline to transport oil from Prudhoe Bay to Valdez, Alaska, the northernmost ice-free port in North America. The pipeline cost an estimated $8 billion to build and opened in 1977. Since that time, more than fifteen billion barrels of oil have been successfully transported. With the pipeline in place, Alaskan oil production reached a peak in 1988 at over two million barrels per day and has declined sharply with depletion of the Prudhoe Bay oil fields. In 2011, Alaskan oil production was down to 572,000 barrels per day.

In recent years, U.S. oil production has been enhanced by development of new technologies. Horizontal drilling and fracking have made it

Table 6.4   Crude Oil Production by Location and Average Productivity per Well in the United States, 1955–2011

Year	48 States	Alaska	Total	Average Well Productivity
	(Thousand Barrels Per Day)			(Barrels Per Day)
1955	6,807	0	6,807	13.0
1960	7,034	2	7,036	11.9
1965	7,774	30	7,804	13.2
1970	9,408	229	9,637	18.1
1975	8,183	191	8,374	16.8
1980	6,980	1,617	8,597	15.7
1985	7,146	1,828	8,974	13.9
1990	5,582	1,773	7,355	12.2
1995	5,076	1,484	6,560	11.4
2000	4,851	970	5,820	10.9
2005	4,314	864	5,178	10.4
2011	5,090	572	5.662	10.6

Source: Energy Information Administration, U.S. Department of Energy

economically feasible to produce "light tight" oil from shale formations. This same technology has also dramatically impacted natural gas production, which is discussed later. Utilization of these "unconventional" strategies has allowed development to occur in the Bakken and other shale formations. The Bakken Field is centered in North Dakota, but extends into Montana and Saskatchewan and Winnipeg, Canada. Resulting from the emergence of fracking, North Dakota oil production increased from 29 million barrels in 2003 to 153 million barrels in 2012. The Energy Information Administration projects that fracking will greatly increase U.S. energy production and thus reduce the need for energy imports.

Depletion of U.S. oil fields makes apparent the first problem of a fossil fuel-based economy: fossil fuels are not a renewable resource. Fossil fuels developed over geologic time, and when they are used, they are gone. The fossil fuels we use today will simply not be available for our children or grandchildren (Catton 1980). Resource depletion does not occur overnight. Rather, a process of "economic decline" occurs. As demand grows, efforts are made to locate additional supplies and to efficiently extract these resources. Discovery of previously unknown resources or technological breakthroughs which allow previously unusable supplies to be brought into production can increase supplies. Eventually as non-renewable resources are used, supplies necessarily dwindle. The cheapest supplies diminish first and then other more expensive and difficult to obtain supplies are brought into use. As this occurs, costs inevitably increase. Higher costs then put a damper on demand. Over time, increasingly expensive supplies will result in higher prices and demand will diminish. Eventually, costs will become so high that resource use will virtually discontinue. How much driving would the typical American do if gasoline cost four dollars, ten dollars, or 100 dollars a gallon?

As supplies diminish and costs increase, alternatives are sought. This includes fossil fuel supplies that were previously too costly to use and non-fossil fuel resources. The extent to which alternatives can be found is one of the great questions of our age. Thus far, the United States has been able to avoid extreme costs and other problems associated with resource depletion by importing oil from counties with greater supplies. However, when dealing with a finite resource, even international supplies must eventually become depleted, especially considering the rate at which fossil fuels are being used. In time, as costs increase, it may become cost effective to utilize oil shale and other products that are too expensive now. While these additional resources may postpone the inevitable, in time, even these resources will become depleted. Whether in fifty, one hundred, or one thousand years from now, our descendants are going to have to deal with the fact that we left them with a fossil fuel bag that is approaching empty. An economy based on fossil fuels has allowed extensive population growth. To what extent and at what level will we be able to support this population on other energy resources?

With respect to oil production and resource depletion, a common term is "peak oil." Peak oil is the date of maximum oil production. The United States reached "peak oil" in about 1970. When "peak oil" from a global perspective will be reached is a critical question that is influenced by new discoveries and technological breakthroughs.

Ever-increasing resource use obviously speeds up the resource depletion process. The world's population is growing and people are getting wealthier, both of which lead to increased consumption. Like Americans, as people around the world become wealthier, they desire to translate their higher incomes into an improved standard of living, which includes consumption of vastly greater amounts of energy. For example, with rapid economic growth, it is expected that incomes in China will achieve parity with the United States in about 2031. Today, the number of cars per capita in China is about the same as that in the United States in 1912. Assuming that Chinese citizens transform their new wealth into the same rates of car ownership as Americans, there would be more than twice as many cars in the world today. To show that this time is drawing closer, the number of cars purchased annually in China already surpasses the number of cars purchased in the United States (Yergin 2011). If Chinese were to drive these cars as much as Americans drive their cars, it would require all of the oil that the world currently produces, plus an additional fifteen million barrels per day, to make this possible. Then there is India, which has a population nearly as large as China and an economic growth rate not far behind (McKibben 2007). Obviously, something has to give.

Oil shale is a fossil fuel with massive reserves that may be a critical resource in the future. Oil shale generally refers to any sedimentary rock that contains solid bituminous materials called kerogen that are released into petroleum-like liquids as the rock is heated. Oil shale is very different from oil that is trapped in shale formations, such as the Bakken, in that it more closely resembles coal. This oil shale can be mined and processed to generate oil similar to oil that is pumped from conventional wells. While oil shale is found in many places throughout the world, by far the largest known deposits are found in the Green River Formation in Colorado, Utah, and Wyoming. Estimates of recoverable oil from the Green River Formation are three times greater than proven oil reserves in Saudi Arabia. Extracting oil from oil shale is more complex as it has to be mined and then heated and is thus more expensive. Additionally, current oil shale recovery technologies utilize extensive amounts of water, which is an obvious problem in the water-scarce West. Because of these problems, present utilization of oil shale is minimal. Should oil prices get high enough or extraction techniques more efficient, oil shale could play a significant role in meeting energy needs of the future. Oil shale, however, is a fossil fuel and when it is used supplies diminish and emissions contain greenhouse gasses.

U.S. Dependence on Foreign Supplies

As is apparent from petroleum production and consumption, the United States remains heavily dependent on foreign oil. This is the second problem with our current fossil fuel-based economy. Foreign oil dependence is problematic for several reasons. First, when the United States imports foreign oil, it results in transfer of massive wealth to major oil producing countries. This leads to balance of trade concerns. Furthermore, many oil exporting countries use oil wealth to maintain non-democratic governments and suppress human rights. Finally, for the United States, dependence means vulnerability.

One way to decrease dependence on foreign oil is to increase production of the more plentiful energy resources that do exist in this country. While oil shale is one such resource, coal is the most prominent resource that is currently cost effective. Known coal deposits in the United States contain more energy than all the world's known oil reserves. Of course, with current technology, coal cannot be effectively transformed to liquid fuel to be used in the transportation sector and so the overall capacity of coal to replace oil is limited. Table 6.5 presents data showing coal production in the United States from 1950 to 2011. This table indicates that coal production has increased substantially since 1960. Much of this increased coal production came following the OPEC embargo of the 1970s. This embargo made the vulnerability and dependence of the United States on foreign energy sources apparent, and resulted in significant efforts to increase domestic production to help achieve energy independence.

Table 6.5   Coal Production in the United States by Mining Method and Location, 1950–2011
(Million Short Tons)

Year	Mining Method		Location		Total
	Underground	Surface	East of Mississippi	West of Mississippi	
1950	421.0	139.4	524.4	36.0	560.4
1955	358.0	132.8	464.2	26.6	490.8
1960	292.6	141.7	413.0	21.3	434.3
1965	338.0	189.0	499.5	27.5	527.0
1970	340.5	272.2	567.8	44.9	612.7
1975	293.5	361.1	543.7	110.9	654.6
1980	337.5	492.2	578.7	251.0	829.7
1985	350.8	532.8	558.7	324.9	883.6
1990	424.5	604.6	630.2	398.9	1,029.1
1995	396.6	636.9	544.8	488.7	1,033.5
2000	373.6	700.0	507.5	566.1	1,073.6
2005	368.6	762.9	493.8	637.7	1,131.5
2011	345.5	748.8	455.8	638.5	1,094.3

Source: Energy Information Administration, U.S. Department of Energy

Table 6.5 also shows that through the years, there have been major changes in mining methods and location of coal production. In 1950, 75 percent of coal produced in the United States was from underground mines, and most (93.6 percent) was taken from mines east of the Mississippi. Most significant coal mining areas at mid-century were in the Appalachian regions of West Virginia, eastern Kentucky, and western Pennsylvania. Substantial amounts of coal continue to be mined using underground methods and in the eastern states. However, dramatic increases have occurred in the amount of coal obtained from surface mines and from mines in the West. With modern technology, surface mining is far cheaper and western coal deposits are more amenable to surface mining. With surface mining, massive machines can be used to move the soil and other materials covering the coal, remove coal, and then transport it to power-generating facilities. By 2011, 68.4 percent of U.S. coal was obtained from surface mines and 58.3 percent was from the West. Wyoming is now the nation's leading coal-producing state, and Campbell County, Wyoming, is the nation's top coal producing county, mining more than one million tons of coal per day. In Campbell County and the Powder River Basin, coal seams from 65 to 100 feet thick are located near the surface and are thus relatively easy and cheap to mine. In some cases, power plants are located at the mouths of the mine and the electricity that is generated is carried by transmission lines to distant cities. At other mines, the coal is loaded onto trains which then carry the coal to power plants located throughout the country.

Another option to reduce foreign dependence is increased production of natural gas. Natural gas consists of methane and other hydrocarbons that are naturally occurring and found in deep underground rock formations. At one time, natural gas was considered a relatively worthless by-product of oil production. If markets could not be found near oil wells, natural gas was simply burned off at the oil field. In recent years, markets for natural gas have expanded greatly and gas-to-liquid technologies make transporting natural gas economically feasible.

Today, natural gas is a tremendously valuable resource that is widely used for heating, electricity generation, and increasingly as a transportation fuel. An added benefit is that natural gas releases lower levels of greenhouse gasses than coal. Table 6.6 provides data on natural gas production in the United States from 1950 to 2011. Natural gas production increased rapidly from 1950 to 1970, and then leveled off for the next 30 years. In the past decade natural gas production has increased significantly. This is largely a consequence of recent developments in production technology, which include horizontal drilling and fracking. These technologies have greatly increased the amount of natural gas that

Table 6.6 Natural Gas Production in the United States by Type of Well, 1950–2011 (Million Cubic Feet)

Year	Gas Wells	Oil Wells	Coal Bed Wells	Shale Wells	Total
1950	NA	NA	0	0	8,479,650*
1960	NA	NA	0	0	15,087,911*
1970	18,594,658	5,191,795	0	0	23,786,453
1980	17,572,526	4,297,166	0	0	21,869,692
1990	16,053,566	5,469,055	0	0	21,522,621
2000	17,726,056	6,447,820	0	0	24,173,876
2007	14,991,891	5,681,871	1,999,748	1,990,145	24,663,655
2011	12,291,070	5,907,919	1,779,055	8,500,983	28,479,027

* Figures reflect gas and oil wells combined.
Source: Energy Information Administration, U.S. Department of Energy

can be economically produced by allowing access to gas that is trapped in shale formations. These unconventional natural gas technologies have been a real game changer. Table 6.6 shows that shale gas production has gone from nothing in 2000 to about 30 percent of all production in 2011. Currently, the highest producing shale formations include Haynesville (Louisiana and Texas), Marcellus (Pennsylvania, West Virginia, New York, and Ohio), Barnett (Texas), and Fayetteville (Arkansas). Greatly increased supplies made available by fracking have also resulted in substantial reductions in natural gas prices.

Climate-Changing Greenhouse Gas Emissions

Unfortunately, even if the United States is able to increase fossil fuel production, serious problems remain. The third problem of a fossil fuel economy is climate change. Increasingly, scientists are in agreement that climate change is occurring and is a result of human activities, especially the burning of fossil fuels. Burning fossil fuels have increased the amount of carbon dioxide and other greenhouse gasses such as methane and nitrous oxide in the atmosphere. Coal is the worst of the fossil fuels in terms of the amount of greenhouse gasses emitted, but burning any fossil fuel releases greenhouse gasses. As fossil fuels are burned and greenhouse gasses accumulate in the atmosphere, they allow light from the sun to enter, but then trap a portion of outward-bound infrared radiation, which makes air temperatures increase (Speth 2004). In the nineteenth century and before, carbon dioxide levels in the atmosphere were about 284 parts per million (ppm) (Emanuel 2007; IPCC 2007; Speth 2004). Carbon dioxide levels increased from 316 ppm in 1959 to 395 ppm in January 2013, an increase of 25 percent in 54 years. Also significant is that the rate of increase has become larger as progressively larger amounts of fossil fuels are being burned each year. The carbon dioxide problem is made more severe as deforestation practices reduce the capacity of the world to absorb carbon.

Evidence of climate change abounds throughout the West and the rest of the world. On average earth's temperature has increased by 1.2 degrees Fahrenheit in the past century (Emanuel 2007). The year 2012 was the hottest year on record, and each of the first twelve years of this new millennium was among the fourteen hottest years on record. Numerous visible signs of climate change exist. For example, in the nineteenth century, there were 150 named glaciers in Glacier National Park in Montana.

Today this number is down to 26, and several of these are mere remnants of their former selves. Estimates are that all of the glaciers in the park will be gone by 2020. Consequences are even more dramatic in Arctic regions where average temperatures have increased at almost twice the rate of the rest of the world in recent decades (Gamble et al. 2011; Hassol 2004; Karl et al. 2009; Walsh et al. 2008). As a result, there is widespread melting of glaciers and sea ice. Overall, the geographic extent of arctic sea ice has decreased by 15 to 20 percent. The Columbia Glacier in Alaska, which discharges into Prince William Sound, has shrunk by nine miles since 1980 and is discharging nearly two cubic miles of ice annually. Decreasing sea ice, associated with melting of glaciers, especially in Greenland and Antarctica, are resulting in rising sea levels. Further, arctic snow cover has declined and river flows have increased as the length of frost-free seasons has increased by as much as 50 percent; permafrost is melting and its southern limit has moved north by a significant amount. As a result, vegetation zones are shifting northward, frequency and intensity of forest fires and insect disturbances have increased, and a number of marine species that are dependent on sea ice, including polar bears, seals, and walruses, are declining and some may face extinction (Hassol 2004).

In other parts of the world, oceans have begun to rise and the temperature of the oceans is increasingly leading to more frequent and more severe storms. Further, temperature changes shift vegetation community boundaries, centers of distribution for various species have changed, and globally the area affected by drought has increased since the 1970s. These changes make some habitats and some species extremely vulnerable (Chou et al. 2008; Emanuel 2007; IPCC 2007). The Intergovernmental Panel on Climate Change (IPCC) Fourth Assessment Report (2007) concludes with high confidence that these changes are influenced by human activities.

If current trends continue, the amount of greenhouse gasses in the atmosphere will continue to grow, and consequences could be disastrous (Stern 2007). If CO_2 levels can be sustained at 450 ppm, projections indicate that the eventual temperature rise will be between 1 and 3.75 degrees Celsius. Under these circumstances, deserts are likely to spread, crops fail, the number of people affected by hunger will grow, melting of the Greenland ice sheet will be irreversible, cities such as Tokyo, New York, and London will be threatened by rising seas, and there will be a substantial increase in hurricane damage in the United States. Should CO_2 levels increase beyond this level, consequences could be progressively more catastrophic (IPCC 2007). Obviously the best way to avoid these scenarios is to reduce fossil fuel use. How to do this without massive economic implications is a significant question with no easy answers.

Environmental Consequences of Fossil Fuel Extraction and Transport

By its very nature, extraction of fossil fuels is environmentally disruptive, which is the fourth problem of a fossil fuel-based economy. Fossil fuels are underground and soil and rocks must be removed, tunnels dug, or wells drilled to reach them. The Appalachian coal mining industry has come under fire for what is called "mountain top removal," where tops of mountains are removed to provide access to coal seams below. With this approach, much cheaper surface mining techniques can be used. Laws require that land disrupted by mining be reclaimed. Reclamation, however, has its limitations and the disruption and biodiversity losses have long-term consequences. Amenity and water quality concerns are also substantial.

In April 2010, a massive oil spill occurred in the Gulf of Mexico following an explosion at a BP well. The explosion caused a drill rig to sink at sea, killing eleven workers and injuring seventeen others. An estimated 19,000 barrels of oil per day were released. Before the flow could be stopped several months later, more than 120 million gallons of oil had been spewed into the gulf, making it the worst oil spill in world history. In 1989, the wreck of supertanker *Exxon Valdez* in Alaska's Prince William Sound resulted in 260,000 barrels of oil being spilled. Implications of oil spills for wildlife and biodiversity are extensive and last for years. An additional concern with fossil fuel mining is that the sought-after resources are mixed with impurities and other unwanted materials that have to be removed. Disposing of these unwanted by-products is a significant problem.

Concerns about environmental consequences of fossil fuel development have resulted in significant political controversy. For example, in the 1960s another major oil reserve was discovered east of Prudhoe Bay along Alaska's north shore, where an additional estimated ten billion barrels of oil are stored. This reserve, however, is located within boundaries of the Arctic National Wildlife Refuge (ANWR). Questions about utilization of these oil reserves have resulted in a classic clash of resource development versus preservation. At issue is the fact that oil underlies the primary calving grounds for North America's largest caribou herd, and the region provides critical habitat for other arctic animals. The battle over ANWR oil has raged for more than thirty years. Other similar battles have been and will be fought.

Reducing Fossil Fuel Dependence

Problems associated with a fossil fuel economy have fueled interest in decreasing our dependence on fossil fuels. Two major approaches for reducing fossil fuel consumption include increased alternative energy use and conservation.

Alternative Energy

Two major sources of non-fossil fuel energy are nuclear power and renewable energy. Nuclear power is generated by a nuclear fission process where reactors heat water to produce steam, which is used to turn turbines to generate electricity. Nuclear power plants have been constructed since the 1950s, and have always been surrounded by controversy. Consequently, no new nuclear plants have been brought online in the United States since 1996. At present, there are 104 operating nuclear reactors in the United States. In recent years, major problems confronting the fossil fuel industries have led to a renewal of the debate about nuclear power. Proponents of nuclear energy argue that nuclear power is sustainable because uranium supplies are projected to last much longer than fossil fuels, nuclear power generation emits no climate-changing greenhouse gasses, and nuclear power can decrease U.S. dependence on foreign energy.

Opponents contend that nuclear power poses significant threats because of nuclear wastes that can remain dangerous for millennia, the risk that technology and materials can be used to build nuclear weapons, and concern that nuclear power poses the risk of major nuclear accidents such as those that occurred at Chernobyl and Three Mile Island. These fears were renewed when a devastating earthquake hit Japan on March 11, 2011, which led to a partial meltdown of a nuclear reactor at the Fukushima Daiichi Plant and the threat of another major nuclear accident. There are also serious concerns associated with the mining of uranium, the fuel source for nuclear power. Uranium mining, like all mining endeavors, leaves tailings that often leach acids and heavy metals into nearby water supplies (Stiller 2000; Wilshire et al. 2008). Worries about leaching from uranium mines are compounded because of the radioactivity involved. While nuclear power has the potential to generate significant amounts of energy, major problems must be dealt with and overcome.

The other major alternative energy source is renewable energy. As opposed to nonrenewable fossil fuels, renewable energy is generated from naturally replenishing resources (IPCC 2011). Historically, five major sources of renewable energy have been biomass, water, wind, geothermal, and solar. Table 6.7 presents data on renewable energy production from 1950 to 2011. In 2011, 83 percent of renewable energy produced in the United States came from biomass (49 percent) and water (mostly hydroelectric; 34 percent). In recent years, renewable energy production has increased substantially. Growth has been especially pronounced in wind. Hydroelectric power production has been mostly stable. Increasing hydroelectric production will be difficult in an environment where most of the best dam sites are already taken, existing dams are losing capacity as they fill with silt, and the cultural and political climates generally oppose construction of additional dams. In fact, several existing dams are slated for removal to enhance biodiversity, especially salmon survival (Clark 2009). Obviously, as dams are removed, hydroelectric generation will decline.

Table 6.7 Renewable Energy Production by Type in the United States, 1950–2011 (Quadrillion BTU)

Year	Hydroelectric Power	Geothermal	Solar	Wind	Biomass
1950	1.415	-	-	-	1.562
1955	1.360	-	-	-	1.424
1960	1.608	0.001	-	-	1.320
1965	2.059	0.004	-	-	1.335
1970	2.634	0.011	-	-	1.431
1975	3.155	0.070	-	-	1.499
1980	2.900	0.110	-	-	2.476
1985	2.970	0.198	-	-	3.018
1990	3.046	0.336	0.060	0.029	2.737
1995	3.205	0.294	0.070	0.033	3.103
2000	2.811	0.317	0.066	0.057	3.010
2005	2.703	0.343	0.066	0.178	3.120
2011	3.171	0.226	0.158	1.168	4.511

Source: Energy Information Administration, U.S. Department of Energy

Increased energy from biomass is a result of developments in ethanol and other biofuels. A major advantage of biofuels is that they can be used to produce liquid fuels, which can then be used in the transportation industry. Greenhouse gasses emitted from the burning of biofuels are offset by carbon sequestered by growing plants before conversion to fuel (Coyle 2007; McCarl 2008). The National Energy Act of 1978 gave ethanol blends an exemption on federal motor fuels tax. Biodiesels also have a federal tax break (Duffield and Collins 2006). In September 2007, U.S. ethanol production consisted of 128 manufacturing plants with a capacity of seven billion gallons per year (Carolan 2009). Production potential tripled from 2000 to 2007, but still accounts for less than three percent of global transportation fuel (Coyle 2007). A substantial concern with biofuels is that diverting food crops into fuel has a major impact on agricultural markets and food prices, and significant energy must be utilized to grow crops that become biofuels (Elam 2008). Thus, efforts are under way to efficiently convert cellulosic materials (such as wood chips or switch grass) into biofuels. At present, the process is more complex. While potential benefits of renewable energy are great, significant problems remain. Most fundamentally, producing renewable energy is generally more expensive than producing fossil fuel energy—unless externalities are considered. For example, producing electricity from coal that is plentiful and cheap to mine is simply more cost efficient than producing energy from wind or solar resources—especially if the costs of greenhouse gas emissions are not considered. In many cases programs and policies are needed to support renewable energy development as technology continues to develop. As policies emerge that require various energy producers to pay the true cost of their product, renewable energies will become much more competitive. In this regard, the Supreme Court ruled in 2007 that the Environmental Protection Agency (EPA) had authority to regulate greenhouse gas emissions. As a result, Congress is considering several policies that would provide incentives to reduce fossil fuel use and thus encourage alternative and renewable energy and cleaner forms of fossil fuel energy. Renewable energy industries need consistent policies and program so they can develop long-term strategies.

There are other problems that plague the renewable energy industry. Perhaps most troubling are problems of consistency and predictability. The wind doesn't always blow, and cloudy and rainy days reduce capacity of solar energy. As a result, renewable energy is generally used in conjunction with fossil fuel energy generation, where fossil fuels are used to make

Renewable energy production. *istockphoto.com*

up the difference when renewable sources are unable to meet demands. I was visiting a power plant in Gillette (Campbell County), Wyoming, on what happened to be a windy day. The power plant received word from corporate headquarters that they only needed to produce at about two-thirds of capacity because windmills were spinning and generating significant energy. The benefits are obvious. Less coal is burned, thus preserving a nonrenewable resource, and fewer greenhouse gasses are emitted into the atmosphere. However, because the wind is unpredictable, the power plant had their full labor force on hand and was unable to fully capture potential savings. These unneeded labor costs are then passed on to consumers. While visiting Fresno, California, I learned that this part of the Central Valley is in high demand for solar energy production because of the consistency and predictability of sunshine. The Mediterranean climate makes rainfall virtually unheard of and clouds are rare during summer months, thus providing energy companies with consistent and predictable supplies of renewable energy. This allows coal plants to more effectively plan on how much energy they will need to produce. Until these consistency and predictability issues can be more thoroughly addressed, renewable energy use will always face limitations.

The renewable energy industry also faces energy transmission problems that are made more complex by the vast stretches of publicly owned land in the West. At present, there is strong opposition and extensive red tape slowing development on public lands. There are also amenity and biodiversity concerns. Some people prefer not to have ridge tops covered with windmills and there is concern that spinning windmills have significant negative implications for wildlife.

Two wind energy projects in Utah provide relevant examples of the potential future of renewable energy. One is a smaller project to generate energy to be used locally, while the other is a much larger project where wind energy is transmitted hundreds of miles to cities in Southern California. In the mouth of Spanish Fork Canyon in Utah County, nine wind towers generate electricity that is used in the nearby communities of Spanish Fork, Springville, and Mapleton. Each wind tower when operating at full capacity generates power for about 12,000 homes. Towers are located at the mouth of the canyon where the wind often blows but still requires working in cooperation with plants using fossil fuels to generate electricity when there is little or no wind. The project not only reduces coal and natural gas utilization, but also creates local jobs, and money used to pay utility bills stays in the local community rather than being sent to a faraway corporation.

A much larger project has been constructed in Millard and Beaver Counties in southwest Utah. Here, a company called "First Wind" has constructed a wind farm with ninety-seven turbines that generate about 203.5 megawatts of energy (each MW is capable of supplying power for 800 homes). From the wind farm, a ninety-mile transmission line to Delta, Utah, has been constructed where wind energy ties in with existing power lines from Intermountain Power Project's (IPP) coal-fired power plants. The electricity is then transmitted to Burbank and Pasadena, California.

Conservation and Efficiency

An absolute necessity to assure a reasonable energy future is improved conservation. Vast amounts of energy could be saved if cars achieved better gas mileage and were driven fewer miles, if public transportation was more widely available and used, if we all walked more, and if homes were smaller and better insulated. Table 6.8 shows evidence of improvements in energy efficiency. The amount of energy consumed per person declined by 10.9 percent from 2000 to 2011. Even though we are living in larger homes and using more electrical gadgets, we are actually consuming less energy because of improvements in efficiency. Additionally, energy

Table 6.8 Energy Consumption Per Person and Per Real Dollars of GDP in the United States, 1950–2011

Year	Energy Consumption Per Person (Million BTU)	Energy Consumption Per Real Dollars of GDP*
1950	227	17.27
1955	242	16.09
1960	250	15.94
1965	278	14.98
1970	331	15.91
1975	333	14.76
1980	344	13.38
1985	321	11.16
1990	338	10.52
1995	342	10.02
2000	350	8.81
2005	339	7.94
2011	312	7.31

*Thousand BTU per claimed in 2005 dollars
Source: Energy Information Administration, U.S. Department of Energy

consumption per real dollar of GDP has steadily declined, indicating better energy efficiency in all segments of American life.

Obviously there remains much room for improvement. One problem is the size of our homes. The average home built in the United States in the twenty-first century is more than twice as large as the average home built prior to 1970 (McKibben 2007). All else equal, a larger home obviously requires more energy to heat and cool than a smaller home. Another sector with potential for vast improvements is transportation. Energy efficiency improvements in transportation are especially vital because transportation requires liquid fuels which cannot be offset by nuclear, wind, geothermal, solar, or other alternative or renewable energy sources (unless electrical cars become more widely used). Table 6.9 shows motor vehicle mileage and fuel rates in the United States from 1950 to 2010. This table shows that the number of miles driven per vehicle steadily increased until there was a decline since 2005. Also, since 1970 there has been a slow but steady increase in miles per gallon. Certainly, there is capacity for vast improvements. Without harming national productivity, it is possible to significantly reduce the number of miles driven and to improve fuel rates of our vehicles. Americans have long loved driving

Table 6.9 Motor Vehicle Mileage and Fuel Rates in the United States, 1950–2010

Year	Passenger Cars		Vans, Pickup Trucks & SUVs		Trucks		All Motor Vehicles	
	Miles Per Vehicle	Miles Per Gallon	Miles Per Vehicle	Miles Per Gallon	Miles Per Vehicle	Miles Per Gallon	Miles Per Vehicle	Miles Per Gallon
1950	9,060	15.0	-	-	10,316	8.4	9,321	12.8
1955	9,447	14.6	-	-	10,576	8.2	9,661	12.7
1960	9,518	14.3	-	-	10,693	8.0	9,732	12.4
1965	9,603	14.5	-	-	10,851	7.8	9,826	12.5
1970	9,989	13.5	8,676	10.0	13,565	5.5	9,978	12.0
1975	9,309	14.0	9,829	10.5	15,167	5.6	9,627	12.2
1980	8,813	16.0	10,437	12.2	18,736	5.4	9,458	13.3
1985	9,419	17.5	10,506	14.3	20,597	5.8	10,020	14.6
1990	10,504	20.2	11,902	16.1	23,603	6.0	11,107	16.4
1995	11,203	21.1	12,018	17.3	26,514	6.1	11,793	16.8
2000	11,976	21.9	11,672	17.4	25,617	5.8	12,164	16.9
2005	12,510	22.1	10,920	17.7	26,235	6.0	12,082	17.1
2010	10,649	23.5	15,463	17.2	26,609	6.4	11,853	17.5

Source: Energy Information Administration, U.S. Department of Energy

cars, and especially big cars. Many of our cities are not constructed in ways that are conducive to mass transit and we seem to have an aversion to carpooling. Behavioral change will be motivated by higher energy costs, but perhaps people will be motivated by factors other than cost as we move into an era where concerns with fossil fuel energy increase.

Energy and Economics

Development and use of fossil fuels has had dramatic economic consequences. By increasing the capacity of farm and factory workers, fossil fuels have contributed to the growth of our nation's GDP and our personal incomes. Efficiencies gained by the use of fossil fuels in the production of food and other necessities have helped release many people to be artists, academics, and athletes, adding to our quality of life. The fossil fuel industry provides numerous jobs. The coal industry alone, for example, provides over one million jobs in the United States. Transformations in the energy industry will make some job skills obsolete, create the need for new job skills, and change the location of many jobs.

A significant advantage of renewable energy is that it has potential to be produced at an individual or community scale as noted in the Spanish Fork, Utah, example. While it is not feasible for an individual or a community to develop and operate a coal fired power plant, it is possible for a community or farm to have their own windmill and individuals can place solar panels on their homes. There is even progress being made on small scale hydroelectric generation where turbines are placed anywhere there is moving water, even in irrigation canals. The greater the local production, the greater amount of money that remains in the local economy. Further, local production is simply more sustainable, and policy and other efforts should be implemented now to move development in that direction.

Energy and the Rural West: Campbell County, Wyoming

Campbell County is located in the northeastern portion of Wyoming. Historically, Campbell County was economically dependent on ranching and for decades had experienced gradual economic and demographic decline. The 1930 census counted 6,720 residents in the county; by 1960 this number had been reduced to 5,861. Campbell County and the Powder River Basin then became the heart of the nation's coal development efforts. Numerous coal mining jobs emerged, and were quickly followed by construction jobs and employment in power plants. Between 1960 and 1970, Campbell County population more than doubled to 12,957, and then nearly doubled again to 24,370 in 1980. The 2010 census lists the population of Campbell County at 46,133. Coal mining and electricity generation had transformed Campbell County and its primary city, Gillette, from a sleepy ranching community to the nation's most important coal-producing county.

Initially, rapid growth resulting from energy development during the 1970s led to the City of Gillette earning the reputation as a boomtown. A term was coined to describe social disruptions that occur when the population grows too rapidly and the community is unable to respond adequately. Throughout the West during the 1970s and 1980s, communities were described by the extent to which they were experiencing the "Gillette Syndrome." Symptoms of the Gillette Syndrome include high crime rates, high rates of alcohol and drug abuse, degraded mental health, and weakened social and community bonds (Kohrs 1974). Gillette is no longer afflicted by boomtown growth. It is now a thriving community with good schools and good community services. Many existing jobs in the energy industry in Campbell County require significant skills and pay very well. In fact, in 2009 the median household income in Campbell County was higher than in any other nonmetropolitan county in the West with the exception of Los Alamos, New Mexico. This same process has occurred in other western energy boomtowns (M. Smith and Krannich 2000), and communities dependent on the energy industry are among the most prosperous in the West. Significant changes in the energy industry could have major economic and demographic implications for communities such as Gillette.

Conclusions

The utilization of fossil fuel energy has completely transformed the world in which we live. A fossil fuel economy, however, is unsustainable. Finite resource supplies are being depleted and global climate consequences of fossil fuel use are potentially catastrophic. Thus, efforts to enhance production of alternative and renewable energy are vital and time is of the essence. Improved energy conservation is also essential. Educational programs and policy alternatives to reduce dependence on fossil fuels should be a top priority. The West has the potential to be a major producer of renewable energy, with the resulting expansion of employment opportunities and other economic benefits. Many rural communities have the potential to reap major benefits by becoming producers of renewable energy at the local level. The sun and wind that are so pervasive throughout the West may become major economic assets. An advantage of sun and wind, compared to fossil fuels, is that these energy sources are infinite.

CHAPTER SEVEN

Biodiversity, Rangelands, Forests, and Minerals

The search for traditional natural resources was the magnet that attracted residents to the West throughout the isolation era. Because the water, soil, and climate essential for agricultural production were lacking in much of the West, residents turned to other resources such as rangelands for grazing livestock, commercially valuable trees, minerals, and energy resources for their economic livelihoods. Policy and cultural values placed high priority on development of these traditional resources so that they could support more families and communities. Policies, circumstances, and attitudes began to change during the mass society era and are transforming even more dramatically with the global society era. Consequently, resource concerns have become much more complex, are fraught with controversy, and policy outcomes have dramatic implications for the residents and communities of the rural West (Davis 2001; Nie 2008). As such, resource issues were the first priority defined by the rural roundtable participants. The previous two chapters have described resource issues associated with water and energy. In this chapter, several other resource issues are described.

Biodiversity in the Global Society Era

We live on a beautiful yet extremely complex and fragile planet. The array of living organisms and ecological systems is remarkable. Yet the world in general, and the United States in particular, confront major challenges if we wish to retain current living standards. Some argue that human-caused changes to our planet even threaten our survival as a species (Speth 2008).

Continued life on earth is made possible because a large number of species provide critical biological services. For example, many organisms are involved in cleaning the air and water, creating soil, pollinating flowers, preventing erosion, and countless other essential activities. Plants sequester carbon from the atmosphere and transform the sun's energy into energy forms that we can use. Biodiversity is the term that is used to define the variation of life forms that exist within a given ecosystem, biome, or for the entire earth. Examination and measures of biodiversity are often used to determine the health of biological systems. A major source of reduced biodiversity is human activity, as humans change the environment to make it more conducive for themselves. As habitats conducive for humans expand, the extent of habitat available for other species generally declines. Relationships are interwoven and complex and our actions often have unintended and unforeseen consequences for a variety of organisms. As habitats are altered, affected organisms often experience population declines and thus their ability to perform critical biological services is impaired (Anderson et al. 2008). A growing concern is that if we continue to take bricks out of the wall, the wall will eventually collapse.

Biodiversity loss resulting from human activity is a consequence of two major factors—the size of the human population, and lifestyles or consumptive patterns of these populations. The number of humans on the planet has grown rapidly in modern times. It took from human beginnings until 1800 for the world's population to reach one billion. It then took only 130 years, to 1930, to add a second billion. The population of the world then increased to three billion in less than thirty years. Growth rates exploded as the world's population doubled in only forty years, growing from three billion in 1959 to six billion in 1999. The world's population reached seven billion in 2012, and it is projected that nine billion people will inhabit the earth by the middle of this century. More people obviously consume more resources. All else being equal, seven billion people consume seven times more resources than one billion people.

But all is not equal. Perhaps even more significant than population size are the lifestyles of human populations. Americans, with their high standard of living, consume massive amounts of resources from energy to food, water, and precious metals. The global footprint of the average American is thirty-two times greater than for the average Kenyan. When Americans were about the only people on earth who were living like Americans, consequences for the world were more manageable. However, economies and income levels around the world have grown rapidly, especially in heavily populated countries such as China and India. In recent decades, millions of people around the world have moved from a subsistence existence to the middle class. Like Americans, people around the world desire to translate their higher incomes into an improved standard of living, which includes consumption of vastly greater amounts of energy and other resources. Still, half of the world's population lives on two dollars or less per day. As economic growth reaches even more of the world's population, resource consequences will expand. Additionally, a number of our current ecological problems are global in nature. Whether the impact occurs in Chicago, China, or the Congo, consequences are felt throughout the world (Speth 2004).

Biodiversity loss is of particular concern in the West. There is little doubt that the environment cannot sustain present lifestyles in western communities indefinitely. For example, current water and energy use patterns resulting from millions of people living in arid and semi-arid climates cannot continue long-term without fundamental changes. Some resource problems facing the American West were created intentionally as people attempted to make a living from a harsh and unforgiving environment. Some problems were created accidentally. In either case, there was little scientific understanding of the complexity of nature, and people were unaware that environmental disruptions would have unintended and sometimes disastrous consequences for later generations.

A common approach for discussing the threats to biodiversity is to use the HIPPO model. From this perspective, the major threats to biodiversity are Habitat destruction, Invasive species, Pollution, human Populations, and Overharvesting. Each is briefly discussed below as it pertains to the West. Of course, it should be remembered that many of the threats are interactive and involve multiple causes.

Habitat Destruction

Upon arrival, new American settlers began altering the region so that it would better meet their food, safety, and habitation needs. European transplants were not unlike the native inhabitants in their efforts to control or manage nature to attain a more comfortable living. However, their views about nature were different, their technology was more advanced (which allowed them to have a larger impact), their populations grew quickly, and they brought with them species of plants and animals that were not native to the West. All of these factors led to greater ecological impacts than were occurring prior to their arrival. Trees were cut both to clear farm land and to be used as lumber, prairie sod was plowed, swamps were drained, rocks were removed, and rivers and streams altered to provide irrigation water for their farms. Cattle and sheep by the millions were imported to graze on the western range. Implementation of agriculture can be seen as an attempt to achieve a monoculture where biodiversity is intentionally reduced. Herbicides and pesticides are used to eliminate unwanted weeds, insects, and rodents, and fences are built to keep larger animals away from crops. Some of the most productive land in the West is located in valleys near streams. Much of this land is now used for homes and communities and much is covered by concrete. Roads and power lines can disrupt migration patterns and provide pathways for invasive species. Hillsides were dug away in an effort to find valuable minerals. All of these changes have altered the areas in which plants and animals grow, breed, seek shelter, and find food. To a large extent, these changes made the environment more comfortable for humans but less accommodating for many native plant and animal species and thus greatly reduced biodiversity.

Conservation biologists speak of "keystone species," organisms so central to the functioning of an ecosystem that their removal can have far-reaching, even devastating consequences. Such keystone species often play a key role in local human culture as well. In the Pacific Northwest and throughout coastal Alaska, several species of salmon have played this keystone role. For thousands of years prior to the arrival of Europeans, Native American tribes of the Pacific Northwest had economies based heavily on the annual spawning migration of salmon. Each year, millions of salmon would return from the oceans and migrate upstream to the place of their birth to reproduce and the cycle would begin anew. It is estimated that prior to European contact, the number of fish migrating up the Columbia River alone each year was between eleven and sixteen million.

Since the nineteenth century, salmon numbers have declined precipitously as a result of human activities. Agriculture, mining, and logging all led to erosion and increased sediments in rivers and streams. Metropolitan and industrial activities also resulted in higher pollution levels. Fish were overharvested by both commercial fisheries and sportsman. Most significantly, numerous dams have been constructed along northwest rivers, effectively blocking 75 percent of original salmon spawning grounds and making salmon migration vastly more difficult on many other rivers and streams (Robbins 2004; Taylor 1999). As early as 1937, there were 174 dams in the Columbian Basin alone. As historian Richard White (1995) put it, although the river's architects continually expressed their concern for salmon, they "quite consciously made a choice against the conditions that produce salmon." Only recently have efforts been made to equip these dams with ladders and implement other techniques to improve the likelihood that migrating salmon will reach their destination. These techniques have had somewhat limited success. Improving salmon numbers with hatcheries has also proven to have numerous problems (Taylor 1999). With survival of some species of salmon in some watersheds in question, more aggressive approaches are now being implemented which include removal of some dams and ongoing discussion about removal of others. Thus through the years, the environment has been altered to make it more comfortable for humans with serious negative implications for salmon.

Another of the many species that had their numbers plummet as their prime habitat was converted to homes and farms was the tule elk, smallest of the North American elk species. Prior to settlement by Europeans, tule elk roamed in vast numbers in California, specifically in the Central Valley. During the 1800s their numbers were reduced to near extinction as their native habitats were converted to agriculture and because of excessive hunting. At one point during the 1890s it was believed that only twenty-eight tule elk remained. Since then, tule elk have been protected from hunting, and habitat preserves have been set aside to meet their ecological needs. Their numbers have rebounded and are now estimated to be about 2,700. Numerous other examples of species large and small could be cited. Without question, human activities have negatively impacted organisms that we are not even aware of.

Invasive Species

In 1540, Francisco Vazquez de Coronado led an expedition of Spanish soldiers and Indian allies northward from Spanish settlements in Mexico in search of the famed "Seven Cities of Gold." The expedition eventually entered what is now the American Southwest. Party members saw the Colorado River where it now represents the Arizona-California border, they gazed in wonder at the Grand Canyon, and wandered across the grass-covered plains of Kansas where they found the ocean of grass so vast and featureless that they had to navigate with a sea-compass. One of the explorers later wrote, "Who could believe that 1,000 horses and 500 of our cows and more than 5,000 rams and ewes and more than 1,500 men, in traveling over those plains, would leave no more trace when they had passed than if nothing had been there—nothing." While it may be true that footprints of the Coronado expedition were soon erased, other remnants of the expedition remained and changed the West forever. Not only did the expedition bring exotic animals, but they carried grain and other plants that were not native to the Americas. Through importation of non-native species, and often conscious efforts to help these species become established, biodiversity of the West has been drastically and irreversibly altered.

Within a few decades of the Coronado expedition, Spanish settlers had permanently moved to the American Southwest and established communities along the Rio Grande in modern day New Mexico. Settlers brought with them more horses, cattle, sheep, goats, dogs, cats, and other animals. They also brought wheat and other grains and fruit trees that were not native to the Americas. Their purpose was simply to try to survive and thrive in a land that is rather inhospitable for humans. Some of their domesticated plants and animals escaped into the wild. Over time, additional plants and animals were brought unintentionally as stowaways on ships or as seeds mixed with grain. In many cases the non-native species did extraordinarily well, increased in number, and often out-competed native species. Non-native species were often aided by settlers who were intentionally altering the environment to make it more conducive for non-native crops and livestock they had brought with them. Additionally, some transplanted species are, often for the first time in their existence, in a climatically suitable habitat in the absence of most or all of their natural predators, parasites, and competitors (Low and Berlin 1984). Changes wrought by the invasive species often initiate a complex chain of events. As the environment alters, it becomes more suitable for some species and less suitable for others. Over time, other indirect changes allow some species to prosper while others diminish. Thus, not only are there direct changes, but ongoing and complex indirect changes as the environment continues to evolve.

By the 1800s when English speaking settlers were moving into what would become the American West, herds of wild horses roamed the plains and invasive plants had spread. Horses had been domesticated and were widely used by the Plains Indians. Even today, thousands of wild horses and burros roam public lands of the West. By the time English speaking Europeans arrived in the Southwest, sheep and peach trees were an important part of Navajo subsistence. Ecological transformation of the West gained momentum in the 1800s as new English speaking settlers built homes, roads, and mines, and attempted widespread farming. Ranches were established with non-native livestock imported to graze on the open range. Soon millions of cattle and sheep were scattered across the Great Plains and throughout the West, and much of the range was seriously overgrazed within a few years.

Imported cows, sheep, horses, and burros graze and browse differently than native bison, deer, elk, antelope, or even rabbits, tortoises, and prairie dogs. As a result, some plant species declined as a result of changing grazing patterns while others thrived, which made the altered environment less hospitable for some herbivores and more hospitable for others. Changing populations of herbivores then dramatically alters predator populations.

Whether introduced intentionally or unintentionally, invasive species can do great damage to an ecosystem. Consider cheatgrass, perhaps the most serious invasive species problem that currently exists in the West. Cheatgrass was inadvertently imported with wheat or other grains from the trans-Caspian steppes during the 1890s or early 1900s. It did very well in the Intermountain West and spread extremely rapidly, especially as native plants were weakened by overgrazing. Cheatgrass now dominates millions of acres, especially in the Great Basin, and its coverage is continually expanding (Pellant 1996). Cheatgrass does well because it produces a large number of seeds, it adapts to drought or other environmental conditions, and perhaps most importantly, has changed the fire ecology of areas where it grows. Cheatgrass grows quickly in spring and then dries much earlier in summer than other grasses. As a result it is palatable for both livestock and wildlife for only a very short period of time. Because it dries early, it acts like tinder that burns quickly and easily. Before the infestation, it is estimated that areas in the Intermountain West would experience wildfire only once every thirty to seventy years; cheatgrass-infested areas now see wildfires up to once each five years. Such high fire frequencies make survival most difficult for many native plant species, making the area even more susceptible to increased domination by cheatgrass.

Cheatgrass decreases the value of grazing land for livestock because it can only be grazed for a short time in spring and it pushes out more nutritious grasses. Likewise, many native wild animals are threatened as their traditional food sources are eliminated. Spread of cheatgrass has functionally altered both sagebrush and pinion-juniper biomes. Alteration of the sagebrush biome has led to such serious reductions of sage grouse populations that they are being considered for protection under the Endangered Species Act. Despite extensive research, options for dealing with cheatgrass are few.

Pollution

Human actions have led to pollution problems throughout the West. Mining has resulted in high levels of heavy metals and acids being leached into water supplies. Agriculture and logging increase erosion that clog waterways with silt. Fertilizers, herbicides, and pesticides are washed into rivers and streams and threaten aquatic biodiversity. Many western cities battle severe air pollution problems resulting from auto emissions, heating and cooling homes, and operating industry, businesses, and public buildings. Resulting winter inversions are both dangerous and ugly.

Perhaps the most serious pollution problem threatening biodiversity is increased levels of greenhouse gasses accumulating in the atmosphere resulting in climate change as described in Chapter Six (Gore 2006). While consequences of climate change are especially severe in Arctic regions, parts of the West are struggling with an epidemic of mountain pine beetles, a native insect of western U.S. pine forests. Pine beetles have killed millions of trees in the Rocky Mountains and interior British Columbia in recent years. Similarly, a spruce beetle epidemic is killing millions of spruce trees in Alaska. This epidemic is widely believed to be exacerbated by climate change in two respects. First, increased temperatures in northern parts of the region and at higher elevations have allowed beetles to infest areas that were previously not susceptible to infestation because beetles were unable to survive the winter cold in sufficient numbers. Second, regional droughts resulting from climate change have made more trees vulnerable to beetle attacks. Additionally, clearcut logging and reforestation has resulted in forests of uniform age which are more susceptible to beetle damage. There is concern that the beetle may spread across jack pine forests of northern Canada and may even reach eastern pine forests. Much beetle-killed timber could be used for lumber or for biomass energy, but the substantial volume of timber available far exceeds existing capacity to use the wood. Not only has increased global warming enhanced the severity of the pine beetle outbreak, but the outbreak is contributing to climate change. Dead trees release carbon dioxide as they rot, and dead trees fail to sequester carbon dioxide as they would if alive.

Human Populations

The population of the American West has grown rapidly in recent decades. More people mean more homes, more roads, more schools, and more malls, all of which translate to reduced habitat for plants and animals. Much of the population has become richer, which allows them to live in larger homes, own more things, and travel more, all of which devour greater amounts of energy, natural resources, land, and water, and emit climate-changing greenhouse gasses. In the amenity-rich areas of the West, greater numbers of people are living in exurbs and more remote rural areas, often residing in previously undisturbed locations (Jackson-Smith et al. 2006). Brown et al. (2005) report that areas of low-density, exurban development beyond the urban fringe occupy nearly fifteen times the area of higher density urbanized development. Exurban development reduces native species richness and increases exotic species and human-adapted native species (Hansen et al. 2005). These low-density population patterns also increase dangers from and the severity of wildfires (Travis 2007). In sum, growing human populations increase the proportion of the environment being used by humans, reduce the extent to which the environment is available to other species, and generally result in biodiversity reductions.

Overharvesting

Much biodiversity loss can be attributed to overharvesting, both intentional and unintentional. From the time of their initial entry in the West, European-based settlers have overharvested some species, leading to the demise of that species and often upsetting ecological balances. Early mountain men overharvested beaver, for example. The biological impacts of invasive species, including cattle and sheep as described earlier, become even more dramatic when too many livestock are placed in an environment and overgrazing occurs. An ecology text describes the outcomes of overgrazing:

> Grazing animals that are foreign to the community are used to harvest a larger share of its primary productivity than under natural conditions. Some of the plant species native to grassland [are] unable to survive this increased harvest. Effects of overgrazing appear first in the decline of these species (decreasers). Meanwhile other species (increasers), that are more tolerant of grazing and are now relieved of the competition of the decreasers, expand their coverage. At the same time the biomass, height, and total coverage of the grassland decrease.

Continued overgrazing can overharvest and reduce the increaser species, while still other species (invaders) that are not part of the undisturbed community appear. These may then increase in coverage, and in time the grassland may become a weed field dominated by them. With...continued overgrazing and trampling, the weeds, in turn, can be reduced in coverage and the soil further exposed to erosion. The final result of overgrazing to its limit may be a virtual non-community—a mud field or eroded rocky slope, depending on location. (Cited in Donahue 1999, 43)

Sometimes broad efforts were made to intentionally overharvest and eliminate animals that were felt to have a harmful effect on agricultural enterprises or other human endeavors. Bison were hunted to near extinction in the 1800s, partly to make more room for cattle to graze on prairies and to subdue Native American tribes. In 1915, the federal Bureau of Biological Survey was assigned responsibility for predator control. The agency then hired 175 to 300 hunters and trappers to carry out their work of wiping out "pests" and "varmints." In 1931 Congress passed the Animal Damage Control Act, which authorized the Secretary of Agriculture to conduct campaigns for destruction of animals injurious to agriculture including mountain lions, wolves, coyotes, bobcats, prairie dogs, gophers, ground squirrels, and jack rabbits (Merrill 2002). Of major concern were predators that killed livestock. From 1937 through 1983, approximately 26,000 bears, 500,000 bobcats, 3.7 million coyotes; 50,000 red wolves, 1,600 gray wolves, and 8,000 mountain lions were killed under the Animal Damage Control Act.

Some rodents were also targeted as they ate crops and damaged farm land. Among those were prairie dogs, burrowing rodents that live in large colonies that sometimes cover several hundred acres. Attempts were made to remove these colonies through hunting and poisoning so the land could be used more efficiently for farming (Donahue 1999).

The culture of the West, based on the Human Exceptionalism Paradigm, encouraged elimination of animals felt to be harmful to humans. It was believed that animals that were defined as economically harmful or those providing no economic value should be eliminated so that humans and beneficial plants and animals could live their lives more abundantly. For years bounties were paid for coyotes, bobcats, and other predators. In his classic book, *A Sand County Almanac*, Aldo Leopold (1949) described an experience while he was a young Forest Service employee in New Mexico. He wrote:

We were eating lunch on a high rimrock, at the foot of which a turbulent river elbowed its way. We saw what we thought was a doe fording the torrent, her breast awash in white water. When she climbed the bank toward us and shook out her tail, we realized our error: it was a wolf. A half-dozen others, evidently grown pups sprang from the willows and all joined in a welcoming melee of wagging tails and playful maulings. What was literally a pile of wolves writhed and tumbled in the center of an open flat at the foot of our rimrock. In those days we had never heard of passing up a chance to kill a wolf. In a second we were pumping lead into the pack, but with more excitement than accuracy: how to aim a steep downhill shot is always confusing. When our rifles were empty, the old wolf was down, and a pup was dragging a leg into impassable slide-rocks. We reached the old wolf in time to watch a fierce green fire dying in her eyes. I realized then, and have known ever since, that there was something new to me in those eyes—something known only to her and to the mountain. I was young then, and full of trigger-itch; I thought that because fewer wolves meant more deer, that no wolves would mean hunters' paradise. But after seeing the green fire die, I sensed that neither the wolf nor the mountain agreed with such a view.

Extermination efforts were very successful. Wolves were eliminated in forty-seven of the forty-eight contiguous states, and other predators' numbers have been greatly reduced. Among rodents, prairie dog numbers have been drastically cut and this has led to the near-extinction of the black-footed ferret, a small predator in the weasel family whose diet is based heavily on prairie dogs. But human actions were not universally successful. While some animals have been driven to near extinction, other animals have adapted to environmental changes wrought by humans. Coyotes, for example, adapt well to human-disrupted environments and despite efforts to eliminate them, they are now perhaps more numerous than ever before.

Consequences of Biodiversity Change

Efforts of humans to remake the environment to better suit their needs often has severe unintended consequences. Leopold (1949) describes what happens to a mountain when wolves are eliminated.

Since then I have lived to see state after state extirpate its wolves. I have watched the face of many a newly wolfless mountain, and seen the south-facing slopes wrinkle with a maze of new deer trails. I have seen every edible bush and seedling browsed, first to anemic desuetude, and then to death. I have seen every edible tree defoliated to the height of a saddlehorn...In the end the starved bones of the hoped-for deer herd, dead of its own too-much, bleach with the bones of the dead sage, or molder under the high-lined junipers. I now suspect that just as a deer herd lives in mortal fear of its wolves, so does a mountain live in mortal fear of its deer. And perhaps with better cause, for while a buck pulled down by wolves can be replaced in two or three years, a range pulled down by too many deer may fail of replacement in as many decades.

With improved scientific understanding and evidence of the consequences of biodiversity loss, there have been efforts to recreate biodiversity by reintroducing species that were previously eliminated. A case that generated much controversy was the reintroduction of wolves into Yellowstone and central Idaho. Wolves historically occupied a wide range of habitats throughout much of North America north of the twentieth parallel in Mexico (Schullery 1996). From colonial days, efforts were made to eliminate wolves. Eventually, wolves were eliminated from 99 percent of their original habitat. Outside of Alaska, only in northern Minnesota have populations of wolves continually persisted since European settlement (Nie 2003). In 1926 the last wolves in Yellowstone were killed. Consequently, over succeeding decades, populations of elk and other large herbivores soared, and new-growth vegetation suffered as a result. Soon deciduous woody plants such as aspen and cottonwood died off as a result of overgrazing. A number of plans were implemented to limit elk numbers, none very effectively. This ecological imbalance affected many other species as well. Coyote numbers soared as they attempted to fill the void left by wolves. Coyotes, however, are not large enough to harvest very large herbivores, and their growing numbers had a negative effect on other species such as the red fox.

After decades of study, public hearings, and lawsuits, sixty-six wolves captured in Mackenzie Valley of Alberta, Canada, were released in greater Yellowstone and central Idaho in 1995. Ten years later, it was estimated that there were 325 wolves in Yellowstone and 565 in central Idaho. As a result, the Yellowstone elk population had been reduced by half, but there have been numerous confirmed reports of livestock depredation. Thus, the controversy continues. In Arizona, the five last-known wild Mexican grey wolves were captured in 1980 in order to save the critically endangered subspecies. Since then, a captive breeding program has brought the Mexican wolves back from the brink. In March 1998, some of these wolves were reintroduced into the Apache–Sitgreaves National Forest in Arizona.

There is no doubt that the long-term success of rural communities in the west requires that we live sustainably. Sustainability requires that the range of species that perform vital ecological services that make life on earth possible be retained. We also must remember that we live in a complex world, and human understanding of this complexity is lacking. Our actions often have unintended consequences. Thus, it is essential that resources be used in a manner that will leave them available to our descendants. To achieve this objective, many things must be done very differently than in the past.

Rangelands in the Global Society Era

Prior to the global society era, western rangelands had been managed largely as grazing land for livestock. Much western land held such little plant life that its value even for livestock grazing was minimal. The Bureau of Land Management (BLM) was created primarily to manage livestock grazing on public rangelands of the West; the Forest Service also managed grazing lands. Change began during the mass society era with passage of legislation such as NEPA and the Endangered Species Act. Forces of change have intensified during the global society era. Issues of controversy on western rangelands are basically the same as issues associated with other western resources such as water, forests, and minerals. Simply put, it is no longer sufficient to consider only immediate economic benefits; rather it is essential to regard amenities, biodiversity, and overall ecosystem health. Increasingly, it is necessary to consider rangeland and other resources from the NEP perspective rather than from the HEP perspective alone.

From a rangelands perspective, transition to the global society era can generally be pinpointed to when Congress passed the Federal Land Policy and Management Act (FLPMA) in 1976. This act was the culmination of efforts of environmental groups to widen the expressed purposes of public grazing lands managed by the BLM. FLPMA authorized consideration of recreational and wildlife interests in making range policy. Two years later, Congress passed the Public Rangeland Improvement Act (PRIA), which required the consideration of the ecological health of the land when making grazing policy. With these safeguards in place, a number of groups began pushing for livestock reductions on public lands (Merrill 2002). The Carter administration used these laws as the basis for proposals to reduce the number of livestock grazing on western public lands. In some cases calls were even made for the total elimination of public land livestock grazing (Donahue 1999).

Arguments to limit or eliminate livestock grazing on public lands have been based on ecological, aesthetic, and economic grounds. Ecologically, it is maintained that livestock grazing potentially alters species composition by enhancing conditions for some species and diminishing habitat for others (Fleischner 1994). In most cases, the final result is reduced biodiversity as described earlier in this chapter. For the most part, arid and semi-arid lands of the West are not naturally adapted to grazing by herds of large ungulates. Sparse and erratic rainfall, thin soils, and steep slopes make these lands highly susceptible to damage from grazing, and make recovery slow, if not impossible. Aesthetically, western rangelands include millions of acres of spectacular desert, mountain, and canyon landscapes, vistas, and open spaces that are enjoyed by millions of Americans each year. What was once considered largely useless land because it lacked traditional natural resources is now recognized as having great aesthetic value. Some argue that these aesthetics are damaged by livestock grazing which alters landscapes and makes areas appear less pristine and natural. Economically, it is maintained that benefits from livestock grazing on western public lands are relatively small and these lands actually make only a small contribution to the nation's beef supply. Thus, the economic benefits of grazing are generally insufficient to offset the ecological and aesthetic costs.

On the other hand, proponents of continued livestock grazing on public lands have several strong arguments. First, public land grazing is essential to economic survival for many western ranching operations. Most of these ranches have insufficient pasture land to feed cattle throughout the year, and without public land grazing the economic survival of the ranch would be at risk. Often, nearby rural communities are economically dependent on area farms and ranches. Some also argue that survival of ranches can also play a role in protection of open spaces. From this perspective, if the ranch is not doing well economically, the rancher is more likely to sell to developers who may subdivide into small acreage ranchettes. Gosnell and Travis (2005) found that when ranches were sold in the post-1990 era, a majority were purchased by amenity and out-of-state buyers. Consequently, what was once open rangeland becomes a maze of roads and power lines leading to homes which are often only periodically lived in. Increased development then detracts from open space and amenities and is disruptive to wildlife habitat. Other problems faced by ranchers increase the likelihood that a ranch will be sold. These include concerns about the profitability of ranching—beef prices remain low while production costs steadily increase, environmental concerns and regulations, and invasive plants (Holechek 2001). Some argue that livestock grazing is one of the few, and perhaps the most effective, means of dealing with ecological concerns such as invasive cheatgrass. Livestock grazing can also be done in a way that may enhance biodiversity. Obviously, decisions regarding livestock grazing on public lands will have significant consequences. No doubt, more and better science and public deliberation are needed.

Western Forests in the Global Society Era

Entering the global society era, the western timber industry faced several significant obstacles. The initial concern was that for the first time ever the industry was experiencing production reductions because of the depletion of timber resources. For decades, trees had been cut at a much faster rate than they could grow—a pattern that, of course, could not continue indefinitely. The timber industry had historically relied heavily on old-growth forests where massive trees that had taken centuries to grow were being harvested. By the global society era, 90 percent of these old-growth forests had been removed and, with increased reliance on the much smaller second- and third-growth trees, the industry was simply unable to produce board feet at the same pace. While the Forest Service had always maintained that sustainability was one of their core principles, they had often placed a higher priority on providing jobs and economic stability in timber-dependent rural communities. As a result, even on Forest Service land trees had often been cut at a faster rate than they could grow back. Sustainable practices were even less common on privately owned forest lands. Through the nineteenth century and early decades of the twentieth century, the timber industry would often "cut and run," and then allow the land to revert to public ownership by failing to pay taxes (LeMonds 2001). By the global society era, however, sustainable harvesting and replanting were taking place even on most private land.

A second obstacle confronting the timber industry was growing pressure to practice "ecological" forestry, an example of HEP views being replaced by NEP concerns. Ecological forestry places emphasis on the overall health of the forest, biodiversity, and the thousands of species comprising the forest community, rather than solely on the few species of commercially valuable trees (Fortmann and Fairfax 1991; Hays 2007;

2009). In 1990 the impact of ecological forestry came to the forefront when the northern spotted owl was placed on the endangered species list. Spotted owls live primarily in old-growth forests, which are now limited in size and geographically fragmented. Thus, court orders and subsequent management plans emphasized protection of remaining old-growth forests. In 1994, a federal court upheld a plan that reduced logging to one billion board-feet per year in the Pacific Northwest, less than 25 percent of timber harvests in the 1980s, and protected two-thirds of remaining old-growth forests. In 1995, the Supreme Court ruled that spotted owl protection laws could be applied to private land. As a consequence, in many cases the timber industry could not harvest trees in old-growth forests even when these forests were on privately owned land.

Controversy surrounded the northern spotted owl ruling. Widespread protests erupted throughout the Pacific Northwest because of concerns about lost jobs and economic decline. Proponents of spotted owl protection maintained that preserving remaining old-growth forests was essential to prevent extinction of a species. They also argued declines in the timber industry were not all a result of spotted owl protection. Rather, such declines were going to occur anyway because of decades of unsustainable overharvesting. Opponents contended that the economic livelihood of individuals and families and viability of rural communities should be considered, and maintained that people were more important than owls. Additionally, strong challenges were made to the science behind the endangered species classification. There are three subspecies of spotted owls—northern, California, and Mexican (Hobbs 2007). Some maintain that the spotted owl should be classified as one species without subspecies. If classified as a single species, overall spotted owl numbers may be sufficient to avoid endangered species classification. Opponents also argue that declining numbers are not entirely due to the timber industry but are also a consequence of the invasion of the barred owl, an aggressive relative of the spotted owl that has moved west after historically only living in eastern forests. Increasingly, barred owls are claiming areas that were once the habitat of spotted owls. Thus, aggressive timber harvesting reductions may not save the spotted owl from extinction. It should also be apparent that this controversy is much deeper than simply jobs vs. owls. In many ways, spotted owls are merely surrogates in the much larger debates over public land, environment, and the place of humans in nature in a global world (Nie 2008).

Reduced production resulting from both resource depletion and implementation of ecological forestry led to reductions in the number of workers employed in the timber industry (Sherman 2006; 2009). Workforce reductions were exacerbated by steadily improving technology as machines replaced human labor in the production process (LeMonds 2001). As people lost their jobs and companies were forced to close, there was increased pressure on the Forest Service to open more lands for timber harvest. It was hoped that federal land management agencies could play their historic role of assuring jobs and economic viability of rural communities. However, logging on federal land virtually ceased after the spotted owl ruling. Nearly every proposal for a timber harvest on federal land was challenged on ecological grounds, and litigation became commonplace. Consequently, the amount of timber harvested from national forest lands declined dramatically.

The economic, social, and cultural repercussions of dramatic reductions in the logging industry have been devastating for rural logging communities throughout the West. Unemployment rates with attendant problems skyrocketed, timber-related businesses closed, and many people moved elsewhere to seek employment. Persons not directly employed in the timber industry were often dependent on timber-related businesses and employees. Thus, as populations declined and as many of the people who remained had lower incomes, the economic effects were felt more widely. Eventually, many businesses not directly involved in the timber industry began to falter. City and county tax revenues shriveled, which significantly affected the ability of communities to support schools and provide other public services.

As economic viability of timber-based communities continued to erode, there were legislative efforts to aid declining rural communities. Local and state governments have never been able to get property tax revenues from federally owned land, which is a significant concern when so much of the land in the West is federally owned. However, throughout most of the twentieth century, federal laws allowed county governments to get 25 percent of the revenue generated from timber leases on Forest Service and other federal land. Many counties in Washington, Oregon, and other western states with significant timber industries had become dependent on these funds to provide for local schools and other government services. As the amount of logging on Forest Service land declined, these revenues declined as well. For example, Oregon's Lake County received $5.3 million a year in federal timber revenue in 1987 and 1988. In

1998, the county collected only $300,000 (LeMonds 2001). In April 2000, a bill sponsored by Oregon Democrat Ron Wyden and Idaho Republican Larry Craig provided $576 million per year to rural western counties suffering from the loss of timber revenues through 2006. This legislation was intended to provide funds to communities as a bridge to allow them to develop other industries and sources of employment. When funding expired in 2006, efforts to extend the program were defeated in Congress.

In addition to economic problems, timber industry decline had significant social and cultural impacts as well. In many ways, the very fabric that was holding some logging communities together was ripped. For decades logging had been at the heart of community life. For generations, forests had provided the primary source of employment, income, and definition of place (Sherman 2005). Communities were recognized by both residents and nonresidents alike as logging towns. In addition, working in the forests provided local males with an identity. Logging was an occupation in which "real men" worked. Men would enter the forests carrying their chain saws to cut down massive trees. Others had jobs where they would climb tall trees or cut them into boards that could be used to build homes or businesses. It was physically demanding and dangerous work. Losing these jobs and finding employment in the service sector was simply not very appealing to many rural men who had spent a lifetime in the woods. Further, skills that allowed one to gain respect and earn a living in the woods did not translate readily into skills where one could gain respect and earn a livable income in other sectors. Relatively well-paid and respected workers in the timber industry were often forced to take low-skill, low-pay work in another sector because the logging jobs were gone. The transition was difficult both economically and emotionally (Brown 1995; LeMonds 2001).

Impacts of declines in the timber industry were felt well beyond the Pacific Northwest. Commercially valuable trees have historically been found in other places in the West, especially in the Rocky Mountains and Sierra Nevadas, and many rural communities have been dependent on the timber industry to varying degrees. Private timber land is relatively uncommon in western states outside of the Pacific Northwest and thus the timber industry was more heavily dependent on federal lands, and especially lands managed by the Forest Service. With growth of ecological forestry, declining timber harvests from Forest Service land largely eliminated the timber industry in many communities as there usually were no private timber lands to fall back on. Issues leading to timber industry declines were largely the same as in the Pacific Northwest—in some places resources had been depleted and in other places growing demands of ecological forestry were reducing timber harvests.

Even in the few places where a viable timber industry existed on nonfederal land, it was often impacted by demands of ecological forestry. At one time, ponderosa pine was being sustainably harvested to provide employment and generate revenue on the Navajo Reservation in Arizona, an area historically plagued by high rates of poverty and unemployment. Then in 1993 the Mexican spotted owl was declared as threatened under the Endangered Species Act. Again, this decision led to efforts to protect old-growth forest habitat. Consequently, many logging operations in the Southwest have been forced to close, including those operations on the Navajo Reservation.

The Future of Logging Communities

The timber industry is not going to come back the way it was. Never again will logging provide employment opportunities to the level they did in the past. James LeMonds (2001, 182) stated, "if you are looking for the past, you should refer to books and photographs. Only a fool would expect it to come around again." Communities must generate other sources of revenue, and individuals who were employed or who wished to be employed in the forests need to develop marketable skills that will allow them to obtain high quality employment in other sectors. There are options and opportunities. For the most part, communities that have been historically dependent on the timber industry have advantages that provide avenues for success in the global society era. Specifically, these communities are often very aesthetic. Trees and mountains that are ubiquitous to timber communities are often high on the list of amenities that people enjoy. Communities with extensive amenity resources are often in good position to attract or build employment opportunities. With amenities as a high priority, spotted owls and salmon migrations that were instrumental in the decline of the timber industry can become significant attractions for tourists and become attributes that make communities desirable places of residence. These resources can thus become the attractions on which a new economy is built. Finding ways of replacing the relatively high paying jobs that have been lost, however, will be difficult and will be discussed in later chapters.

It is also important that the timber industry does not simply cease to exist in western states. Timber is a renewable resource and there are advantages for our nation remaining at least somewhat timber self-sufficient. Dependency means vulnerability. For the United States to remain timber self-sufficient, trees from the West need to play a role. In addition, as a renewable resource, forests need to play a significant role as a source of bioenergy as our nation seeks to become energy independent and as we seek to reduce emissions of climate-changing greenhouse gas. Of course, continued forest use must be done sustainably.

Also, a viable timber industry can play a critical role in maintaining forest health and reducing dangerous wildfires. In recent years, as pine beetle epidemics have destroyed millions of trees throughout the West, there was a need to eradicate infested trees and remove other trees in order to establish a buffer between infected and uninfected trees. Often these preventive management tasks were not performed because the timber industry had declined to the point that there were no longer operations with capacity to remove trees and because getting permission to cut trees on federal lands was very difficult to obtain. Similarly, removal of trees is often an important strategy in protecting homes and communities from dangerous wildfires. Again, such work cannot be efficiently done without a viable timber industry.

Minerals in the Global Society Era

Many of the minerals extracted from western mines continue to be critical for products such as computers, cell phones, televisions, and cars. Beginning in the mass society era, environmental laws and improved mining techniques have been engaged to prevent some of the more serious environmental problems. Most environmentally harmful mining practices were outlawed and new approaches were prescribed as a means of limiting the spread of toxins and other pollutants. While representing a vast improvement over previous approaches, these new methods do not eliminate all problems. Removal of minerals is not now, nor never will be, sustainable. Further, mines from previous eras continue to wreak havoc. In many cases, responsible individuals and companies are no longer around and cannot be held financially accountable. To attempt to cope with some of the more critical environmental problems, the Comprehensive Environmental Response, Compensation and Liability Act (CERCLA) of 1980 (better known as Superfund) requires the Environmental Protection

Agency to clean up and alleviate problems resulting from toxic waste sites that threaten human health. Many Superfund sites are abandoned mines in the west. The most expensive Superfund site is the Butte/Anaconda region of Montana.

During the global society era, mining lacks the universal support it once generated and now produces substantial controversy. Demand for minerals remains high, but this demand is offset by widespread concern for resulting environmental problems. The HEP perspective is now severely challenged by the NEP perspective. Greater pressure is placed on mines to cover the complete cost of their efforts, including damage to the environment and human health. With these additional costs taken into account, a growing number of mines are no longer economically viable. Unlike the past, each new potential mining development goes through an extensive evaluation process. NEPA requires that potential environmental damage be listed, and means taken to alleviate this damage.

Conclusions

The presence of traditional natural resources was the magnet that attracted settlers to areas where available resources would allow them to earn an economic livelihood. The relative lack of such resources resulted in sparse human settlements throughout the West. Now during the global society era, perceptions of which resources are important and how resources should be used have changed dramatically. To fully take advantage of global era opportunities, it is critical that communities recognize these changes in their policy decisions. It is also vital that resources be used sustainably and in ways that preserve biodiversity.

CHAPTER EIGHT

Improving Employment Opportunities Through Place-Based Economic Development

A fundamental concern of rural communities over time has been inadequate employment opportunities. In comparison to urban areas, rural areas have been beset by lower incomes and higher rates of unemployment and poverty (D. Albrecht 2012; D. Albrecht et al. 2000). Lack of jobs and low pay for existing jobs has been the primary reason for rural-to-urban migration (Kandel and Brown 2006). Thus, it is not surprising that the second issue that emerged from the rural roundtables was the need to create more and higher quality employment opportunities in rural communities.

In some respects, problems associated with the lack of quality jobs in rural areas have been exacerbated in the global society era by major declines in the traditional primary sources of rural employment: agriculture, natural resource industries, and manufacturing. In addition, rural communities are plagued by other significant and long-term economic problems that are discussed in this chapter. While transition to the global society era has presented challenges to rural areas, it has also created vast new economic opportunities that simply did not exist in the past.

Increasing the Number of High-Quality Jobs

Communities have always, to one degree or another, been concerned about increasing the number and quality of employment opportunities. During the isolation era, when most jobs were in agriculture and natural resources industries, community development efforts tended to focus on increasing the supply of or demand for natural resource products. These included irrigation projects or other means of enhancing agricultural production, efforts to locate minerals or fossil fuels, and improved transportation to allow easier access to markets and supplies. Many communities remain convinced that resource jobs are vital to their economy (Power 1996; Power and Barrett 2001). With the decline of employment in natural resource industries and increased manufacturing employment, the most common approach for communities seeking to increase the number of high-quality jobs has been to induce some industrial firm to build or relocate in their community. Competition for firms was cutthroat and tax incentives and other benefits were offered by communities to potential candidates. This "buffalo hunt" approach made sense during the mass society era as manufacturing was the growth industry and success meant a community could attain a significant number of stable, middle-income jobs that often matched the skill set of the local labor force.

Circumstances are vastly different after the transition to the global society era. With employment in agriculture and natural resource industries continuing to decline, both opportunities for and economic benefits of the types of resource development utilized in the past are limited (Baden and Snow 1997; Power and Barrett 2001). Further, the manufacturing sector is no longer the growth industry. In the global society era, when a new industrial plant is built or when one decides to relocate, the recipient location is often international. Subsequently, the hunt for industrial firms is more costly, odds of success are greatly reduced, and overall this approach is much less effective as a community development strategy than it was in the past.

Rural communities continue to face additional economic development concerns. An extensive literature from economic geography (e.g., Fujita et al. 1999; Krugman 1991; Venables 2003) and agglomeration and central place theory (e.g., Kanbur and Rapoport 2005) has sought to understand the economic advantages of centralization where larger cities are greatly advantaged relative to smaller cities and rural areas. This research has shown that centralization and urbanization have two major economic advantages, location and population size. With respect to location, centralization means that transportation costs are reduced by being near markets and suppliers and a pooled market for workers with industry-specific skills ensures both a lower probability of unemployment for workers and a lower probability of a labor shortage for industries (Krugman 1991).

As cities became larger, a second advantage resulting from their greater population size becomes more relevant. Specifically, a larger population base creates opportunities for cities to provide more specialized services in a variety of areas. These advantages can be envisioned by imagining an economic ladder. When the population is larger, this ladder is going to have more rungs at the top which provide opportunities to climb higher. The "economic ladder" advantages of urban areas can be illustrated by looking at health care. Many small towns have a doctor or two and perhaps even a hospital. However these small town doctors are unlikely to be heart surgeons and small town hospitals are unlikely to specialize in heart surgery. The population is simply not large enough to provide sufficient demand to support such specializations. Medical specialties are almost always going to be in large cities where they draw their clientele not only from their larger urban population base but also from surrounding nonmetro areas that do not have this specialization. Such differences become relevant when metro/nonmetro income comparisons are made as urban-based heart surgeons generally have much higher incomes than small town general practitioners because they are on a higher rung of the economic ladder, a rung that doesn't even exist in nonmetro areas. The same metro advantages exist in many other industries including finance, insurance, sports, or politics. Thus, the most prestigious and high-paying positions in medicine, finance, academia, politics, sports, and many other fields remain centered in large cities.

In his book, *Who's Your City?*, Richard Florida (2008) argued that powerful, productivity-enhancing agglomerations are emerging and driving economic growth in mega-cities, both in the United States and worldwide. Mega-cities include New York, London, Tokyo, and the San Francisco Bay area. Florida maintains that even in a global world, individuals and businesses located in these mega-cities have distinct advantages over those located elsewhere. These advantages derive from typical benefits of being near markets and supplies, but more importantly, there are tremendous advantages in the global world of being near other creative individuals who are involved in the same or similar work with whom one can exchange ideas and develop relationships of trust. In previous eras, the key economic factors were generally related to location, which provided advantaged access to resources, supplies, and markets. Florida argues that the key economic factors in the global world have changed. Now the most significant economic factors include talent, creativity, and innovation. No longer does big beat small, but rather it is the fast beating the slow. While in many ways the relevance of location has been reduced, in a world where speed is critical there are great advantages for being near talent, creativity, and innovation and working with individuals that you know and trust.

Under these circumstances, Florida paints a bleak and even ominous future for those areas that are not a part of a mega-city. This includes second- and third-tiered cities such as Cleveland, St. Louis, and Milwaukee, and especially rural areas (Goetz et al. 2009). D. Albrecht (2012) found that the gap between metro and nonmetro incomes was greatest for persons with high levels of education and who were employed in the high-pay service industries. Thus, highly educated individuals and those working in select industries choosing to live in nonmetro areas do so at considerable economic cost. So where does this leave rural America in the global society era?

While there are certainly advantages to being in a location where cutting edge ideas are being shared and where corporate offices of the world's largest companies are located, there is no question that rural America remains relevant. To begin with, food, fiber, and energy that make life possible will continue to come primarily from rural areas. With even the mega-cities dependent on resources derived from rural areas, vast opportunities remain. In many ways there are greater opportunities in rural areas than at any time in the past. By describing potential opportunities for the rural west in the global world, I am not attempting to argue that Sheridan, Wyoming, will replace Silicon Valley as the global center of innovation, or that Fortune 500 companies will move their corporate offices there. I am suggesting, however, that in the global society era, Sheridan, Wyoming, and hundreds of other rural communities have tremendous opportunities for economic development that provide a way for those who wish to live in Sheridan to do so while making a comfortable living.

Rural communities should recognize that significant proportions of the population desire some of the many benefits of rural living. These benefits include escaping congestion, smog, and crime, and being closer to the natural world. In addition, for many a desire to live in a close-knit community near family and friends is becoming even more significant in a fast-paced world. For decades, many Americans have worked increasingly longer hours and moved from one community to another in an effort to climb the ladder of economic success. In pursuit of this economic success, ties to home and family were often weakened. Florida (2008), in fact, argues that a key to success in the global society era is "the strength of weak ties" (Granovetter 1973). In other words, success is better achieved by having numerous "acquaintances" that we occasionally contact (often by text or email or through Facebook and Twitter) that can benefit one's career, while at the same time avoiding extensive time and effort commitments required by close relationships. While such a strategy may be helpful in advancing a career, many people are finding this lifestyle to be unfulfilling. A growing body of empirical research is finding that in the United States we have reached the point where continued economic growth is no longer contributing to our happiness. In fact, our lifestyle of growing affluence tends to isolate us more and we seem to be enjoying it less (McKibben 2007). Rather than wanting to move even more often to gain even more affluence to become even more isolated, many people desire to find a home, sink their roots, and establish close personal relationships. Many believe that these goals are more likely to be achieved in rural communities.

However, having a desire to sink roots, to be next to nature, to escape urban pollution and congestion, or to enjoy other benefits of rural living is simply not enough to prompt many people to relocate. There is also a need for good jobs. With the decline of the traditional mainstays of the rural economy, rural communities need to establish new ways for people to obtain high quality employment. Four major approaches, with considerable overlap between them, for creating high quality employment in rural communities are described below.

Local Production and Value-Added

I am convinced that the key to rural economic development in the global society era is to decisively rebuild local economies, which in many ways means reverting back to some community features that were prominent during the isolation era (McKibben 2007). During the isolation era, communities were dependent on local production of food, energy, and other products by necessity because of transportation and communication inadequacies. As isolation was reduced by technological breakthroughs during the mass society and global society eras, there was a tendency to centralize production of nearly everything because of resulting increases in efficiency. It is time to rethink this process and bring more production back to the local community. In the global society era, this can be done efficiently with the aid of modern information and communication technology.

Advantages of increased local production are many. First, the most fundamental aspect of economic growth involves taking resources and rearranging them in ways that make them more valuable, a process called "value-added." For example, raw materials such as wheat, trees, and cows are transformed into bread, furniture, and hamburgers. The cost of raw material is only a very small share of the finished product. Real economic benefits occur during transformation processes. During the isolation era, much value-added processing was done locally. Then beginning with the mass society era, rural communities lost much of their value-added capacity and have simply become specialized producers of raw materials for use in global production. Now rural residents generally sell raw materials to large corporations and then purchase finished products from large corporations at much higher prices. Money used in these purchases then immediately leaves the community. Bringing value-added production back to local communities could result in creation of many jobs and retention of money in the local economy for much longer. In other words, it could increase the multiplier effect. Further, local production does not necessarily mean small-scale production. In California's Central Valley, for example, large plants hull, shell, and size locally produced almonds while other large plants transform locally produced tomatoes into millions of pounds of tomato paste daily.

Additionally, environmental and resource benefits of local production could be extensive. Centralization was made possible by cheap energy that allowed local raw materials to be transported to large central plants and then transported back to the community as finished products. Energy that made this system possible is no longer cheap and there are growing concerns with other consequences of fossil fuel consumption. Increased local production could result in much more sustainable use of energy.

The most obvious example of the potential for increased local production and corresponding value-added is with respect to food (Mooney and Hunt 2009; Pollan 2006, 2009; Roberts 2008; Sapp et al. 2009). During the isolation era most communities were largely self-sustaining with regard to food production. This meant that each community grew locally most of what community members ate. This has all changed in the global society era. Most regions of the country no longer produce a variety of products for their own consumption, but have become specialized in growing one or two items for the global market. The diversified family farm of the past has almost ceased to exist. Specialized products from all over the world are purchased by a small number of multinational food processing firms that take various products and transform them into a dizzying array of food items that are then sent back to local grocery stores. Results of this global industrial food system are impressive. The variety of food choices in any modern grocery store at any time is astounding. Fruits and vegetables that were once seasonal are now available throughout the year. Exotic tropical fruits that I had never even heard of during my childhood, such as mangoes and guava, are now available at my local grocery store any time. Further, Americans now spend a smaller share of their income on food than at any time in the past, leaving more money for other items that enhance our standard of living and quality of life.

Despite these benefits, there are growing concerns about the global industrial food system. First, communities and regions are no longer self-sufficient and even major farm states, such as Iowa, import the vast majority of their food. This raises serious food security concerns when one considers how easily this system could be disrupted. Also, the global industrial food system uses vast amounts of energy to produce, process, transport, and store food, and a system so dependent on cheap energy is simply not sustainable (Merrigan 2012). The average bite of food has travelled over 1,500 miles before reaching the American dinner plate. Additionally, some communities have become heavily dependent economically on providing a commodity to the global industrial food system. Should that community lose out to another provider in global competition, it could have significant economic implications. At-risk communities include those in the American corn belt that specialize in producing corn and soybeans to those communities in Third World countries, which in turn have become massive export-oriented farms for everything from avocados to zucchini. Finally, with the decline of local production, many people, and especially large numbers of rural residents, live in what are referred to as "food deserts" in that they have limited access to grocery stores and thus to fresh and nutritious food (Morton and Blanchard 2007).

There are growing concerns about health consequences of a diet based on the global industrial food system. Obesity levels and rates of diet-related illnesses such as type 2 diabetes have skyrocketed in the United States in recent years. No doubt these problems are at least partially a result of changes in our food consumption patterns. These changes include regular meals from fast food restaurants and consumption of massive amounts of convenience foods laced with sugar and artificial preservatives. The average American now consumes 25 percent more calories than a generation ago. Other problems faced by the global industrial food system include the fact that highly productive crops, grown largely in monocultures, necessitate using ever greater amounts of fertilizers, herbicides, and pesticides to deal with increasingly resistant pests.

Fertilizers, herbicides, and pesticides then wreak havoc on downstream waterways. Pollution and smell resulting from large-scale animal feedlots and increased danger from highly toxic pathogens are other potentially dangerous consequences emerging from the global industrial food system.

Increased reliance on locally produced foods and more local value-added production for these foods is one way of alleviating some of these problems. In other words, we may do best to revert back to earlier eras. Increased consumption of foods produced locally could greatly reduce the amount of energy used by the food industry, improve freshness, taste, and nutritional content of food, and improve the local economy. Jobs could be created locally, and money that would otherwise leave could remain in the community.

There are numerous examples of value-added opportunities in the food industry. The role of farmers' markets and food hubs has grown dramatically in recent years. Local growers are able to market their produce, and local residents are able to buy food that is more nutritious and tastes better simply because it is fresher and is less likely to have been processed. Additionally, local foods are usually cheaper because the middle-man has been eliminated and transportation costs are lower. There are other systems of enhancing local food production such as "community-supported agriculture" (CSAs), and farm-to-school and farm-to-hospital programs.

Some wheat farmers in the Palouse region of Washington, Idaho, and Oregon began using sustainable farming practices including no-till (now called direct seeding). These producers then joined forces and formed Shepherd's Grain Alliance. The core strategy of Shepherd's Grain is to provide sustainably produced and nutritious flour to consumers with information about where their food comes from and how it is produced. Each package of sustainably produced flour contains a "story" about the farmer and the wheat production process. A web address is provided on the package where consumers can obtain even more information. With this approach, farmers are able to reach a growing market of consumers concerned with sustainability and food production practices. Producers of raspberries in the Bear Lake area of Utah and Idaho are now marketing raspberry jam and other preserves. Cost-wise they cannot compete with major food producing companies, but they can market their name and the value of their product and have successfully created a niche market. Some western cattle ranchers have learned that recent concern with healthy food has led to growing demand for grass-fed beef. Rather than selling their calves to large-scale feedlots that then load these calves with antibiotics, steroids, and other rations that are not compatible with the bovine digestive system, these ranchers are retaining their calves and letting them grow on a diet of grass. Beef is then marketed to specialty sources and ranchers receive a higher return on their investment (Hussa 2009).

While there is no question that the health and financial benefits of locally produced food are noteworthy, there are costs of time and effort. Preparing fresh food simply takes longer and is more difficult than popping a frozen meal into the microwave or stopping at the drive-through window of a fast-food restaurant. It was saving time and convenience that largely led to centralization and emergence of the industrial food system in the first place. We need to be cognizant of the fact that agriculture needs to be productive enough to feed a world population that will soon reach nine billion. Research needs to be conducted and outreach programs implemented so that more of this production can be done locally.

Beyond food, value-added opportunities exist in other segments of the rural economy. Sheridan, Wyoming, has become the heart of a regional leather and related crafts industry. Based on traditions dating back to the nineteenth century when leather was used to make saddles, horse riding attire, shoes, belts, and holsters, leather craft has long been part of the culture and tradition of the area. In the global society era, talented craft workers are stamping complex patterns of wild roses and other designs onto saddles and other leather objects. These crafts have become collectors' items that have been acquired by Queen Elizabeth, Ronald Reagan, and the Crown Prince of Saudi Arabia. In addition to craft workers, other individuals are employed providing supplies and other support. This includes local cattle ranchers who now have an additional market for some of their products. Sales have expanded greatly in recent years because these works of art can be marketed worldwide using the internet. The leather craft industry takes a basic raw material (hide of a cow) and adds value that greatly enhances the economic worth of that product. The end result is that jobs are created and economic benefits remain in rural Wyoming (Rosenfeld 2009b).

Similar opportunities can be created in other parts of the rural West. In rural Nevada, farm families that grew alfalfa for cattle feed are now converting alfalfa into pellets that can be fed to horses and rabbits. This value-added process means that the product can be marketed more broadly, exported for much higher prices, and advertised on the internet. The economic returns to Nevada farmers are thus enhanced.

There are also significant opportunities for local energy production. Under the current system, most of our energy is produced at some centralized, distant location and then vast sums of local money are used to purchase this energy. Of course, there are obstacles to be overcome and change will require cooperation of local utility companies, but communities, farms, and individuals could use windmills, solar panels, or other means of producing energy locally. Canals or other flowing water courses could produce significant amounts of micro-hydroelectric power. Those who produce in excess of their needs could sell energy back to the grid. Locally produced energy could also come from renewable sources. The benefits would range from environmental protection to improving the national balance of trade, creating local jobs, and keeping money in the community.

Entrepreneurial Development

With computers, internet, and cell phones, it is now possible for individuals and firms to be connected to the global world while enjoying the benefits of rural living. Consequently, there are significant opportunities for entrepreneurial development. It is now possible to develop products locally and market them internationally using internet and other technologies. Local development results in many benefits for rural communities. Research reveals a positive relationship between density of locally-owned firms and per capita income growth (Fleming and Goetz 2011). Empirical evidence further suggests that the presence of small firms is correlated positively with subsequent growth, while large firms have a negative effect (Glaeser et al. 2010; Rosenthal and Strange 2003). Small firms benefit local economies because of higher marginal productivity of workers (where each worker is more productive in a small firm than in a large firm) and greater ability to adapt to external shocks (such as economic recession or technology change) (Fleming and Goetz 2011). Some authors also emphasize the destructive effects of large firms on small firms and local jobs (Bonanno and Lopez 2008). Further, locally created businesses, such as northeastern Wyoming's leather crafts industry, are more likely to fit into the local culture and environment and to use locally produced resources.

Locally owned small businesses provide opportunities for people who have a desire to live in a specific rural community. Generally, entrepreneurial people who build their own businesses are committed to stay in the community and help the community thrive. In contrast, for multinational industrial firms profit margin is paramount and many firms will relocate to improve the bottom line regardless of local impacts. An example of this occurred in a rural community in eastern Colorado. After great effort, the community was able to attract a relatively large industrial firm that would create more than 300 new, local jobs. Community leaders were ecstatic. New roads were built, water and sewer systems were expanded, and additions were made to local schools. However, during the 2008 economic downturn, the firm closed, employees lost their jobs, and the community was left with the expenses of unneeded roads, too much water and sewer capacity, and schools with empty classrooms.

There are several steps that communities can take to encourage entrepreneurship (Acs 2008). Much of this can be done by working cooperatively with the local county extension agent. The first is to carefully examine community policies and make sure that they encourage rather than discourage innovation and development. Red tape should be kept to a minimum. Second, a system of roundtables and workshops can be initiated during which people can generate and discuss ideas. When talented and creative people come together, ideas flow more freely, and the end result usually amounts to more than the sum of the parts. This process of developing new ideas through interactions of innovative and talented people is the very principle that gives mega-cities advantages over other areas, as noted by Richard Florida (2002). Third, relevant computer, internet, and other skills can be taught, and assistance can be provided in helping people complete the necessary paperwork. Fourth, many extension or Small Business Development Centers (SBCD) offices offer small business training and workshops that can provide valuable knowledge and skills. Finally, careful and accurate market research is critical. A word of caution should be offered. Many small businesses fail and many others seem to barely survive; average incomes of self-employed workers are significantly lower than average incomes of those who are employees of another organization. Potential entrepreneurs must have the best skills possible.

Attract Creative Class Workers

Another way to take advantage of modern information and communication technology is to encourage individuals with geographically mobile or creative class occupations to establish their homes in rural communities. Such individuals often have significant incomes and skill sets that can benefit the community. Potential targets include employees who wish to work from their home or establish an office away from company headquarters, and persons with creative jobs, such as writers and artists, who can live anywhere they wish. For example, a software engineer who works for a firm in San Jose, California, lives in a small and isolated rural Utah community and is able to do his work over the internet. In the global society era, a growing number of workers no longer need to be in the office every day, and for many of them it may be possible to live in the rural West regardless of where the home office is located.

Of course both attracting creative class workers and encouraging entrepreneurial development assumes that broadband and other modern technologies are available in all locations, which is simply not the case at the present time. In fact, remote areas of the rural west are among locations least likely to have broadband. In the global society era, a community that is not connected to the modern world has little chance. Obviously, an absolute vital first step to rural economic development in the global era is for communities to become connected to the modern world. National and state policies and programs to make this a reality are essential.

Clusters and Regional Development

Another way to create more high quality jobs is to focus on clustering and regional development. It is critical for communities to recognize they are far better off if they consider neighboring communities as partners rather than competitors. By working together as regions, rather than trying to go it on their own, rural communities greatly increase their opportunities. For example, the Stronger Economies Together (SET) program is a collaboration between USDA Rural Development, the Regional Rural Development Centers, and land-grant universities to provide communities in rural America an opportunity to work together to develop economic development plans that strategically build on current and emerging strengths of their regions.

Clustering is an approach to regional development. Porter (2000) defined a cluster as "a geographically proximate group of interconnected companies and associated institutions in a particular field, linked by commonalities and complementarities." A regional clustering approach would involve a number of establishments and would ideally take advantage of the region's culture, history, and locally-produced resources to provide comparative advantages and even branding and name recognition.

Clusters are not simply defined by firms producing similar products that are located in the same area, but by true interrelationships and collaborations. The goal should be innovation, upgrading infrastructure, and improving the labor force (Woodward and Guimaraes 2009). Examples include cheese artisans in Vermont, catfish farming in Mississippi, and folk art in San Luis Valley, Colorado (Rosenfeld 2009a). Shields, Barkley, and Emery (2009) outline three principle advantages of regional clustering that accrue to establishments and their host region:

1. *Industry clusters provide production and marketing cost savings.* Sources of potential cost-savings include access to specialized input and service providers, a larger pool of trained and specialized workers, and public infrastructure investments and financial markets geared to the needs of the industry.

2. *Industry clusters provide a more conducive environment for change.* Establishments have a greater ability to focus on their core activities, production technologies, and organizations. With greater focus on their core activities, and through positive interactions with similar firms, innovation is more likely to occur.

3. *Industry clustering facilitates the development of linkages, cooperation, and collaboration among area firms.* Consequently, new business activity in an industry is positively associated with the region's industry cluster size.

The key to successful clustering is true regional collaboration among both local governments and firms. In a world where emphasis has always been on competition, such collaboration is not always easy. Benefits, however, are many. Rosenfeld (2009b) maintains that regional clustering can achieve a triple-bottom line—having economic, social, and environmental benefits. The economic advantages of jobs and financial benefits are apparent. In addition, regional clustering has the potential of enhancing local culture and history, thus providing social benefits. Finally, by using locally produced products in a sustainable manner, regional clustering provides significant environmental advantages.

Achieving Place-Based Rural Economic Development

To achieve success with any of these place-based rural economic development efforts requires a concerted effort by community members and especially community leaders. Several important points should be considered. First, community development efforts must reflect the values and wishes of local populations (Christenson and Robinson 1989; Theodori 2009). Local people understand their history and culture better than the often ill-informed experts who live beyond community boundaries. Also, efforts must be exerted to involve all segments of the local population, and this requires careful communication and engaging persons who otherwise tend to be less involved, including racial and ethnic minorities and people in all age groups. Additionally, successful community development requires a commitment to consider what is best for the community, rather than potential personal gains for a few community leaders or a few local businesses.

Conclusions

While employment in the goods-producing industries—the traditional primary employers of rural workers—has been declining for decades, there are opportunities for high-quality employment in rural communities that simply did not exist in the past. Improved information and communication technology have greatly increased opportunities for rural communities of the West.

Implementing place-based rural development approaches described in this chapter will be more difficult for some communities than others. Consider the role of amenities. When people are free to locate where they wish, a high proportion of them choose to locate in high-amenity communities. Thus, it seems that in the global society era, aesthetic communities will have distinct advantages over communities lacking high-quality amenities. Additionally, some communities have had declining populations or high rates of poverty for decades and face significant obstacles in turning these trends around. Achieving place-based rural development in these most vulnerable communities will be the topic of the next chapter. It is also critical to remember that place-based rural economic development as described in this chapter cannot work in a vacuum. For communities to receive the full benefit of global society era opportunities there must be a corresponding development of human capacity—a people-based approach to rural development. This people-based approach is the topic of Chapters Ten and Eleven.

CHAPTER NINE

Place-Based Rural Development Among the West's Most Vulnerable Communities

As with other major economic transitions, advent of the global society era has resulted in circumstances where some communities thrive while others struggle with economic and demographic stagnation and decline. The characteristics of thriving or struggling communities are often different from previous eras. During the isolation era, access to traditional natural resources was essential for community vitality, while during the mass society era proximity to metro areas or major transportation routes was strongly related to economic and demographic growth. The critical factors contributing to community vitality are likely to be different during the global society era. The primary objective of this chapter is to understand factors related to whether communities thrive or struggle and then provide a discussion on community development strategies most likely to be effective in addressing concerns of the most disadvantaged communities. Disadvantaged communities discussed in this chapter are starting with obstacles that make it difficult for them to utilize the approaches described in Chapter Eight.

To address the concerns of the most disadvantaged communities, it is first essential to determine characteristics of the most advantaged and most disadvantaged counties to understand factors most strongly related to these economic outcomes. An empirical assessment was made to determine which counties in the nonmetro west were economically advantaged or disadvantaged and characteristics of counties on different sides of this economic spectrum. The first step in this process was to develop an economic advantage scale. An economic advantage measure was developed using three economic variables associated with community vitality: median household income, percent of persons in poverty, and median value of owner-occupied homes. Economically vibrant communities have high incomes, low poverty rates, and high home values which provide residents with a significant source of wealth. Counties in the top 10 percent of western nonmetro counties on each variable were given a score of 6, counties between the 75th and 90th percentiles were given a score of 5, those between the 50th and 75th percentile a score of 4, from the 25th to the 50th percentile a score of 3, from the 10th to the 25th percentile a score of 2 and counties in the bottom 10th percentile were give a score of 1. Scoring was reversed for the poverty variable where having low poverty rates is desired. Possible scores on this economic advantage scale thus range from 3 to 18 with low scores representing the most economically disadvantaged counties and high scores representing the most economically advantaged counties. For a county to earn a score of 18, it had to be in the top 10 percent of all western nonmetro counties in median household income, the fewest percent of residents living in poverty, and home values. To earn a score of 3, the county had to be in the bottom 10 percent on all three variables.

The second step was to empirically explore the characteristics of counties that were the most economically advantaged and disadvantaged. A number of variables were explored that theoretically make sense or that have been found to be important to community vitality in previous research. Variables examined include amenities, the racial/ethnic composition of the population, levels of educational attainment of residents, population size, proximity to metropolitan areas, and proportion of labor force employed in the goods-producing industries. Analysis revealed that three variables were very strongly related to economic advantage scale scores including amenities, race/ethnicity, and educational attainment. Other variables were much less significant. Thus, economically advantaged nonmetro counties in the West tend to have high-quality amenities, small minority populations, and a well-educated populace. The most disadvantaged counties are the opposite—they lack high-quality amenities, have large minority populations, and have lower levels of educational attainment among their residents.

Table 9.1 presents data showing characteristics of counties with various scores on the economic advantage scale. Since income, poverty rates, and home values were used to construct the scale, these variables are obviously strongly related to scale scores. In highly advantaged counties, median household incomes were more than double those in highly disadvantaged counties, poverty rates were less than one-third as high, and home values were about four times higher. Table 9.1 also shows that more advantaged communities have much higher scores on the natural amenity scale score, have a smaller proportion of minority residents, and have higher levels of educational attainment. While other variables

Table 9.1 Relationship Between Economic Advantage Scale and Characteristics of Counties in the Nonmetropolitan West, 2010 (N = 314)

Economic Advantage Scale	Median Household Income	Percent in Poverty	Median Home Values	National Amenity Scale Score	Percent White	Education		Percent Employed in Goods Producing Industry	Population in 2010	Urban Influence Score
						High School Degree (Percent)	College Degree (Percent)			
Highly Disadvantaged (Scores 3–6; N = 46)	$31,194	24.9	$87,389	2.68	54.7	80.9	16.1	30.2	16,455	7.5
Disadvantaged (Scores 7–10; N = 121)	$38,808	17.2	$131,202	2.43	77.3	85.0	18.5	30.3	21,770	7.4
Advantaged (Scores 11–15; N = 110)	$46,680	12.9	$190,143	3.87	80.6	87.4	20.7	30.8	24,322	7.1
Highly Advantaged (Score 16–18; N = 37)	$63,175	8.2	$339,162	5.02	76.4	91.8	30.9	24.4	31,355	6.4
Overall Mean	$43,369	15.7	$170,436	3.22	75.0	86.1	20.4	29.8	23,023	7.2
Correlation with Economic Advantage Scale	.872	-.842	.689	.350	.287	.494	.468	-.117	.170	-.174

Source: Don E. Albrecht

(percent employed in the goods producing industries, population size, and urban influence) are also related to the economic advantage scale, these relationships are much weaker, and the effects of these variables virtually disappear in regression models.

Table 9.2 provides a list of the most advantaged counties (those with scores of 17 or 18) and most disadvantaged counties (those with scores of 3 or 4). Of the eighteen most advantaged counties, fifteen of them are known for being high amenity communities and include Jackson, Wyoming (Teton County); Sun Valley, Idaho (Blaine County); the Lake Tahoe region in Nevada (Douglas County); and the Colorado resort communities of Aspen (Pitkin County), Steamboat Springs (Routt County), Vail (Eagle County), Breckenridge (Summit County), and Telluride (San Miguel County). Also among the most advantaged nonmetro counties

Table 9.2 List of the Most Advantaged and Most Disadvantaged Counties in the Nonmetropolitan West, 2010

Most Advantaged Counties	Most Disadvantaged Counties
Juneau, Alaska	Wade Hampton, Alaska
Ketchikan Gateway, Alaska	Apache, Arizona
Sitka, Alaska	La Paz, Arizona
Eagle, Colorado	Bent, Colorado
Garfield, Colorado	Conejos, Colorado
Gilpin, Colorado	Costilla, Colorado
Ouray, Colorado	Crowley, Colorado
Pitkin, Colorado	Otero, Colorado
Routt, Colorado	Prowers, Colorado
San Miguel, Colorado	Big Horn, Montana
Summit, Colorado	Blaine, Montana
Blaine, Idaho	Glacier, Montana
Douglas, Nevada	Roosevelt, Montana
Los Alamos, New Mexico	Cibola, New Mexico
Wasatch, Utah	De Baca, New Mexico
Campbell, Wyoming	Guadalupe, New Mexico
Sublette, Wyoming	Hidalgo, New Mexico
Teton, Wyoming	Luna, New Mexico
	McKinley, New Mexico
	Quay, New Mexico
	Sierra, New Mexico

Source: Don E. Albrecht

in the west are Los Alamos County, New Mexico (home of Los Alamos National Laboratory), and two major energy-producing counties in Wyoming (Campbell and Sublette Counties).

On the other hand, the twenty-one highly disadvantaged counties tend to be in the Great Plains portion of the region and thus lack high quality amenities; they tend to have large minority populations and have low levels of educational attainment. In fact, thirteen of the twenty-one most disadvantaged counties have populations that are more than 50 percent minority. In the paragraphs that follow, overviews of the most advantaged and most disadvantaged counties are provided to highlight differences between the two groups. A discussion of community development approaches to address the concerns of the most disadvantaged counties is then provided.

Advantaged Communities of the Rural West

The case of Teton County, Wyoming, provides a classic example of highly advantaged nonmetro communities in the west. No question one of the most serenely beautiful views in the world is from the shores of Jackson Lake in Grand Teton National Park. Behind the lake are the rugged peaks of the picturesque Teton Mountains, rising to an elevation of over 13,000 feet. A century ago during the isolation era, Teton Mountain amenities were of little value to those attempting to make a living in the area. Traditional natural resources were limited and thus there were few residents. Because the population was so small, Teton County was not even organized until the 1920s, when it was divided from Lincoln County. In 1930, total population of Teton County was 2,003, with 307 residents living in the county seat of Jackson. Most of the population was striving to earn a living from marginal ranching and farming operations. Crop production was especially difficult because the elevation of Jackson is 6,234 feet and the growing season is short.

Initial proposals to preserve the Teton Mountains as a national park were met with strong local and statewide opposition because of concerns that this would have a negative impact on sheep grazing. Despite opposition, Grand Teton National Park was created in 1929. Even with increased tourism that creation of the park generated, little economic or demographic development occurred for decades. The population of Teton County was only 2,543 in 1940; 2,503 in 1950; and 3,062 in 1960.

Transition from a ranching town to a resort began rather innocuously in the late 1960s with development of two ski resorts. Evidence

Teton Mountains from Jackson Lake. *Don E. Albrecht*

of growth and development resulting from the ski resorts was apparent as the county population increased to 4,823 in 1970. Eventually, skiing blended into year-round tourism, and souvenir shops replaced feed and hardware stores. Then condominiums, rental units, and golf courses emerged. Intended clientele of these establishments was not locals, but visitors and wealthy newcomers who were moving into the valley. Soon, real estate developers realized the potential market and began subdividing ranches into lots where rich and famous could build trophy homes with views of the mountains (Travis 2007). By 2010, the population of Teton County had soared to 21,294. That number would be much higher but home prices are exorbitant and space is scarce as much land is publicly owned. In 2010, average home prices and median household incomes in Teton County were among the highest in the nation. Most long-time residents were no longer able to afford soaring housing prices unless they had made a fortune subdividing and selling their farm or ranch properties. As living costs skyrocketed, low-pay service workers, who are in great demand to take care of wealthy residents and other visitors, could no longer afford to live in Jackson. Many service workers now live in Driggs, Idaho, and make the thirty-mile drive through a difficult mountain pass daily to work in Jackson.

Similar scenarios of population growth and economic change in high-amenity resort communities are apparent in other places in the west. Aspen, Colorado, was originally settled when silver was discovered in 1879. By 1891, Aspen was among the leading silver producing communities in the world, and the population was estimated to be between 10,000 and 16,000. Then the silver mines played out and Aspen went into a tailspin. The 1900 census reported that the population of Pitkin County (where Aspen is located) had a population of 7,020. The 1930 census found only 1,770 residents in the county, most of whom were surviving primarily on marginal ranching and farming operations. Following World War II, a ski resort was built in the area, and transition to a high-income resort community began. By 2010, the population of Pitkin County was 17,148 and the value of owner-occupied homes in the county was even higher than in Teton County, Wyoming. Many long-time residents can no longer afford to live in Aspen, and many service workers commute from Rifle, about sixty-eight miles away. A similar transition has unfolded in other resort communities such as Breckenridge, Steamboat Springs, and Telluride, Colorado, and Park City, Utah. Some communities, such as Sun Valley, Idaho, and Vail, Colorado, have been built as resorts from the ground up.

Other communities in the rural west that have not become world-class resorts are also doing very well economically and demographically. Many of these communities have sufficient amenities to attract creative class workers or service-sector businesses. Additionally, several communities with energy-based economies are also doing extremely well, and two of these, Campbell and Sublette Counties in Wyoming, were among the most advantaged counties listed in Table 9.2. Energy resources provide high paying jobs and a strong tax base that help the entire community prosper. In addition to amenities or energy resources, a common theme with most of thriving communities is that they have a relatively well-educated populace and are predominately white.

Disadvantaged Communities of the Rural West

In contrast to these advantaged communities, other communities in the west contend with significant demographic and economic challenges. In 2009, 57 of 311 nonmetro counties in the west (18 percent) had poverty rates greater than 20 percent. In Crowley County, Colorado, the poverty rate was greater than 50 percent. In ninety-four western nonmetro counties (30 percent), the population declined between 2000 and 2010, and in seventy-eight of these counties, the 2010 population was smaller than the 1980 population. Daniels County in northeast Montana has seen their population plummet from 5,553 in 1930 to 1,751 in 2010, a 68.5 percent decline. Likewise, Wibaux County (along the Montana/North Dakota border), had a 2010 population of 1,017, down from 2,767 in 1930, a decline of 63.2 percent. Further, many western counties have median household income levels that are only a fraction of top amenity and energy counties.

Many disadvantaged rural western communities are in the Great Plains portion of the West and lack high quality amenities (D. Albrecht 1993). Many have large minority populations. For example, in Apache County, Arizona, about two-thirds of the population and over one-half of the land area are comprised of the Navajo Nation, the largest Native American tribe in the United States. The Navajo reservation, like other reservations throughout the country, is plagued by a lack of quality jobs, low incomes, and high poverty rates. Other disadvantaged counties have large Hispanic populations. For example, 80 percent of the residents of Guadalupe County, New Mexico, are Hispanic and the county also faces severe obstacles resulting from a lack of jobs, low incomes, and high poverty rates. Finally, in disadvantaged communities, the populace tends to have low levels of educational attainment. Several western counties deal with several of these obstacles simultaneously. If lack of amenities, minority populations, and educational attainment levels are the factors resulting in disadvantaged communities, then these issues need to be addressed. This is challenging because educational attainment is the only factor that can be dealt with directly.

Amenities

A large and growing literature has found a strong association between amenities and population and economic growth, and as noted earlier, many of the most advantaged rural communities in the west are high amenity communities (D. Albrecht 2004; 2010; Beyers and Nelson 2000; Boyle and Halfacree 1998; Cromartie and Wardwell 1999; Green 2001; Henderson and McDaniel 1998; Hunter et al. 2005; McGranahan 1999; 2009; McGranahan and Wojan 2007; Nelson et al. 2009; Nord and Cromartie 1997; Otterstrom and Shumway 2003; Rudzitis 1999; Saint Onge et al. 2007; Shumway 1997; Shumway and Davis 1996; Shumway and Otterstrom 2001). So where does this leave communities that lack high-quality amenities? There is only one Teton National Park, and intermountain west communities are never going to provide the beaches of Maui.

While the lack of stunning amenities is certainly an obstacle, all is not lost. To begin with, to some extent, amenities exist in the eyes of the beholder and there are no agreed upon features that define a high amenity community. Every community has characteristics that some people are going to find aesthetic. It is important for communities to recognize their special and unique features and find ways to enhance, preserve, and market them. Second, human-built entities, especially those that emphasize history and culture, can contribute greatly to aesthetic appeal of a community. Additionally, there is much that communities can do to make themselves look as good as possible. Cleaning up and adding a coat of paint can do wonders. Finally, every community offers something to some people that no other community in the world can offer—it is home. Recent research shows that many individuals who grew up in small towns and then left for school or jobs are willing to accept career sacrifices in order to go home. And this is just not any community, it is their hometown. A major benefit being sought by those coming home is the chance to raise their children in a familiar, small-town environment (von Reichert et al. 2011).

Racial/Ethnic Composition of the Population

From the time of initial settlement of the West by persons of European descent, minority populations, on average, have had much lower incomes and much higher poverty rates than majority white populations. Generations of discrimination have a powerful effect. Under these circumstances, it is not surprising that communities with large minority populations have been among the most disadvantaged in the country (D. Albrecht et al. 2005). Severe economic problems in communities with large minority populations have existed for decades and are deeply entrenched. Overcoming them will require substantial effort from both inside and outside of the community and extensive progress is not likely to happen overnight. However, the goal of improving circumstances for minority people is critically important to the long-term vitality of this country.

While significant Asian- and African-American minority populations reside in the west, most of these individuals live in urban areas. Rural minority residents are predominately Native American or Hispanic.

Further, all economically disadvantaged nonmetro counties in the west that have large minority populations tend to have either large Native American or Hispanic populations or both.

Native Americans and Disadvantage

For centuries prior to the arrival of whites, the west was occupied by a wide variety of Native American tribes who subsisted by hunting, fishing, and gathering, with some agricultural production. Following arrival of European Americans, Native Americans were forced onto reservations where they were stripped of their culture and traditional means of livelihood. Often these reservations were located in areas that lacked apparent traditional natural resources and often lacked amenity resources as well. Typically, the reservation was only a small proportion of the land that the tribe traditionally lived on. From the outset, these reservations have been beset by extremely high unemployment levels, poverty rates, and other social problems. Educational opportunities have been limited and job availability inadequate (Bordewich 1996). In fact, on most reservations, there is a complete lack of a functioning economy (R. Miller 2012). Thus it is not surprising that several of the most disadvantaged counties in the west listed in Table 9.2 are the homes of Native American reservations. This list includes Apache County, Arizona; McKinley County, New Mexico; and Blaine, Glacier, Big Horn, and Roosevelt Counties in Montana.

This chapter is concerned with community-level factors associated with disadvantage and so will focus on communities on Native American reservations. Individual-level considerations are discussed in Chapter Eleven. Several factors must be considered when discussing economic development among Native American populations living on reservations. The first problem is very low levels of educational attainment. The combination of large minority populations and low levels of educational attainment has been a sure recipe for economic disadvantage. A lack of educational attainment means that communities have a work force that lacks skills and training essential for high quality employment. The root of educational problems on reservations can be traced to generations of inadequate funding for primary and secondary schools, which has resulted in outdated equipment and poorly paid teachers. The lack of high quality jobs on reservations held by individuals who can provide role models of the benefits of education is another problem, as are cultural traditions that have not placed a high priority on education. Further, for individuals living on reservations, colleges tend to be distant, expensive, and can require a difficult cultural transition. Attempts to overcome these educational obstacles include creation of tribal colleges and universities located on tribal lands. Since 1994 these colleges have been a part of the land-grant university system. Current and past efforts, however, remain inadequate, and development of new programs to make reservation schools better and more accessible is essential.

A second major problem is that the very structure of tribal lands provides a major impediment to economic development. Land on American Indian reservations cannot be privately owned and thus cannot be bought and sold. Land is held in trust by the federal government on behalf of the tribes. If a tribe or tribal member wants to build a house or business on tribal land, the Department of the Interior must first approve a "lease" of the land. Prior to consideration by the department, approval from the tribe is often required. This process is slow and cumbersome and most Native Americans feel that the requirement of seeking federal approval to build a home or business is paternalistic. Additionally, since individuals do not own the land on which they wish to build a home or business, finding bank loans or insurance is difficult because of the lack of security. The consequence has been a tremendous drag on development. Streamlining this process is essential.

Hispanics and Disadvantage

In the sixteenth century, well before settlement of Jamestown and Plymouth, Spanish-speaking people moved north from Mexico to settle along the Rio Grande Valley in present-day New Mexico, where they established Albuquerque, Santa Fe, and other communities. Then in the eighteenth century, other Spanish settlements (such as San Diego, Los Angeles, and San Francisco) were built along the California coast. Following the Mexican-American War of 1848, all or parts of the present-day western states of California, Nevada, Arizona, New Mexico, Colorado, Utah, and Wyoming were ceded from Mexico to the United States as a result of the Treaty of Guadalupe Hidalgo. With the stroke of a pen, some 50,000 Mexican citizens were transformed from being a majority in their own country to a minority in an alien land (Massey 2007). Today, thousands of American citizens of Hispanic descent can trace their ancestry in this country to before the Mayflower and many of them live in communities that were settled before the eastern colonies.

During the ensuing decades, periodic labor shortages in agriculture and manufacturing lead to efforts by employers to recruit minority workers to the West. As a result, a number of Asian- and African-Americans moved west, in most cases to urban areas. The major target for workers among western employers, however, was Mexico. This was especially true for seasonal and generally low-pay jobs in agriculture. A "bracero program" was developed in the early 1940s to encourage Mexican residents to come and work, but then return to Mexico when work was completed. The bracero programs continued until the Civil Rights Movement of the 1960s resulted in efforts to eliminate racism from the immigration system. Consequently, immigration laws allowed for legal entry of people from Latin American countries. However, the number of people who were allowed legal entry was relatively small while demand for workers remained much greater. The result was a vast increase in the number of illegal residents who entered the United States seeking employment.

From the 1960s until 1985, movement of illegal immigrants from Latin America to the United States was somewhat circular and predictable. Mostly young men would come, primarily as seasonal agricultural workers, and then return to Mexico to see their families during the off-season. During this era, crossing the border without authorization became a somewhat ritualized game of "cat and mouse." Immigrants would try to avoid detection when crossing the border. Those who were caught were simply sent back to Mexico where, most likely, they would try again to cross the border. This pattern was ended with passage of the Immigration Reform and Control Act (IRCA) of 1986. This act had three major outcomes. First, it authorized legalization of many people who had been living in the United States illegally for a significant amount of time. Second, IRCA sharply increased funding for the Border Patrol, which made crossing the border much more difficult, dangerous, and costly. Under these circumstances, Mexican workers tended to minimize their number of border crossings. Thus, rather than coming to the United States for seasonal work and then returning to Mexico, many men came to the United States, brought their families, and stayed. Consequently, higher levels of funding to the Border Patrol increased rather than decreased the number of illegal residents in the United States. The third outcome of IRCA was that it criminalized the hiring of undocumented workers and made persons doing the hiring legally responsible. As a result, the wage gap between documented and undocumented Hispanic workers became wider.

Because of these events, the number of Hispanic residents of the United States in general, and the West in particular, increased dramatically. During the three decades from 1980 to 2010, the number of Hispanic residents in the West increased from 6.3 million to 20.6 million, an increase of over 14.3 million people or 229 percent. In comparison, the white population increased by only 6.2 million people or 19 percent during this same period. Hispanic and other minority populations tend to be relatively young and thus their numbers are likely to continue to grow rapidly in the future. Of the residents of the West who are eighteen years of age or older, 56.9 percent are white while only 24.8 percent of this age group is Hispanic. In contrast, the number of white and Hispanic residents among the population who are seventeen or younger is relatively even (40.6 percent white and 40.1 percent Hispanic). In California, the 2010 census found that there were 4.8 million Hispanics ages seventeen and younger compared to 2.5 million whites in the same age group. In 1980, nearly three-fourths (73.8 percent) of the residents of West were white. By 2010, the proportion had declined to barely one-half (52.8 percent). In 1980, the population was more than 90 percent white in six Western states. By 2010, none of the states in the west had populations that were more than 90 percent white. In fact, in three western states (California, Hawaii, and New Mexico), the 2010 population was more than 50 percent minority.

Hispanic populations have been increasing rapidly in many counties throughout the West, even in areas where there have been no Hispanic residents in the past. In several western nonmetro counties of the Southwest there are large numbers of Hispanic residents, many of whom can trace their ancestry to early Spanish settlement. Unfortunately, several counties with large Hispanic populations (such as Conejos and Costilla, Colorado, and Guadalupe, Hidalgo, and Luna, New Mexico) are on the list of the most disadvantaged counties (Table 9.2).

Economic development in communities with extensive Hispanic populations must confront two major obstacles. First is education. Hispanic adults, on average, have lower levels of educational attainment than any other racial or ethnic group in the United States. Consequently, many Hispanics lack skills and training to obtain high quality employment, and many communities with large Hispanic populations lack a workforce with the education and skills to attract global era businesses looking to relocate. The low educational attainment of Hispanic adults is a function of large numbers of recent immigrants from parts of the world where educational levels tend to be lower, and of the fact that schools in the United States with large Hispanic populations have historically tended to be poorly funded. If our country does not do a better job of educating Hispanic residents, the consequences will be detrimental for the entire country.

A second obstacle to economic development in communities with extensive Hispanic populations is language barriers. Greater effort must be made by a variety of organizations to provide more material in Spanish. This includes information from schools, programs about business development and retention, and much more. Additionally, more Hispanic residents need to recognize that learning English is an essential first step to opening many doors in this country.

Educational Levels

While low levels of education are problematic in communities with large Native American and Hispanic populations, any community that has a populace with low levels of educational attainment faces significant obstacles in their economic development efforts. The problem stems from fundamental changes in economic structure associated with the transition to the global society era. While college-educated workers have always earned higher incomes than their less-educated counterparts, this gap has increased substantially in recent years. Data from the American Community Survey, presented in Table 9.3, indicate that individuals with college degrees have incomes that are much higher than those of persons with high school degrees or less.

There are things that communities can do to improve educational attainment levels among residents. First, public education is heavily funded by local property taxes and much of what occurs in schools is under local prerogative. Communities can assure that their schools have high priority in the budget process and are adequately funded to meet the needs of students in the global society era. It is also essential that educational efforts reach a broad segment of the population, serving, in particular, racial and ethnic minorities who often lag behind the majority white population in measures of educational attainment. Communities can strive to assure that schools with high minority enrollment are adequately staffed and supplied so that all students get an education that adequately prepares them for the world in which they will live. In many rural communities there needs to be a cultural change about

Table 9.3 Median Incomes by Educational Attainment for Persons Age 25-65 with Full-Time Employment, 2009

Educational Attainment	Median Income
Less Than High School	$24,001
High School Graduate	$34,500
Some College	$40,338
College Graduate	$56,164
Post-Graduate Degree	$75,020

Source: United States Census Bureau, Current Population Survey, 2009

education. Many rural parents never attended college and were still able to find adequate employment. Without knowledge of global economic trends, these parents often place less emphasis on their children's schooling. Research on rural youth indicates that their parents are more likely than urban parents to encourage youth to get full-time jobs, attend trade schools, or enter the military rather than attend college (Carr and Kefalas 2009). Communities have a vital role in helping residents understand the changing global world, the increasing importance of formal education in that world, and the need to bridge the cultural gap so that the college world is less alien to their youth.

Conclusions

The most disadvantaged communities in the rural west face significant obstacles as they seek to adjust to a global era world. Many communities are disadvantaged as a result of large minority populations or a lack of amenities. These are obstacles that are difficult for communities to address. The other key factor related to community disadvantage is education. This is something more amenable to change and improving educational levels should be a high priority at the local, state, and federal policy levels. The importance of education will also be addressed in discussions of people-based rural development in the next two chapters.

CHAPTER TEN

Enhancing Human Capacity Through People-Based Economic Development

I t is a story that has been replayed countless times. Shortly after gradu-ating from the local small town high school, a young person packs his or her bags and moves away to college. Upon completing college, this person obtains rewarding and relatively high paying employment in the city. High-quality jobs necessary to lure him or her back home are simply not available. Soon the former small-town resident and his or her family are a major asset to their new community as they pay taxes and support local businesses, schools, and youth and civic organizations. Eventually visits home are largely limited to seeing Mom and Dad at Christmas.

While common, this scenario is troubling to small towns for many reasons. Of course families and friends miss local young people who move away. The young people that parents, relatives, teachers, and friends have invested so much time and effort into raising now live elsewhere and, in effect, the community receives little direct return on their investment. Perhaps most significantly, the young people who leave are not drawn randomly from the youth of the community. Those who leave tend to be the brightest, best educated, most motivated, and best nurtured both physically and emotionally (Domina 2006a; 2006b; Fuguitt et al. 1989; F. Wilson 1987; Zuiches and Brown 1978), while those who stay are more likely to be "the undereducated and the unskilled" (Lichter et al. 1995). These trends lead to concerns of a "rural brain drain" and fears about reduced human capacity levels and the future of towns left behind (Carr and Kefalas 2009).

While significant proportions of rural young have always migrated from their hometowns to the city (Fuguitt 1971), reasons for concern are amplified in the global society era. In previous decades, young people who stayed in their rural hometowns could take over the family farm or find employment that provided solid middle-class incomes in manufac-turing or the natural resource industries of forestry, fisheries, or mining (the goods-producing industries). Most jobs in these industries did not require a college education and so their lack of advanced training was not a major hindrance. With solid and seemingly stable middle-income jobs, some of these young people would eventually become pillars of the community.

Not only have many of the most talented young people moved away, but many remaining rural residents find skills that once allowed them to earn a comfortable living have become outdated. Consequently, there is a pressing need for people-based rural economic development to improve talents, knowledge, and skill levels of many rural residents. Among human capacity concerns identified by the rural roundtable participants are levels of educational attainment and workforce and leadership skills. This chapter provides a discussion about addressing these individual-level human capacity concerns through people-based rural economic development. Improved human capacity must be accompanied by place-based rural economic development as described in Chapters Eight and Nine as better education and work force skills are of little value without the corresponding high-quality jobs. I begin by outlining some major human capacity problems in rural areas and consequences of these problems. Some potential approaches for addressing these issues are then described.

Human Capacity Problems

Inadequate Education

Educational attainment levels in nonmetro areas lag significantly behind educational levels in metro areas. Data in Table 10.1 show that for more than half of nonmetro adults, the highest level of educational attainment is a high school degree or less. Further, only 21.7 percent of nonmetro adults have a college education compared to 32.9 percent of metro adults. Of special concern are low levels of educational attainment for young

Table 10.1   Educational Attainment for Adults (Age 25 or More) by Metro and Nonmetro Residence in the Western United States, 2009

Highest Level of Educational Attainment	Metro (%)	Nonmetro (%)
Less Than High School	12.4	12.0
High School Graduate	30.4	39.4
Some College	24.3	26.9
College Graduates	20.5	14.3
Post-Graduate Degree	12.4	7.4

Source: American Community Survey

males. An examination of Table 10.2 indicates that for persons age 55 and older, educational attainment levels for males surpassed educational attainment levels for females. For persons from 45 to 54 years of age, educational attainment levels for males and females were very similar. For persons ages 44 and younger, female educational attainment levels surpass those of males, and differences become greater for younger individuals. Low levels of educational attainment, especially for males, is problematic because the economic transition leading to the global society era is resulting in fewer well-paying jobs for workers without a college degree. This transition has been most pronounced for males who traditionally held most well-paying jobs in the goods-producing sector. As a result, there is a large and growing income gap between the college educated and those who lack a college degree (D. Albrecht and S. Albrecht

Table 10.2   Educational Attainment by Age and Gender in the Western United States, 2009

Age and Gender	Educational Attainment (%)				
	Less than High School	High School Graduate	Some College	College Graduate	Post-Graduate Degree
18-24					
Male	16.1	47.9	29.6	6.0	0.4
Female	11.4	41.6	36.1	10.2	0.7
25-30					
Male	12.6	34.6	25.6	21.3	5.9
Female	9.5	28.2	27.0	26.3	9.0
31-34					
Male	13.1	31.3	23.7	21.5	10.4
Female	11.5	26.1	25.4	24.1	12.9
35-44					
Male	13.7	30.6	23.4	20.1	12.2
Female	11.9	27.7	25.5	22.6	12.3
45-54					
Male	11.6	32.6	24.7	18.9	12.2
Female	10.5	31.2	27.9	19.7	10.7
55-64					
Male	9.0	27.2	27.2	20.5	16.1
Female	10.0	32.0	26.7	18.6	12.7
65 or More					
Male	14.8	32.0	20.7	17.1	15.4
Female	17.2	42.6	20.8	12.2	7.2

Source: American Community Survey

2009; Card and DiNardo 2002; McCall 2000; Mishel et al. 1997). It is vital that communities recognize that employment in the goods-producing industries will continue to decline, and persons lacking the advanced education, training, or skills needed for high-quality employment will be forced to take jobs in the low-wage service sector. Obviously, improving educational levels, especially for males, needs to be a high priority for leaders and residents of rural communities.

Inadequate Workforce Skills

In many western communities, there are numerous residents who suddenly find themselves unemployed or underemployed as economic structure changes continue to unfold. Workers who have earned a comfortable living by carrying a chain saw into the woods each day, or who were employed in similar occupations, often find that their skills and training are insufficient as they seek well-paying employment in a vastly different world (Sherman 2006; 2009). Many of these workers are older or have young families, and returning to school to obtain needed training and skills is not a viable option. In such an environment, emphasis should be placed on providing programs that improve and update workforce skills of rural workers.

Inadequate Leadership Skills

A simple definition of leadership is the art of motivating people to act in a way that will help achieve goals. Leadership includes a clear vision of the goal to be accomplished and the ability to communicate that vision with others so that they will follow, devise methods to reach the goal, and coordinate and balance conflicting interests of group members or stakeholders. It has been said that people will follow those who know where they are going. While there are many potential leaders, many rural communities lack quality leadership. Hustedde (1991) listed three factors that inhibit leadership potential of rural communities. First is community size, where there are simply fewer people to draw upon; second, rural communities must rely on volunteers with limited resources and other responsibilities that demand significant amounts of their time, while urban communities can hire staff; and third, rural communities tend to be geographically isolated from potential help and knowledge bases, such as universities. As a result, rural community leaders often lack training, experience, and time. Rural leaders may not understand global trends, or be aware of changing state and federal policies. They may not be aware of effective programs used elsewhere for dealing with community problems. Continuing down paths trod in previous eras will generally not solve the issues confronting communities in the global world. Fortunately, many leadership skills can be taught, and providing training programs that enhance these skills should be a high priority of rural communities. Emery and Flora (2006) maintain that improving social capital skills such as leadership is the best place to begin and leads to "spiraling up" of other community assets.

Consequences of Human Capacity Inadequacies in Rural Areas

Many rural communities confront a variety of significant problems that result from low educational levels, outdated workforce skills, and inadequate leadership abilities. Most directly, these human capacity problems result in inadequate employment for many rural residents which, of course, leads to low incomes, high rates of poverty, and growing inequality. Low quality employment refers to more than simply jobs with low wages. It also means jobs that lack stability, provide few benefits, and perhaps don't give workers an intrinsic sense of self-worth. As the proportion of residents who lack quality employment grows, an expanding array of community problems emerges. Most obviously, lower incomes mean declining tax revenues that reduce the capacity of the community to provide public services and a higher quality of life. Lower incomes mean that community residents have less money to spend to support local businesses. The continuing downward spiral that results is difficult to reverse.

In addition, a growing body of research indicates that inadequate employment, low incomes, poverty, and inequality then initiate a complex set of events that result in major obstacles for communities. Urban scholar William Julius Wilson observed how the basic fabric holding the community together seemed to tear apart in central cities as a decline in manufacturing employment occurred (1987; 1996). Wilson maintains that the decline of manufacturing employment and subsequent rise of low-wage service sector employment resulted in a dramatic rise in the number of jobs that pay wages insufficient to support a family. Because service sector employment is heavily dependent on female workers, this leads to especially high rates of unemployment and underemployment for males and thus a shrinking pool of men able to financially support a family. Marriage thus becomes less attractive and less available to poor women, unwed childbearing increases, and female-headed households proliferate. At the same time, middle-class persons abandon poor communities for places with better opportunities, leaving behind destitute communities that lack institutions, resources, and values necessary for success in a global world.

While Wilson's initial research was conducted in urban areas, subsequent research has found support for this model in both urban (Eggers and Massey 1992) and rural areas (D. Albrecht et al. 2000). In rural areas, the loss of many quality jobs in the goods-producing industries that were held by men is being accompanied by declining educational attainment levels by rural males that further reduce their capacity to obtain high quality employment in the global world. The pattern of community decline described by Wilson then becomes even more problematic. Research indicates that a troubling trend accompanying community dissolution is growing rates of substance abuse, which are now even greater in rural areas compared to urban communities (Pruitt 2009).

Changing family structures are a critical factor of the community declines noted in the above mentioned studies. Higher proportions of female-headed households are a common outcome of community decline. Family structure research indicates that men, women, and children in single-adult families all experience extensive disadvantages relative to their counterparts in married-couple or committed-relationship families (Popenoe 1996). Of the long list of disadvantages, only a few will be mentioned here (D. Albrecht and C. Albrecht 2004). Single-adult families experience much higher levels of poverty, especially for females, with all of its attendant problems (Corcoran et al. 1992; McLanahan 1985; McLanahan and Bumpass 1988). Under such circumstances, people are less likely to have the time, interest, or leadership skills to be involved in and help community institutions succeed. This includes institutions ranging from Little League and Boy or Girl Scouts to churches and schools.

Children who grow up with only one parent have significantly lower educational achievements. These young people are much less likely to graduate from high school and to attend and complete college, and are much more likely to be "idle" (defined as being neither employed or in school) (McLanahan and Sandefur 1994). Girls from one-parent families are much more likely to become pregnant as teenagers than girls from married-couple families, while boys are much more likely to become delinquent (McLanahan and Sandefur 1994; Wells and Rankin 1991). These differences remain even when economic considerations are controlled (Popenoe 1996). The advantages of two-parent households are apparent for adults as well as children. In a variety of ways, both men and women are healthier, happier, and more economically prosperous when married (Lichter and Graefe 2001; Waite 1995; Nock 1998; Haveman et al. 2001). As family structures change, communities are often left to cover the costs and pick up the pieces.

Solutions to Human Capacity Problems

Increasing human capacity is vital to rural community development efforts. Such efforts improve quality of life but are also necessary if the community wishes to be competitive in attracting global era employers and in meeting and confronting problems that emerge. There is no question that programs to increase human capacity are more difficult to implement than place-based community development programs. This is because ultimate success is dependent on the choices of individuals and beyond the control of community leaders. The range of choices, however, can be enhanced through community efforts. I am convinced that when people understand global era circumstances, and when programs are provided to address human capacity needs, many individuals will make choices that will ultimately benefit themselves and their families. Significantly, however, such programs must be initiated and driven by community leaders. In this section, improving human capacity is discussed relative to three areas—educational attainment, workforce development, and leadership development.

Educational Attainment

With a large and growing gap between incomes of college educated persons and those lacking a college education, it is essential to increase formal education levels among nonmetro workers. In the global society era, a higher proportion of employers need skills developed in school. Rural communities with an educated and trained workforce are in much better position to attract or grow businesses that have potential to slow down or perhaps even reverse the "brain drain" problem that has plagued many rural communities for decades.

There are, however, major obstacles that must be overcome before the goal of significantly improved education levels can be achieved in rural communities. First, it is essential that education and training efforts reach a broad segment of the population. In particular as mentioned in Chapter Nine, racial and ethnic minorities often lag behind in educational attainment. In addition, even within the majority group, an extensive literature has found that children from advantaged backgrounds, compared to those from more disadvantaged backgrounds, tend to aspire to higher educational goals (Sewell and Shah 1968), receive better grades, perform better on standardized tests, and are more likely to complete high school and to attend and complete college (De Graaf et al. 2000; G. Duncan et al. 1998; Elman and O'Rand 2004; Ishida et al. 1995; Kingston 2001; Lucas 2001; Mayer 1997; Peters and Mullis 1997). A much higher proportion of rural people come from disadvantaged backgrounds and thus may have a tendency to not attain the full benefits of their educational opportunities.

In many cases there is also a need for a culture change in views toward educational institutions in rural communities, and residents need to understand that the importance of education has greatly increased in the global society era. Of course, money is often a critical factor and the rapidly increasing costs of college education combined with the significantly lower average incomes of rural residents often provides a major obstacle to college attendance (Carr and Kefalas 2009; R. Cobb et al. 1989; Kane 2004). While some programs seek to help underserved populations, much more is needed.

Additionally, many rural youth lack the cultural capital (Bourdieu 1977) that contributes to educational success. Educational cultural capital refers to the widely shared, high status cultural signals that include attitudes, preferences, formal knowledge, linguistic styles, and behaviors that are generally appreciated and rewarded by teachers. These cultural signals tend to be learned through activities such as the theater, museum attendance, literature, and travel, and are most likely to be exhibited by children from highly educated and socially advantaged families, which precludes a high proportion of rural people (De Graaf et al. 2000; DiMaggio 1982; Farkas 1996; Lamont and Lareau 1988; Roscigno and Ainsworth-Darnell 1999; Rothstein 2004). Thus, schools are not neutral institutions where all students start on equal footing, but are institutions where the preferences, attitudes, and behaviors of the "dominant class" are valued and rewarded. Children, including many rural children, are often unfamiliar with this type of environment and are more likely to view schools as hostile environments (Tyson 2003). Improved training and creating instructors with greater sensitivity are needed. Similarly, less biased measures of student progress are needed.

Further, there are major concerns about the quality of many rural schools. Public education is primarily funded by property taxes, and rural areas have lower property values and a lower tax base, making it difficult to afford supplies and to pay wages sufficient to attract top teachers. Rural schools, on average, have lower expenditures per student than urban schools (Green 2007). Additionally, rural schools have problems with economies of scale. Many technologies or programs have a substantial initial cost, whether the technology or program is used by 10 students or 5,000 students. Urban schools obviously have advantages because their cost per student is much lower. Larger urban schools generally have several teachers for each subject, while there is often only one teacher per subject in smaller rural schools. With multiple teachers, students have a greater chance of finding high quality teachers who can motivate them and prepare them for college. In contrast, if the only math teacher in a rural school is not a good teacher, then students from that school are going to be disadvantaged in math aptitude tests and in college math courses.

There are programs and opportunities available in the global world to increase educational opportunities in rural communities. This includes distance education from land-grant and other universities, and regional campuses of these universities. In this way, educational programs can reach rural residents in a much more efficient and timely manner. These distance education programs allow rural adults, who are simply not in a position to move to the university town, to obtain university credit. For these and other efforts to be truly successful, it is necessary that they be a high priority of community leaders.

Workforce Development

It is also essential to help workers with outdated job skills obtain the skills that are in demand in the global economy. The simple fact is that the demand for tractor drivers or chain-saw operators has been on the decline for decades and this demand is not going to return. The same is true for many other skills that could be used to obtain employment in the goods-producing industries. At the same time there is a growing need for people with computer skills and there always seems to be demand for persons who can access, interpret, and manipulate information. Green (2007) notes that having a workforce with skills that are in high demand allows the community to achieve what he calls "flexible specialization." That is, the community is prepared for the ebbs and flows of the economy and industry fluctuations. Again, training programs are available which will help rural community residents attain important workforce skills.

Entrepreneurial skills are always valued. Communities, working in part-nership with universities (especially extension), community colleges, and other organizations could reap great benefits by providing opportunities for such training programs to their residents.

Leadership Development

There is a great need for leadership training programs in rural commu-nities. This leadership training must be based on an awareness of, and thus preparation for, trends occurring in the broader world. An effective leader must recognize that programs and policies that worked in the past may not work in the global society era. Effective leadership must be based on integrity and transparency, and must include concern for all segments of the population, including minorities and other groups that generally lack power. Again, communities, working in partnership with universities (again especially extension), community colleges, and other organizations could reap great benefits by providing such training.

Conclusions

During the isolation and mass society eras, virtually anyone who was willing to work hard could find employment in rural areas of the West. While most of these jobs would not necessarily lead to great wealth, pay was generally sufficient to support a family living frugally. A majority of available jobs were in agriculture, natural resource industries, and manufacturing. Circumstances have changed. For decades, jobs in the goods-producing industries have been steadily declining, and these jobs have been replaced by increased employment in the much more diverse service sector. Quality employment is increasingly dependent on advanced education and training, and the wage gap between the col-lege educated and those without a college degree is getting progressively larger. Persons without a college degree earn significantly less working in the service sector than in the goods-producing industries. As a result of these global changes, the human capacity or skill-levels of many rural residents is problematically low. To a greater extent than ever before, it is critical that programs be instigated in rural communities to increase educational attainment levels, improve workforce skills, and develop leadership capacity. Community development programs of previous eras are simply inadequate to meet rural community needs in the global society era.

CHAPTER ELEVEN

People-Based Rural Development Among the West's Most Vulnerable Populations

People-based rural development to increase human capacity, as described in the previous chapter, is made more complex because large numbers of people in the rural west face significant obstacles or challenges. Among the more significant obstacles are spending one's childhood living in poverty or in a low income family, residing in a single-parent family, being a member of a minority group, or residing in a community with inadequate schools or employment opportunities. A long line of social science research has found that people in these circumstances are less likely to obtain education, employment, or the skills typically needed to become economically stable. In most cases, these challenges are not a result of choices made by individuals, but rather result from circumstances of birth. Concerns have become more pronounced in the global society era as economic, demographic, and social changes have led to increases in the number of people who are in these most vulnerable groups. In particular, there has been a major increase in minority population, and changing family structures have resulted in many more people living in single-parent families than in the past. The purpose of this chapter is to discuss people-based rural development among these vulnerable populations. The chapter begins with a discussion of poverty and inequality. More in-depth discussion is then provided on efforts to change the circumstances of persons who are most disadvantaged.

Poverty in the Global Society Era

Beginning with the "War on Poverty" initiated by President Lyndon B. Johnson in 1964, broad efforts have been made to eliminate or reduce poverty in the United States. When the "War on Poverty" was launched, scholars and public officials were confident that poverty in the United States could largely be eliminated by the beginning of the twenty-first century (Ropers 1991). After emerging from the Great Depression and two world wars, it was believed that booming productivity of American industry and rapid developments in science and technology, with help from carefully implemented social programs, would result in an affluence that would reach all Americans. In his much acclaimed book *The Affluent Society*, economist John Kenneth Galbraith (1958) wrote that widespread poverty would soon largely be a thing of the past, and that only "pockets" of poverty would remain.

Nearly five decades later, in 2009, the number of Americans living in poverty (43.6 million) surpassed the number living in poverty in 1965 (33.2 million). Obviously, poverty has proven to be much more persistent and entrenched than once believed. Over the past five decades, a variety of social programs intended to reduce poverty have been implemented, adjusted, and sometimes discarded when they were felt to be ineffective. Economic trickle-down theories and a variety of affirmative action programs have been tried, yet poverty remains. Since the 1960s, there has been considerable economic growth in the United States, and average incomes—even in constant dollars—have increased significantly. However, incomes of households at the bottom of the economic ladder have grown very little, while incomes of those at the top have grown substantially. Thus, the gap between the economic well-being of the affluent and those in poverty has greatly increased. Although much research has been conducted, it is apparent that our understanding of causes of poverty is insufficient, and at least partly as a result, policy efforts have been inadequate.

While individuals who aid persons living in poverty and those who seek to understand poverty are engaged in a noble effort, living in poverty is anything but noble. The toll of poverty on the lives of individuals and on communities is extensive. First, persons in poverty live shorter lives, have higher infant mortality rates, and experience more health problems than persons who are not in poverty. This is largely a consequence of the poor eating a less nutritious diet and having limited access to medical care (Wolfe 1994). Persons in poverty face major economic constraints when attempting to purchase nutritious food and are much less likely than other Americans to have health insurance (DeNavas-Walt et al. 2010).

Second, children growing up in poverty have significantly fewer educational opportunities than children from more affluent families (Murnane 1994). Persons in poverty often live in low-income neighborhoods and communities. Because public schools are heavily dependent on local property taxes, schools in low-income neighborhoods and communities are underfunded and often fail to prepare or motivate students for either a college education or the job market. The cost of a college education provides major obstacles to young people from low-income families. Children growing up in poverty are less likely than others to graduate from high school and less likely to attend and complete college (C. Albrecht and D. Albrecht 2011; Murnane 1994). From an intergenerational perspective, limited education often means limited employment opportunities, which then puts the next-generation family in a position where educational opportunities of their children are subsequently limited, and the cycle continues (Gottschalk et al. 1994; Haveman et al. 2001).

Finally, many of the costs of poverty are psychological. Living in poverty means living with constant fear and stress. Stress of wondering how next month's rent and utility bills will be paid is staggering. Costs associated with feelings of inferiority when interacting with others is incalculable. In general, positions in the status hierarchy are strongly related to opportunities and obstacles, and these opportunities and obstacles are often a result of ascribed characteristics. Thus, life chances are largely determined by one's birth rather than by one's ability or effort (C. Duncan and Tickamyer 1988; Lichter and Eggebeen 1992; Lichter and McLaughlin 1995; W.J. Wilson 1987). High levels of poverty and the subsequent inequality that exists in the United States, especially considering the cross-generational nature of poverty and inequality, raise important questions of social justice.

Even the wealthiest members of our society pay costs that result from poverty (Danziger and Gottschalk 1994; Danziger et al. 1994). Poverty rates in a community are positively associated with crime rates. Financial costs from criminal damage and from police, court, and prison system are immense. Further, fear of crime is one of the major concerns of Americans and detracts significantly from quality of life. As noted earlier, poverty reduces educational opportunities, which subsequently reduces worker productivity. As a result, ownership and management suffer. Medical treatment for poor people who lack health insurance is often passed on to the general public.

Income levels in the United States have been steadily increasing. Not all Americans, however, have enjoyed the fruits of this growth and income and poverty levels still vary widely from one geographic area to another and among people with different characteristics. Table 11.1 presents median household incomes from 1967 to 2009. Income data prior to 2009 are shown in constant 2007 dollars. From this table it is

Table 11.1 Median Household Income and Income Distribution,[a] 1967–2009

Year	Number of Households (thousands)	Median Household Income	Under $9,999	$10,000-$24,999	$25,000-$49,999	$50,000-$74,999	$75,000-$99,999	$100,000 and Over
					Percent			
1967	60,813	$38,771	11.5	19.5	35.3	20.6	7.7	5.4
1970	64,778	$41,620	10.5	18.8	31.9	22.3	9.7	6.8
1975	72,867	$41,348	8.8	21.3	30.3	21.8	10.4	7.4
1980	82,368	$42,429	8.8	20.5	29.1	21.4	10.8	9.4
1985	88,458	$43,402	8.9	19.8	28.4	20.0	11.4	11.5
1990	94,312	$46,049	8.4	18.5	27.6	19.9	11.7	13.9
1995	99,627	$46,034	7.8	19.3	27.0	19.1	11.6	15.2
2000	108,209	$50,557	6.9	17.1	25.7	18.5	12.5	19.3
2003	112,000	$48,835	7.6	18.2	25.2	17.9	11.8	19.3
2009	117,538	$49,777	7.2	17.6	24.9	18.2	11.9	20.2

[a] In 2007 dollars

Source: De Navas-Walt et al. 2010

apparent that the U.S. economy has been growing as average incomes increased from $38,771 in 1967 to $49,777 in 2009. The proportion of households with low incomes has declined while the proportion of households earning $100,000 or more has increased from 5.4 percent to 20.2 percent. Incomes, however, are unevenly distributed.

Table 11.2 shows income distributions and poverty levels by region. This table shows that median household incomes are lowest in the South ($45,615) and highest in the West ($53,833). The South also has the highest proportion of their population living in poverty (15.7 percent),

Table 11.2   Median Household Income, Number of People (in Thousands), and Percent of People in Poverty by Region, 2009

Region	Median Household Income	Total Population	Poverty Number in Poverty	Percent in Poverty
Northeast	$53,073	54,571	6,650	12.2
Midwest	$48,877	65,980	8,768	13.3
South	$45,615	112,165	17,609	15.7
West	$53,833	71,103	10,542	14.8
Total	$49,777	303,319	43,569	14.3

Source: De Navas-Walt et al. 2010

but poverty levels are higher in the West than in the Northeast or Midwest. Relatively high poverty rates in the South indicate a pattern of low income. Relatively high poverty rates in the West, where median incomes are highest in the country, indicate high levels of inequality and a pattern of duality in the West.

Table 11.3 shows that poverty levels have historically been, and continue to be, higher in nonmetro counties than in metro counties (D. Albrecht et al. 2000; Snyder and McLaughlin 2004; Struthers and Bokemeier 2000; Summers 1995). The gap, however, has declined considerably. In 1967, nearly one-fourth (23.6 percent) of nonmetro residents were living in poverty, compared to only 10.9 percent of metro residents. At that time, more than half of the total population that was living in poverty resided in nonmetro counties. Since that time, the proportion of the population that is nonmetro has steadily declined from 31.8 percent of the total population in 1967 to only 15.7 percent in 2009. At the same time the gap in the percentage of people living in poverty in nonmetro and metro areas has decreased. In 2009, 16.6 percent of nonmetro residents were living in poverty compared to 13.9 percent of metro residents. The proportion of nonmetro residents living in poverty is now lower than the proportion of people residing in central cities of metro counties who are living in poverty. Because of these changes, in 2009, only 18.2 percent of Americans who were living in poverty were residing in nonmetro counties.

Table 11.4 explores the relationship between race/ethnicity and poverty. From this table it is apparent that poverty rates are much higher among Black and Hispanic populations than among the white population. In 2009, the percent living in poverty was 9.4 for the white population, compared to 25.8 percent for the Black population, and 25.3 percent for the Hispanic population. With a significant growth in minority populations, poverty is becoming increasingly a minority issue in the United States. In 1973, the number of white people living in poverty (12.9 million) surpassed the number of Blacks (7.4 million) and Hispanics (2.4 million) in poverty combined. Between 1973 and 2009, the total white population increased by 26.7 million, or 15.6 percent. In comparison, during this same time, the Black population increased by 15.0 million or 64.0 percent, while the Hispanic population grew by 38.0 million or 352.2 percent. Thus, by 2009, the number of whites living in poverty had increased to 18.5 million. These numbers were substantially surpassed by the combined numbers of Blacks (9.9 million) and Hispanics (12.4 million) who were in poverty. If poverty rates among minority

Table 11.3 Number (in Thousands) and Percent of Individuals in Poverty by Residence, 1967–2009

Year	Nonmetropolitan			Metropolitan Central City			Metropolitan Suburban			Metropolitan Total			Overall Total		
	Total Number	In Poverty	Percent in Poverty	Total Number	In Poverty	Percent in Poverty	Total Number	In Poverty	Percent in Poverty	Total Number	In Poverty	Percent in Poverty	Total Number	In Poverty	Percent in Poverty
1967	58,990	13,936	23.6	57,660	8,649	15.0	69,107	5,183	7.5	126,767	13,832	10.9	185,757	27,786	15.0
1970	57,165	12,103	21.2	57,169	8,118	14.2	73,225	5,199	7.1	130,394	13,317	10.2	187,559	25,420	13.6
1975	58,370	10,529	18.0	60,600	9,090	15.0	82,355	6,259	7.6	142,955	15,349	10.7	201,325	25,878	12.9
1980	53,864	11,251	20.9	61,884	10,644	17.2	89,963	7,377	8.2	151,847	18,021	11.9	205,711	29,272	14.2
1985	53,492	9,789	18.3	74,616	14,177	19.0	108,298	9,097	8.4	182,914	23,274	12.7	236,406	33,063	14.0
1990	55,988	9,075	16.2	75,021	14,254	19.0	117,874	10,255	8.7	192,895	24,509	12.7	248,883	33,584	13.5
1995	51,814	8,083	15.6	78,976	16,269	20.6	132,659	12,072	9.1	211,635	28,341	13.4	263,449	36,424	13.8
2000	55,450	6,978	12.6	85,401	13,257	15.5	140,581	11,346	8.1	225,982	24,603	10.9	281,432	31,581	11.2
2003	52,782	7,495	14.2	83,149	14,551	17.5	151,824	13,816	9.1	234,973	28,377	12.1	287,755	35,872	12.5
2009	47,792	7,914	16.6	97,725	18,261	18.7	158,302	17,394	11.0	256,027	35,655	13.9	303,820	43,569	14.3

Source: DeNavas-Walt et al. 2010

Table 11.4   Number (in Thousands) and Percent of People in Poverty by Race, 1973–2009

	Non-Hispanic White			Non-Hispanic Black			Hispanic		
Year	Total Number	In Poverty	Percent in Poverty	Total Number	In Poverty	Percent in Poverty	Total Number	In Poverty	Percent in Poverty
1973	170,488	12,864	7.5	23,512	7,388	31.4	10,795	2,366	21.9
1975	172,417	14,883	8.6	24,089	7,545	31.3	11,117	2,991	26.9
1980	179,798	16,365	9.1	26,408	8,569	32.5	13,600	3,491	25.7
1985	183,455	17,839	9.7	28,485	8,926	31.3	18,075	5,236	29.0
1990	188,129	16,622	8.8	30,806	9,837	31.9	21,405	6,006	28.1
1995	190,951	16,267	8.5	33,740	9,872	29.3	28,344	8,574	30.3
2000	193,691	14,366	7.4	35,425	7,982	22.5	35,955	7,747	21.5
2003	194,595	15,902	8.2	35,989	8,781	24.4	40,300	9,051	22.5
2009	197,164	18,530	9.4	38,556	9,944	25.8	48,811	12,350	25.3

Source: DeNavas-Walt et al. 2010

populations are not reduced, the prevalence of poverty in this country with all of its attendant problems will increase substantially.

Another factor strongly related to poverty levels is family structure. Table 11.5 shows data comparing poverty levels among different types of families. The census defines a family as two or more related individuals residing in the same household. A home resided in by only one person or by unrelated individuals is called a nonfamily household. The proportion of married-couple families (5.8 percent) in poverty is much lower than the percent of female-headed (29.9 percent) and male-headed families (16.9 percent) in poverty. Further, because female-headed and male-headed families have been increasing in number, poverty is coming much more heavily from these nontraditional and especially female-headed families. The increasing share of poverty victims coming from female-headed families is a process called the feminization of poverty (Lichter and Eggebeen 1992; Wu and Wolfe 2001). Between 1975 and 2009, the number of married-couple families increased by 38.8 percent, while the number of female-headed families grew by 197.6 percent and the number of male-headed families increased by 373.5 percent (from a much lower base). In 1975, more than half of all families in poverty were married-couple families. By 2009, the number of female-headed families in poverty (4.4 million) far exceeded the number of married-couple families in poverty (3.4 million).

Finally, Table 11.6 examines the relationship between age and poverty. As is apparent from this table, the age group most likely to be in poverty is children. The table indicates that 20.7 percent of those under the age

Table 11.5 Number (in Thousands) and Percent of Families in Poverty by Type of Family, 1965–2009

Year	Married Couple			Female-Headed			Male-Headed			All Families		
	Total Families	In Poverty	Percent in Poverty	Total Families	In Poverty	Percent in Poverty	Total Families	In Poverty	Percent in Poverty	Total Families	In Poverty	Percent in Poverty
1965	42,107	-	-	4,992	1,916	38.4	1,149	-	-	48,248	6,721	13.9
1970	44,739	-	-	,001	1,952	32.5	1,487	-	-	52,227	5,260	10.1
1975	47,318	2,904	6.1	7,482	2,430	32.5	1,445	116	8.0	56,245	5,450	9.7
1980	49,294	3,032	6.2	9,082	2,972	32.7	1,933	213	11.0	60,309	6,217	10.3
1985	50,933	3,438	6.8	10,211	3,474	34.0	2,424	311	12.8	63,568	7,223	11.4
1990	52,147	2,981	5.7	11,268	3,768	33.4	2,907	349	12.0	66,322	7,098	10.7
1995	53,570	2,982	5.6	12,514	4,057	32.4	3,513	493	14.0	69,597	7,532	10.8
2000	56,598	2,637	4.7	12,903	3,278	25.4	4,277	485	11.3	73,778	6,400	8.7
2003	57,725	3,115	5.4	13,791	3,856	28.0	4,717	636	13.5	76,233	7,607	10.0
2009	58,424	3,409	5.8	14,857	4,441	29.9	5,582	942	16.9	78,863	8,792	11.1

Source: DeNavas-Walt et al. 2010

of 18 were living in poverty in 2009. In comparison, 12.9 percent of individuals between 18 and 64 years of age, and 8.9 percent of those 65 years old and older, were living in poverty. Poverty rates among children have historically been relatively high, while poverty rates among those in traditional working ages have always been relatively low. In contrast, poverty rates among elderly have declined rapidly since the 1960s, indicating success of war on poverty programs. Additionally, since the 1960s, the age structure of the U.S. population has changed dramatically. The number of persons under 18 has remained remarkably stable, but children as a proportion of the total population have declined from 36 percent to 24.5 percent. With aging of the "baby boom" generation, the proportion of people in working ages has increased from 54.7 percent to 62.7 percent. Persons over 65 have also increased as a proportion of the total population from 9.3 percent to 12.7 percent. As a result of these demographic shifts, persons living in poverty are increasingly drawn from the working age population. In 1967, 38.6 percent of persons living in poverty were between 18 and 64 years old; by 2009, this proportion had increased to 56.7 percent. As the baby boom generation continues to age, an increasingly large proportion of the population will be elderly, and programs to keep poverty rates low among elderly populations will become even more important, but progressively costly.

Table 11.6   Number (in Thousands) and Percent of People in Poverty by Age, 1967–2009

	Under 18			18–64			65 and Older		
Year	Total Number	In Poverty	Percent in Poverty	Total Number	In Poverty	Percent in Poverty	Total Number	In Poverty	Percent in Poverty
1967	70,408	11,656	16.6	107,024	10,725	10.0	18,240	5,388	29.5
1970	69,159	10,440	15.1	113,554	10,187	9.0	19,470	4,793	24.6
1975	65,079	11,104	17.1	124,122	11,456	9.2	21,662	3,317	15.3
1980	62,914	11,543	18.3	137,428	13,858	10.1	24,686	3,871	15.7
1985	62,876	13,010	20.7	146,396	16,598	11.3	27,322	3,456	12.6
1990	65,049	13,431	20.6	153,502	16,496	10.7	30,093	3,658	12.2
1995	70,566	14,665	20.8	161,508	18,442	11.4	31,658	3,318	10.5
2000	71,741	11,587	16.2	173,638	16,671	9.6	33,566	3,323	9.9
2003	72,999	12,866	17.6	180,041	19,443	10.8	34,659	3,552	10.2
2009	74,579	15,451	20.7	190,627	24,684	12.9	38,613	3,433	8.9

Source: DeNavas-Walt et al. 2010

Increasing Inequality in the Global Society Era

In addition to relatively high poverty levels, the United States has always been a nation of great inequality, and this inequality has been increasing throughout the global society era. This represents a major change from the mass society era. Beginning in the 1920s, income inequality in the United States commenced a steady decline that lasted for about a half-century. This decline was largely a result of growing manufacturing employment which provided relatively high incomes for a large segment of the population. During this time, the United States became a middle-class society. Then in the 1970s, inequality levels suddenly and unexpectedly reversed (Harrison and Bluestone 1988; Morris and Western 1999). Since that time, researchers have found that inequality in the United States has not only been growing, but growing at an increasing rate (D. Albrecht and C. Albrecht 2007; Chevan and Stokes 2000; Danziger and Gottschalk 1994; 1995; Neckerman and Torche 2007). Since the 1970s, average incomes in the United States have increased significantly. However, most of this increase has gone to the affluent, while incomes of the poor have changed little (D. Albrecht and S. Albrecht 2007). Increasingly, the United States is transitioning from a middle-class to a dualistic society of haves and have-nots.

Research has focused on two major factors to explain increasing levels of inequality in recent decades. First is changing social conditions where increased inequality is thought to be a result of growing proportions of the population in categories most at risk of having low incomes and being in poverty; especially relevant is the growth of minority populations and an increase in the number of female-headed households. The second explanation for increasing income inequality is that it is a function of economic restructuring. From this perspective, increased income inequality results from declining employment levels in the largely middle-income manufacturing sector coupled with increased employment in the more diverse service sector (D. Albrecht and C. Albrecht 2007).

High and growing rates of inequality have profound consequences. Higher levels of inequality, by definition, mean that the gap between the socioeconomically advantaged and disadvantaged becomes wider. As the gap between the advantaged and the disadvantaged widens, it becomes more difficult for the disadvantaged to achieve upward social mobility. Where inequality levels are high, life chances increasingly are determined by one's birth rather than by one's ability, character, or effort.

Additionally, those with greater wealth typically have greater power and can generally assert their political will. Meanwhile the voices of the poor are seldom heard. Further, inequality results in a poverty of dignity, where those with less wealth generally feel less worthy. Frustration and anger are common results of this poverty of dignity.

Data in Table 11.7 make increasing levels of inequality apparent. Data show that between 1967 and 2007, incomes of households in the lowest quintile had their earnings increase from $8,683 to $11,551 (in constant 2007 dollars), an increase of $2,868 or 33 percent. Generally, as income quintile increased, incomes grew at a progressively higher rate. Thus, persons in the highest quintile had their incomes increase from $96,725 to $167,971, an increase of $71,246 or 73.7 percent. With this disparity, the gap between the advantaged and disadvantaged obviously became much greater. Between 1967 and 2007, shares of household income declined for those in lower quintiles and increased for those in upper quintiles. By 2007, nearly 50 percent of the income was being earned by households in the highest quintile. Measures in inequality show steady growth between 1967 and 2007. By 2007, households in the 90th income percentile were earning over eleven times more than households in the 10th percentile, and households in the 80th percentile were earning nearly five times more than households in the 20th percentile. Perhaps the most common measure of inequality is the Gini coefficient. Gini coefficient is determined by measuring the proportion of the total income earned by households in different income categories. A county would have a score of "0" if every household in the county had an equal income, while a score of "1" would mean that one household earned all of the income and all of the other households earned nothing. Between 1967 and 2007, the Gini coefficient steadily increased and grew from .397 in 1967 to .463 in 2007. It should also be noted that this discussion has focused on income inequality. Another measure of economic well-being is wealth. Because wealth can be transferred across generations, it is much more unevenly distributed than income.

People-Based Rural Development Among the Most Disadvantaged Populations

The lack of consistent progress in reducing poverty over the years has led to significant disagreements in the policy arena about the effectiveness of various poverty policies and a lack of consensus about which policies

Table 11.7 Selected Measure of Household Income Inequality, 1967–2007

Year	Mean Household Income by Quintile[a]					Shares of Household Income by Quintile					Income Ratios		Gini Coefficient
	Lowest	Second	Third	Fourth	Highest	Lowest	Second	Third	Fourth	Highest	90/10	80/20	
1967	8,683	24,060	38,415	53,747	96,725	4.0	10.8	17.3	24.2	43.6	9.23	3.95	0.397
1970	9,491	25,713	41,406	58,364	103,326	4.1	10.8	17.4	24.5	43.3	9.22	3.98	0.394
1975	10,194	25,039	41,082	59,693	105,393	4.3	10.4	17.0	24.7	43.6	8.53	4.07	0.397
1980	10,326	25,700	42,408	62,477	111,395	4.2	10.2	16.8	24.7	44.1	9.09	4.21	0.403
1985	10,317	26,144	43,396	65,277	121,935	3.9	9.8	16.2	24.4	45.6	9.69	4.38	0.419
1990	11,020	27,728	45,799	69,053	134,006	3.8	9.6	15.9	24.0	46.6	10.12	4.42	0.428
1995	11,274	27,555	46,075	70,828	147,807	3.7	9.1	15.2	23.3	48.7	10.11	4.52	0.450
2000	12,229	30,535	50,850	79,049	171,297	3.6	8.9	14.8	23.0	49.8	10.58	4.56	0.462
2003	11,269	28,948	49,139	77,782	165,810	3.4	8.7	14.8	23.4	49.8	11.22	4.83	0.464
2007	11,551	29,442	49,968	79,111	167,971	3.4	8.7	14.8	23.4	49.7	11.18	4.93	0.463
Change 1967–2007:													
Dollars	2,868	5,382	11,553	25,364	71,246								
Percent	33.0	22.4	30.1	47.2	73.7								

[a] in 2007 dollars
Source: DeNavas-Walt et al. 2010

would be most effective in the future. At the heart of the issue is a lack of agreement on the root causes of poverty. Theories on the emergence and persistence of poverty generally fall into two major categories: cultural and structural (Baca Zinn 1989; C. Duncan 1996). Adherents to what might be called the "culture of poverty" perspective argue that poverty is largely a result of individuals making poor decisions or being inadequately motivated. Often these poor decisions and lack of motivation are the result of socialization patterns by family, community, and/or culture (Sowell 1994). According to cultural theories of poverty, people are poor because they have a distinctive, culturally determined way of life. Relevant aspects of this "culture of poverty" include a limited time horizon, impulsive need for gratification, low aspirations, and psychological self-doubt (Lewis 1966; Shulman 1990). When taken together, the resulting worldview helps poor people to cope with pervasive hopelessness and despair. Poor families and communities then socialize their young with these values and norms, and consequently limit or obstruct their successful participation in mainstream institutions. The resulting "underclass" thus becomes permanent and is "locked into its own unique, but maladaptive culture" (Baca Zinn 1989: 67; Banfield 1970).

Opinion polls find strong support for this approach among the general public (Bradshaw 2007; Partridge and Rickman 2006; Wright 1993). From this perspective, the solution to poverty is to find ways to increase motivation. It is argued that lack of progress in reducing poverty is evidence that government anti-poverty and other social programs are largely a waste of time and money. In fact, it is argued that such programs may actually make the poverty problems worse by creating a welfare state that contributes to a "culture of poverty." Consequently, it is argued that anti-poverty and other social programs should be eliminated or greatly curtailed, which will then motivate individuals to overcome the faulty traditions they have learned and to then "get off the couch" and get a job.

Since their emergence, cultural theories have received limited empirical support, perhaps partly because of difficulty in measuring attitudes and motivations. Cultural theories have been criticized because of a tendency to "blame the victim" for their poverty; that is they put responsibility on individuals for things that may be beyond the control of that individual (e.g., Baca Zinn 1989; Corcoran et al. 1985; Ryan 1971; Shulman 1990; W. Wilson and Aponte 1985).

The second major category of theories of poverty is summarized in a series of structural perspectives in which the causes of poverty are sought in the social, political, or economic system rather than in the individual (Gordon et al. 1982; Tomaskovic-Devey 1987). From a structural perspective, it is argued that people are poor because racism, sexism, and segregation limit or deny certain categories or groups of people access to education, training, or jobs that are sufficient to maintain an acceptable standard of living or quality of life (J. Cobb 1992; C. Duncan 1999; Maril 1988; Massey and Denton 1993; Rank et al. 2003). In addition, people living in some areas of the country or working in some segments of the economy may lack sufficient access to high-quality jobs or economic opportunities (C. Duncan 1992; Lobao 1990).

Structural theorists maintain that the number of people living in poverty remains high, at least in part because anti-poverty programs have failed to address these fundamental structural concerns. Structural theorists also recognize the intergenerational nature of poverty and that children growing up in poor families are much more likely than others to be poor as adults because of their disadvantaged access to institutions and opportunities (G. Duncan and Brooks-Gunn 1999). Additionally, structural theorists would argue that while poverty programs have been underfunded, they have not been total failures. When poverty reduction programs were initially implemented in the 1960s, poverty numbers declined sharply. Since then, the number of people living in poverty has remained high because support for poverty reduction programs has been inconsistent and because there have been significant increases in the proportion of the population in structural categories most likely to be in poverty (especially racial/ethnic minorities and persons living in single-parent households).

Policy approaches likely to be supported by structural theorists begin with elimination of discrimination, even in its subtle forms. Merely eliminating discriminatory laws, however, is not enough as implications of past discriminatory actions last for generations and parents who are disadvantaged tend to raise children who become disadvantaged as adults (G. Duncan and Brooks-Gunn 1999). Consequently, programs are needed to help the poor gain access to critical institutions and opportunities beyond what their parents could provide (Higgins and Lutzenhiser 1995; Massey 2007). Policies supported by structural theorists may include improved schools in poor neighborhoods and financial assistance to disadvantaged individuals who wish to attend college or start a business.

While there are certainly cases where individuals are poor because of their own decisions, social science research has found that the numbers of such individuals are relatively small. Extensive empirical research has provided strong support for structural theories of poverty and several structural variables have consistently been found to be strong predictors of persons most and least likely to be poor (Wright 1993; Fitchen 1981; Massey 2007; Massey and Denton 1993). Consistently, the strongest of these variables are race/ethnicity, family structure, and educational attainment. Regardless of the relevancy of cultural theories, we do know that there is strong empirical support of structural theories. People-based rural development should begin with policies and programs that will give disadvantaged individuals a lift or a boost and provide opportunities that will allow them to compete on a more level playing field with individuals from more advantaged backgrounds.

Conclusions

To be truly effective, people-based rural development among the most vulnerable populations is going to require a concerted effort among many individuals and agencies and must be based on strong policy support at both the federal and state levels. It is difficult to imagine a scenario where minority populations and communities with long-term persistent poverty make significant progress in overcoming these conditions without substantial help and support. While these efforts may be difficult and perhaps costly, benefits will certainly outweigh the costs.

CHAPTER TWELVE

Conclusions and Policy Recommendations

While Thomas Jefferson may have been disappointed that his vision of the West was not borne out by the expedition of Lewis and Clark, the West was even more spectacular than Jefferson imagined.

Early explorers and settlers found that much of the West lacked traditional resources that allowed people to earn a living during the isolation era. As a consequence, communities were few and far between, and today there remain places where one can drive for hours without seeing a gas station, a farm, or a home. Yet what the West lacks in traditional natural resources, it more than makes up for with amenities. During my travels around the western United States, I have been amazed by the beaches of Maui, the glaciers and ice-covered peaks of Alaska, the rugged mountains of California, Idaho, Montana, Wyoming, and Colorado, the forests of Washington and Oregon, and the stunning red desert cliffs of Arizona, New Mexico, and Utah. I am thrilled by long and lonely drives across the wind-swept plains of Wyoming and barren valleys of Nevada where some people see nothing but desolation. Then of course, there are Yellowstone, Grand Canyon, Yosemite, and the other spectacular national parks.

While residents and communities of the West seem to be struggling with a wide array of problems, participants of our rural roundtables were able to boil these problems down to three major issues and concerns. For rural communities to succeed in the global society era, they must effectively deal with these three issues. Each is briefly reviewed below.

Determining Appropriate Natural Resource Uses

Early settlers of the American West found a dearth of traditional natural resources and so they and their descendants made great efforts to enhance the availability of such resources. They rerouted vast amounts of water; located minerals, fossil fuels, and commercially valuable trees; and developed infrastructure to reach and utilize these resources. Yet, only when the relevance of traditional resources declined and the importance of amenity resources increased did parts of the West begin to prosper and growth rates began to surpass growth rates in other parts of the country. Academic research consistently shows that the factor most strongly related to economic and demographic growth in the global society era is not access to traditional resources, but rather the presence of amenities. After decades of holding the short end of the stick, the West now holds the advantaged position because of their many amenities. Policies and plans at both state and local levels should focus on maintaining amenity advantages. Efforts to get a clearcut or an irrigation project approved are likely to bring fewer economic and demographic benefits to a community than having forests, free-flowing streams, open spaces, or smog-free views of mountains. It is essential in the global society era that communities strive to enhance their amenities and find ways to market their history and culture.

It is vital that resources be used sustainably, which represents a significant change from historical and current use patterns. Certainly it is essential that resources continue to be used for agriculture, logging, or mining. Modern populations and lifestyles are dependent on food produced through commercial agriculture, and on the use of traditional resources such as trees and minerals. Calls to have everyone become vegetarian, or to eliminate pesticides and fertilizers from agriculture, are impractical in light of the necessity of feeding the world's growing population. Food, fiber, and energy for the world must be attained, and the United States needs to play an important role in this provision. However, resource-use decisions should be made carefully and in some cases the lack of development may be the best decision. Further, meeting societal resource needs in a sustainable manner requires knowledge and understanding that we currently lack in many cases. Research and outreach efforts should be devoted to building knowledge and information bases and then sharing this information with farmers and others to help them utilize resources more sustainably. Sustainable resource use may have great benefits for the rural West. In addition to retaining critical jobs in agriculture and natural resource extraction, the West could play a vital role in meeting other societal resource needs. For example, by more efficiently using wind, sun, and plant life, the West could play a major role in providing renewable energy in a way that reduces environmental impacts and yet provides jobs to rural workers.

Coping with Limited Economic Opportunities through Place-Based Rural Development

The global society era has seen a steady decline in employment in agriculture, natural resource industries, and manufacturing—the historical mainstays of the rural economy. Traditional approaches to create high-quality employment opportunities in rural areas are less successful than in the past. When most rural jobs were in agriculture and the natural resource industries, community development efforts focused on enhancing the supply of or demand for natural resources, and included irrigation projects and building roads, bridges, and other infrastructure. With the growth of manufacturing, rural communities sought to attract industrial firms to create jobs and support their economies.

Today, opportunities for resource development are limited, and the traditional "buffalo hunt" for industrial firms is much less effective than in the past as a community development strategy. At the same time, there are development opportunities that did not exist in the past. With computers, the internet, and cell phones, it is now possible for individuals and firms to be connected to the global world while enjoying benefits of rural living. Because of their amenity advantages, the rural West has an opportunity to reap great benefits from these societal changes. The disadvantages of the past have become the advantages of the present.

There are several approaches available for communities to take advantage of opportunities created by modern information and communication technologies. These approaches include increasing local production and developing value-added capacity from traditional agriculture and natural resource materials, encouraging entrepreneurial development, promoting the community as a place for retirees and for persons with creative class or geographically mobile jobs, and supporting clustering and regional development. Local leaders should carefully examine policies to assure they encourage and promote such opportunities and that red tape is kept to a minimum. For these efforts to be successful communities must be connected to the global world with modern information and communication technology. Developing this infrastructure should be a high priority for federal, state, and local governments.

Enhancing Human Capacity through People-Based Rural Development

With a decline in traditional sources of rural employment, rural workers must have access to education, skills, and training needed for high-quality employment in the global society era. In the isolation and mass society eras, there were opportunities for employment that would provide an economic livelihood for individuals with high school degrees or less. Significant global-era reductions in the number of workers in agriculture, natural resources industries, and manufacturing have reduced quality employment opportunities for persons without college degrees. Consequently, the gap in incomes between persons with college degrees and those without has been steadily growing.

Rural communities must seek to improve their K-12 schools to prepare and motivate their youth for advanced education or training, and provide adult education and workforce training programs. Training programs geared toward underserved, low income, and minority populations are especially needed. Communities must foster and improve leadership capacity with leadership training programs. Without strong leaders, communities lack direction and therefore are at a disadvantage when coping with the issues and problems that confront them. A concern that continually emerged from the roundtable discussions was the lack of involvement by young people in leadership positions. Encouraging and training leaders from the younger generation is especially important.

Concluding Thoughts

Every community is unique. The combination of resources varies greatly from one place to another, as do the goals, desires, and talents of community residents. No one understands the assets and advantages or the problems and disadvantages of a community better than their residents. No one understands a community's dreams and goals better than the people who live there. While an understanding of major national and international trends is certainly essential, effective community development has to begin at home and involves defining assets and establishing local goals.

Next, effective community development requires involvement from all segments of the community. Concerted efforts should be made to involve community residents who are not always involved in planning and policy efforts, including low-income, minority, and young people. Planning efforts will be more effective if individuals and groups who have historically been on different sides of an issue learn to sit around the same table and find areas of agreement and places to compromise. By promoting sustainable resource use, seeking to expand employment in high-quality jobs in growing segments of the economy, and enhancing the capacity of their residents, the sky is truly the limit for the residents and communities of the rural West.

References

Acs, Z.J. 2008. "Innovation and the Growth of Cities." *Contributions to Economic Analysis* 266: 635-658.

Albrecht, Carol Mulford and Don E. Albrecht. 2011. "Social Status, Adolescent Behavior and Educational Attainment." *Sociological Spectrum* 31(1): 114-137.

Albrecht, Don E. 1993. "The Renewal of Population Loss in the Nonmetropolitan Great Plains." *Rural Sociology* 58(2): 233-246.

_____. 1998. "The Industrial Transformation of Farm Communities: Implications for Family Structure and Socioeconomic Conditions." *Rural Sociology* 63(1): 51-64.

_____. 2004. "Amenities, Natural Resources, Economic Restructuring and Socioeconomic Outcomes in Nonmetropolitan America." *Journal of the Community Development Society* 35(2): 36-52.

_____. 2007. "Small Town in Global Society." The 2007 Southern Rural Sociological Society Presidential Address, *Southern Rural Sociology* 22(1): 1-14.

_____. 2010. "Nonmetropolitan Population Trends: Twenty-First Century Updates." *Journal of Rural Social Sciences* 25(1): 1-21.

_____. 2012. "A Comparison of Metro and Nonmetro Incomes in a Twenty-First Century Economy." *Journal of Rural Social Sciences* 27(1): 1-23.

Albrecht, Don E. and Carol Mulford Albrecht. 2004. "Metro/Nonmetro Residence, Nonmarital Conception, and Conception Outcomes." *Rural Sociology* 69(3): 430-452.

_____. 2007. "Income Inequality: The Implications of Economic Structure and Social Conditions." *Sociological Spectrum* 27(1): 1-17.

Albrecht, Don E., Carol Mulford Albrecht, and Stan L. Albrecht. 2000. "Poverty in Nonmetropolitan America: Impacts of Industrial, Employment, and Family Structure Variables." *Rural Sociology* 65(1): 87-103.

Albrecht, Don E., Carol Mulford Albrecht, and Edward Murguia. 2005. "Minority Concentration, Disadvantage, and Inequality in the Nonmetropolitan United States." *The Sociological Quarterly* 46(3): 503-523.

Albrecht, Don E. and Scott G. Albrecht. 2007. "The Benefits and Costs of Inequality for the Advantaged and Disadvantaged." *Social Science Quarterly* 88(2): 382-403.

_____. 2009. "Economic Restructuring, the Educational Income Gap and Overall Income Inequality." *Sociological Spectrum* 29(4): 519-547.

Albrecht, Don E. and Steve H. Murdock. 1990. *The Sociology of U.S. Agriculture: An Ecological Perspective.* Ames: Iowa State University Press.

Anderson, Terry L. and Laura E. Huggins. 2008. "Homegrown Property Rights for the Klamath Basin." Chapter 5 in Terry L. Anderson, Laura E. Huggins, and Thomas Michael Power (eds.), *Accounting for Mother Nature.* Stanford, CA: Stanford University Press.

Anderson, Terry L., Laura E. Huggins, and Thomas Michael Power (eds.) 2008. *Accounting for Mother Nature*. Stanford, CA: Stanford University Press.

Arrington, Leonard J. 2005. *Great Basin Kingdom*. Urbana: University of Illinois Press.

Baca Zinn, Maxine. 1989. "Family, Race, and Poverty in the Eighties." *Signs* 14: 856-874.

Baden, John A. and Donald Snow (eds.). 1997. *The Next West*. Washington, DC: Island Press.

Banfield, Edward C. 1970. *The Unheavenly City*. Boston: Little, Brown.

Barca, F., P. McCann, and A. Rodriguez-Pose. 2012. "The Case for Regional Development Intervention: Place-Based Versus Place-Neutral Approaches." *Journal of Regional Sciences* 52(1): 134-152.

Barker, Rocky. 1997. "New Forestry in the Next West." Chapter 2 in J.A. Baden and D. Snow (eds.) *The Next West*. Washington, DC: Island Press.

Barrows, Benjamin H. 1894. *Irrigation: Its History,, Methods, Statistics and Results*. San Francisco: Union Pacific Company.

Bartolino, J.R. and W.L. Cunningham. 2003. *Groundwater Depletion Across the Nation*. Restin, VA: U.S. Geological Survey.

Beale, Calvin L. 1993. "Salient Features of the Demography of American Agriculture." Pp. 108-127 in D.L. Brown, D. Field, and J.J. Zuiches (eds.), *The Demography of Rural Life*. Publication #64. University Park, PA: Northwest Regional Center for Rural Development.

Bealer, R.C., F.K. Willits, and W.P. Kuvlesky. 1965. "The Meaning of Rurality in American Society: Some Implications of Alternative Definitions." *Rural Sociology* 30: 255-266.

Beaulieu, Lionel J. 2002. *Creating Vibrant Communities and Economies in Rural America*. Mississippi State University: Southern Rural Development Center.

Bender, T. 1975. *Toward an Urban Vision: Ideas and Institutions in Nineteenth Century America*. Lexington, KY: University of Kentucky Press.

Beyers, W. and P. Nelson. 2000. "Contemporary Development Forces in the Nonmetropolitan West: New Insights from Rapidly Growing Communities." *Journal of Rural Studies* 16: 459-474.

Bluestone, Barry and Bennett Harrison. 1982. *The Deindustrialization of America*. New York: Basic Books.

_____. 2000. *Growing Prosperity: The Battle for Growth With Equity in the Twenty-First Century*. Boston: Houghton Mifflin.

Bonanno, A. and R.A. Lopez. 2008. "Wal-Mart's Monopsony Power in Local Labor Markets." (Working Paper). Retrieved from ageconsearch.umn.edu/bitstream/6219/2/469304.pdf.

Bordewich, Fergus M. 1996. *Killing the White Man's Indian: Reinventing Native Americans at the End of the Twentieth Century*. New York: Doubleday.

Bourdieu, Pierre. 1977. "Cultural Reproduction and Social Reproduction." Pp. 487-511 in Jerome Karabel and A.H. Halsey (eds.), *Power and Ideology in Education*. New York: Oxford University Press.

Boyle, P. and K. Halfacree. 1998. *Migration into Rural Areas.* Chichester, UK: Wiley.

Bradshaw, Ted K. 2007. "Theories of Poverty and Anti-Poverty Programs in Community Development." *Community Development* 38(1): 7-25.

Brower, David. 1966. *The Place No One Knew: Glen Canyon on the Colorado.* San Francisco: Sierra Club.

Brown, Beverly A. 1995. *In Timber Country.* Philadelphia: Temple University Press.

Brown, Daniel G., Kenneth M. Johnson, Thomas R. Loveland, and David M. Theobald. 2005. "Rural Land-Use Trends in the Conterminous United States, 1950-2000." *Ecological Applications* 15(6): 1851-1863.

Card, D. and J. DiNardo. 2002. "Skill-Based Technological Change and Rising Wage Inequality: Some Problems and Puzzles." *Journal of Labor Economics* 20: 733-783.

Carolan, Michael S. 2009. "A Sociological Look at Biofuels: Ethanol in the Early Decades of the Twentieth Century and Lessons for Today." *Rural Sociology* 74(1): 86-112.

Carr, Patrick J. and Maria J. Kefalas. 2009. *Hollowing Out the Middle: The Rural Brain Drain and What it Means for America.* Boston: Beacon Press.

Carson, Rachel. 1962. *Silent Spring.* Boston: Houghton Mifflin.

CAST (Council for Agricultural Science and Technology). 1988. *Effective Use of Water in Irrigated Agriculture.* Report No. 113. Ames, IA.

Catton, William R., Jr. 1980. *Overshoot: The Ecological Basis of Revolutionary Change.* Urbana: University of Illinois Press.

Catton, William R., Jr. and Riley Dunlap. 1978. "Environmental Sociology: A New Paradigm." *The American Sociologist* 13: 41-49.

_____. 1980. "A New Ecological Paradigm for Post-Exuberant Sociology." *American Behavioral Scientist* 24: 15-47.

Chevan, A. and R. Stokes. 2000. "Growth in Family Income Inequality, 1970-1990: Industrial Restructuring and Demographic Change." *Demography* 37: 365-380.

Chou, W.W., W.L. Silver, R.D. Jackson, A.W. Thompson, and B. Allen-Diaz. 2008. "The Sensitivity of Annual Grassland Carbon Cycling to the Quantity and Timing of Rainfall." *Global Change Biology* 14(6): 1382-1394.

Christenson, James A. and Jerry W. Robinson Jr. 1989. *Community Development in Perspective.* Ames: Iowa State University.

Clark, Bradley T. 2009. "River Restoration in the American West: Assessing Variation in the Outcomes of Policy Change." *Society and Natural Resources* 22: 401-416.

Cobb, James C. 1992. *The Most Southern Place on Earth: The Mississippi Delta and the Roots of Regional Identity.* New York: Oxford University Press.

Cobb, Robert A., Walter G. McIntire, and Phillip A. Pratt. 1989. "Vocational and Educational Aspirations of High School Students: A Problem for Rural America." *Research in Rural Education* 6(2): 11-16.

Corcoran, Mary, Greg J. Duncan, Gerald Gurin, and Patricia Gurin. 1985. "Myth and Reality: The Causes and Persistence of Poverty." *Journal of Policy Analysis and Management* 4: 516-536.

Corcoran, M., R. Gordon, D. Laren, and G. Solon. 1992. "The Association between Men's Economic Status and Their Family and Community Origins." *Journal of Human Resources* 27: 575-601.

Coyle, William. 2007. "The Future of Biofuels." *Amber Waves* 5(5): 24-29.

Cromartie, John B. and John M. Wardwell. 1999. "Migrants Settling Far and Wide in the Rural West." *Rural Development Perspectives* 14(2): 1-8.

Danziger, S. and P. Gottschalk. 1994. *Uneven Tides: Rising Inequality in America.* New York: Russell Sage Foundation.

_____. 1995. *America Unequal.* Cambridge, MA: Harvard University Press.

Danziger, S., G.D. Sandefur, and D.H. Weinberg (eds). 1994. *Confronting Poverty: Prescriptions for Change.* Cambridge, MA: Harvard University Press.

Davis, Charles (ed). 2001. *Public Lands and Environmental Politics, Second Edition.* Boulder, CO: Westview.

deBuys, William. 2001. *Seeing Things Whole: The Essential John Wesley Powell.* Washington, DC: Island Press.

De Graaf, Nan Dirk, Paul M. De Graaf, and Gerbert Kraaykamp. 2000. "Parental Cultural Capital and Educational Attainment in the Netherlands: A Refinement of the Cultural Capital Perspective." *Sociology of Education* 73(April): 92-111.

DeNavas-Walt, Carmen, Bernadette D. Proctor, and Jessica C. Smith. 2010. *Income, Poverty, and Health Insurance Coverage in the United States: 2009.* Current Population Reports, P60-238. Washington, DC: U.S. Government Printing Office.

DeVoto, Bernard. 2000. *The Western Paradox.* New Haven, CT: Yale University Press.

DiMaggio, Paul. 1982. "Cultural Capital and Social Success: The Impact of Status Culture Participation on the Grades of High School Students." *American Sociological Review.* 47:189-201.

Domina, Thurston. 2006a. "Brain Drain and Brain Gain: Rising Educational Segregation in the United States, 1940-2000." *City and Community* 5(4): 387-407.

_____. 2006b. "What Clean Break? Education and Nonmetropolitan Migration Patterns, 1989-2004." *Rural Sociology* 71(3): 373-398.

Donahue, Debra L. 1999. *The Western Range Revisited.* Norman: University of Oklahoma Press.

Dorner, P. 1983. "Technology and U.S. Agriculture." Pp. 73-86 in G.F. Summers (ed.), *Technology and Social Change in Rural Areas: A Festschrift for Eugene A. Wilkening.* Boulder, CO: Westview Press.

Duffield, James A. and Keith Collins. 2006. "Evolution of Renewable Energy Policy." *Choices* 21(1): 9-14.

Duncan, Cynthia M. 1992. *Rural Poverty in America.* New York: Auburn House.

_____. 1996. "Understanding Persistent Poverty: Social Class Context in Rural Communities." *Rural Sociology* 61:103-124.

_____. 1999. *Worlds Apart: Why Poverty Persists in Rural America.* New Haven: Yale University Press.

Duncan, Cynthia M. and Ann R. Tickamyer. 1988. "Poverty Research and Policy for Rural America." *American Sociologist* 19: 243-259.

Duncan, Greg J. and Jeanne Brooks-Gunn (eds). 1999. *Consequences of Growing up Poor.* New York: Russell Sage Foundation.

Duncan, Greg J., W. Jean Yeung, Jeanne Brooks-Gunn, and Judith R. Smith. 1998. "How Much Does Childhood Poverty Affect the Life Chances of Children?" *American Sociological Review* 63:406-421.

Eggars, M.L. and D.S. Massey. 1992. "A Longitudinal Analysis of Urban Poverty: Blacks in U.S. Metropolitan Areas between 1970 and 1980." *Social Science Research* 21: 175-203.

Elam, Thomas E. 2008. "Food or Fuel? Choices and Conflicts." *Choices* 23(3): 12-15.

Elman, Cheryl and Angela O'Rand. 2004. "The Race is to the Swift: Socioeconomic Origins, Adult Education, and Wage Attainment." *American Journal of Sociology* 110(1): 123-160.

Emanuel, Kerry. 2007. *What We Know About Climate Change.* Boston: MIT Press.

Emery, Mary and Cornelia Flora. 2006. "Spiraling-up: Mapping Community Transformation with Community Capitals Framework." *Community Development* 37(1): 19-35.

England, L. and R.B. Brown. 2003. "Community and Resource Extraction in Rural America." Chapter 24 in D.L. Brown and L.E. Swanson (eds.), *Challenges for Rural America in the Twenty-First Century.* University Park: The Pennsylvania State University Press.

Falk, W.F., M.D. Schulman, and A.R. Tickamyer. 2003. *Communities of Work: Rural Restructuring in Local and Global Context.* Athens: Ohio University Press.

Family Farm Alliance. 2007. *Water Supply in a Changing Climate.* Klamath Falls, OR: Family Farm Alliance.

_____. 2008. *Western Water Policy: The Challenges and Opportunities of Our Times.* Klamath Falls, OR: Family Farm Alliance.

Farm Foundation. 2008. *The 30-Year Challenge: Agriculture's Strategic Role in Feeding and Fueling a Growing World.* Oak Brook,IL: Farm Foundation.

Farkas, George. 1996. *Human Capital or Cultural Capital? Ethnicity and Poverty Groups in an Urban School District.* New York: Aldine de Gruyter.

Ferguson, N., C.S. Mair, E. Manela, and D. J. Sargent (eds.). 2010. *The Shock of the Global: The 1970s in Perspective.* Cambridge, MA: Harvard University Press.

Fernandez-Cornejo, Jorge. 2007. "Farmers Balance Off-Farm Work and Technology Adoption." *Amber Waves* 5(1): 23-27.

Fitchen, Janet M. 1981. *Poverty in Rural America: A Case Study.* Boulder, CO: Westview.

Fleishner, Thomas L. 1994. "Ecological Costs of Livestock Grazing in Western North America." *Conservation Biology* 8(3): 629-644.

Fleming, David A. and Stephan J. Goetz. 2011. "Does Local Firm Ownership Matter?" *Economic Development Quarterly* 25(3): 277-281.

Flora, Cornelia Butler and Jan L. Flora. 2008. *Rural Communities: Legacy and Change* (Third Edition). Boulder, CO: Westview Press.

Florida, Richard. 2002. *The Rise of the Creative Class.* New York: Basic Books.

_____. 2008. *Who's Your City?* New York: Basic Books.

Fortmann, Louise and Sally K. Fairfax. 1991. "Forest Resource Policy." Chapter 22 in Cornelia B. Flora and James A. Christenson, *Rural Policies for the 1990s.* Boulder, CO: Westview Press.

Fradkin, Philip L. 1995. *A River No More.* Berkeley: University of California Press.

Friedland, W.H. 2002. "Agriculture and Rurality: Beginning the 'Final Separation'?" *Rural Sociology* 67: 350-371.

Friedman, Thomas. 2007. *The World is Flat.* New York: St. Martins Press.

Frink, Maurice, W. Turrentine Jackson, and Agnes Wright Spring. 1956. *When Grass Was King.* Boulder: University of Colorado Press.

Fuglie, Keith O., James M. MacDonald, and Eldon Ball. 2007. *Productivity Growth in U.S. Agriculture.* Washington, DC: United States Department of Agriculture, Economic Research Service.

Fuguitt, G.V. 1971. "The Places Left Behind: Population Trends and Policy for Rural America." *Rural Sociology* 36(4): 449-470.

Fuguitt, G.V., D.L. Brown, and C.L. Beale. 1989. *Rural and Small Town America.* New York: Russell Sage.

Fujita, M., P. Krugman, and A. Venables. 1999. *The Spatial Economy: Cities, Regions and International Trade.* Cambridge, MA: MIT Press.

Galbraith, John Kenneth. 1958. *The Affluent Society.* Boston: Houghton Mifflin.

Gamble, Brook, Sarah Trainor, and Nancy Fresco. 2011. "Assisting Arctic Inhabitants in Responding to a Changing Climate." *Rural Connections* (June): 39-44.

Glaeser, E., S. Rosenthal, and W. Strange. 2010. "Urban Economics and Entrepreneurship." *Journal of Urban Economics* 67: 1-4.

Goe, W.R., S.A. Noonan, and S Thurston. 2003. "From Extraction to Amenities: Restructuring and (In)conspicuous Consumption in Missoula, Montana." Chapter 5 in W.F. Falk et al. (eds.), *Communities of Work: Rural Restructuring in Local and Global Context.* Athens: Ohio University Press.

Goetz, Stephen J., Steven C. Deller, and Thomas R. Harris. 2009. *Targeting Regional Economic Development.* New York: Routledge.

Gordon, David, Richard Edwards, and Michael Reich. 1982. *Segmented Work, Divided Workers: The Historical Transformation of Labor in the United States.* New York: Cambridge University Press.

Gore, Al. 2006. *An Inconvenient Truth.* New York: Rodale.

Gosnell, Hannah and William R. Travis. 2005. "Ranchland Ownership Dynamics in the Rocky Mountain West." *Rangeland Ecology and Management* 58(2): 191-198.

Gottschalk, P., S. McLanahan, and G.D. Sandefur. 1994. "The Dynamics and Intergenerational Transmission of Poverty and Welfare Participation." Chapter 4 in S.H. Danziger et al. *Confronting Poverty: Prescriptions for Change.* Cambridge, MA: Harvard University Press.

Granovetter, Mark S. 1973. "The Strength of Weak Ties." *American Journal of Sociology* 78(6): 1360-1380.

Green, Gary P. 2001. "Amenities and Community Economic Development: Strategies for Sustainability." *The Journal of Regional Analysis and Policy* 31: 61-75.

_____. 2007. *Workforce Development Networks in Rural Areas*. Northhampton, MA: Edward Elgar.

Green, Gary Paul, David Marcouiller, Steven Deller, Daniel Erkkila, and N.R. Sumathi. 1996. "Local Dependency, Land Use Attitudes, and Economic Development: Comparisons between Seasonal and Permanent Residents." *Rural Sociology* 61(3): 427-445.

Hansen, Andrew J., Richard L. Knight, John M. Marzluff, Scott Powell, Kathryn Brown, Patricia H. Gude, and Kingsford Jones. 2005. "Effects of Exurban Development on Biodiversity: Patterns, Mechanisms, and Research Needs." *Ecological Applications* 15(6): 1893-1905.

Hardin, Garrett. 1968. "The Tragedy of the Commons." *Science* 162: 1243-1248.

Harlan, Sharon L., Scott T. Yabiku, Larissa Larsen, and Anthony J. Brazel. 2009. "Household Water Consumption in an Arid City: Affluence, Affordance, and Attitudes." *Society and Natural Resources* 22: 691-709.

Harrison, Bennett and Barry Bluestone. 1988. *The Great U-Turn: Corporate Restructuring and the Polarizing of America*. New York: Basic Books.

Hassol, Susan Joy. 2004. *Impacts of a Warming Arctic: Arctic Climate Impact Assessment*. New York: Cambridge University Press.

Haveman, Robert, B. Wolfe, and K. Pence. 2001. "Intergenerational Effects of Non-marital and Early Childbearing." Chapter 10 in L.L. Wu and B. Wolfe (eds.), *Out of Wedlock*. New York: Russell Sage Foundation.

Hays, Samuel P. 2007. *Wars in the Woods*. Pittsburgh: University of Pittsburgh Press.

_____. 2009. *The American People, The National Forests*. Pittsburgh: University of Pittsburgh Press.

Henderson, J. and K. McDaniel. 1998. "Do Scenic Amenities Foster Economic Growth in Rural Areas?" *Regional Economic Digest* 1: 11-17.

Higgins, Lorie and Loren Lutzenhiser. 1995. "Ceremonial Equity: Low-Income Energy Assistance and Failure of Socio-Environmental Policy." *Social Problems* 42: 468-492.

Hobbs, Jared. 2007. *Spotted Owls*. Vancouver, BC: Greystone Books.

Holechek, J.L. 2001. "Western Ranching at the Crossroads." *Rangelands* 23(1): 17-21.

Holechek, J.L., R. Cole, J. Fisher, and R.Valdez. 2000. *Natural Resources: Ecology, Economics, and Policy*. Upper Saddle River, NJ: Prentice-Hall.

Hundley, Norris, Jr. 2001. *The Great Thirst*. Berkeley: University of California Press.

_____. 2009. *Water and the West*, Second Edition. Berkeley: University of California Press.

Hunter, Lori M., Jason D. Boardman, and Jarron M. Saint Onge. 2005. "The Association between Natural Amenities, Rural Population Growth and Long-Term Residents' Economic Well-Being." *Rural Sociology* 70(4): 452-469.

Hussa, Linda. 2009. *The Family Ranch.* Reno: University of Nevada Press.

Hustedde, Ronald J. 1991. "Developing Leadership to Address Rural Problems." Pp. 111-123 in Norman Walzer (ed.), *Rural Community Economic Development.* New York: Praeger.

IPCC (Intergovernmental Panel on Climate Change). 2007. *Fourth Assessment Report of the Intergovernmental Panel on Climate Change.* New York: Cambridge University Press.

_____. 2011. *IPCC Special Report on Renewable Energy Sources and Climate Change Mitigation.* New York: Cambridge University Press.

Ishida, Hiroshi, Walter Muller, and John M. Ridge. 1995. "Class Origin, Class Destination, and Education: A Cross-National Study of Ten Industrial Nations." *American Journal of Sociology* 101(1): 145-193.

Jackson-Smith, Douglas, Eric Jensen, and Brian Jennings. 2006. "Changing Land Use in the Rural Intermountain West." Chapter 12 in W.A. Kandel and D.L. Brown (eds.), *Population Change and Rural Society.* The Netherlands: Springer.

Jenkins, Matt. 2009. "Into Thin Air?" Pp. 23-27 in Char Miller (ed.) *Water in the 21st Century West.* Corvallis: Oregon State University Press.

Johansen, Harley E. and Glenn V. Fuguitt. 1984. *The Changing Rural Village in America: Demographic and Economic Trends Since 1950.* Cambridge, MA: Ballinger Publishing Company.

Johnson, Kenneth M. 1989. "Recent Population Redistribution Trends in Nonmetropolitan America." *Rural Sociology* 54: 301-26.

Kanbur, R. and H. Rapoport. 2005. "Migration Selectivity and the Evolution of Spatial Inequality." *Journal of Economic Geography* 5(1): 43-57.

Kandel, William A. and David L. Brown. 2006. *Population Change and Rural Society.* The Netherlands: Springer.

Kane, T.J. 2004. "College-Going and Inequality." In K.M. Neckerman (ed.), *Social Inequality.* New York: Russell Sage Foundation.

Karl, T.R., J.M. Melillo, and T.C. Peterson, eds. 2009. *Global Climate Change Impacts in the United States.* New York: Cambridge University Press.

Kassab, C. and A.E. Luloff. 1993. "The New Buffalo Hunt: Chasing the Service Sector." *Journal of the Community Development Society* 24: 175-195.

Kelly, Erin Clover and John C. Bliss. 2009. "Healthy Forests, Healthy Communities: An Emerging Paradigm for Natural Resource-Dependent Communities?" *Society and Natural Resources* 22: 519-537.

Kemmis, Daniel. 2001. *This Sovereign Land.* Washington, DC: Island Press.

Kennedy, Paul and William I. Hitchcock. 2000. *From War to Peace: Altered Strategic Landscapes in the Twentieth Century.* New Haven, CT: Yale University Press.

Keppen, Dan. 2010. "Tunnel Vision in the Central Valley." *Rural Connections* 4(2): 41-42.

Kingston, Paul W. 2001. "The Unfulfilled Promise of Cultural Capital Theory." *Sociology of Education* 74(Extra Issue): 88-99.

Kohrs, El Dean. 1974. "Social Consequences of Boom Growth in Wyoming." Paper presented at the Annual Meeting of the Rocky Mountain Section of the American Association for the Advancement of Science, Laramie, WY.

Krannich, Richard S., Peggy Petrzelka, and Joan M. Brehm. 2006. "Social Change and Well-Being in Western Amenity-Growth Communities." Chapter 15 in W.A. Kandel and D.L. Brown (eds.), *Population Change and Rural Society*. The Netherlands: Springer.

Krugman, P. 1991. "Increasing Returns and Economic Geography." *Journal of Political Economy* 99: 483-499.

Lamont, Michele and Annette Lareau. 1988. "Cultural Capital: Allusions, Gaps and Glissandos in Recent Theoretical Developments." *Sociological Theory* 6:153-168.

Langston, N. 1995. *Forest Dreams Forest Nightmares: The Paradox of Old Growth in the Inland West*. Seattle: University of Washington Press.

LeMonds, James. 2001. *Deadfall: Generations of Logging in the Pacific Northwest*. Missoula, MT: Mountain Press Publishing.

Leopold, Aldo. 1949. *A Sand County Almanac*. New York: Oxford University Press.

Lewis, Oscar. 1966. "The Culture of Poverty." *Scientific American* 215(4): 19-25.

Lichter, D.T. and D.J. Eggebeen. 1992. "Child Poverty and the Changing Rural Family." *Rural Sociology* 57: 151-172.

Lichter, D.T. and D.R. Graefe. 2001. "Finding a Mate? The Marital and Cohabitation Histories of Unwed Mothers." Chapter 11 in L.L. Wu and B. Wolfe (eds.), *Out of Wedlock*. New York: Russell Sage Foundation.

Lichter, D.T. and D.K. McLaughlin. 1995. "Changing Economic Opportunities, Family Structure, and Poverty in Rural America." *Rural Sociology* 60: 668-706.

Lichter, Daniel T., Diane K. McLaughlin, and Gretchen T. Cornwell. 1995. "Migration and the Loss of Human Resources in Rural America." Chapter 11 in L.J. Beaulieu and D. Mulkey (eds.), *Investing in People: The Human Capital Needs of Rural America*. Boulder, CO: Westview Press.

Lobao, Linda M. 1990. *Locality and Inequality: Farm and Industry Structure and Socioeconomic Conditions*. Albany: SUNY Press.

Low, Bobbi S. and J.A. Berlin. 1984. "Natural Selection and the Management of Rangelands." In Gardner et al., *Developing Strategies in Rangeland Management*. Boulder, CO: Westview Press.

Lucas, Samuel R. 2001. "Effectively Maintained Inequality: Education Transition, Track Mobility, and Social Background Effects." *American Journal of Sociology* 106(6): 1642-1690.

Malin, Stephanie. 2008. "Nuclear Energy and the West." *Rural Connections* 3(1): 20-21.

Maril, Robert Lee. 1988. *Poorest of Americans: The Mexican Americans of the Lower Rio Grande Valley in Texas*. Notre Dame, IN: Notre Dame University Press.

Massey, Douglas S. 2007. *Categorically Unequal: The American Stratification System*. New York: Russell Sage Foundation.

Massey, Douglas S. and Nancy A. Denton. 1993. *American Apartheid*. Cambridge, MA: Harvard University Press.

Mayer, Susan. 1997. "Trends in the Economic Well-Being and Life Chances of America's Children." Chapter 4 in G.J. Duncan and J. Brooks-Gunn (eds.), *Consequences of Growing up Poor*. New York: Russell Sage Foundation.

McCall, Leslie. 2000. "Gender and the New Inequality: Explaining the College/Non-College Wage Gap." *American Sociological Review* 65: 234-255.

McCarl, Bruce A. 2008. "Bioenergy in a Greenhouse Mitigating World." *Choices* 23(1): 31-33.

McGranahan, D.A. 1999. *Natural Amenities Drive Rural Population Change*. Food and Rural Economics Division, Economic Research Service, U.S. Department of Agriculture. Agricultural Economic Report No. 781. Washington, DC.

_____. 2009. "Scenic Landscapes Enhance Rural Growth." *Amber Waves* (June): 9.

McGranahan, D.A. and T.R. Wojan. 2007. "The Creative Class: A Key to Rural Growth." *Amber Waves* (April): 17-21.

McKibben, Bill. 2007. *Deep Economy*. New York: Times Books.

McLanahan, S. 1985. "Family Structure and the Reproduction of Poverty." *American Journal of Sociology* 90: 873-901.

McLanahan, S. and L. Bumpass. 1988. "Intergenerational Consequences of Family Disruption." *American Journal of Sociology* 93: 130-152.

McLanahan, S. and G. Sandefur. 1994. *Growing up with a Single Parent*. Cambridge, MA: Harvard University Press.

Merrill, Karen R. 2002. *Public Lands and Political Meaning*. Berkeley: University of California Press.

Merrigan, Kathleen. 2012. "Beyond Farmers Markets: Why Local Food Belongs on Grocery Shelves." *The Atlantic,* September 6.

Miller, Char. 2009. *Water in the 21st Century West*. Corvallis: Oregon State University Press.

Miller, Robert J. 2012. *Reservation Capitalism*. Santa Barbara, CA: Praeger.

Mishel, Lawrence, Jared Bernstein, and John Schmitt. 1997. *The State of Working America 1996-1997*. Armonk, NY: M.E. Sharp.

Mooney, Patrick H. and Scott A. Hunt. 2009. "Food Security: The Elaboration of Contested Claims to a Consensus Frame." *Rural Sociology* 74(4): 469-497.

Morris, M. and B. Western. 1999. "Inequality in Earnings at the Close of the Twentieth Century." *Annual Review of Sociology* 25: 623-657.

Morton, Lois Wright and Troy C. Blanchard. 2007. "Starved for Access: Life in Rural America's Food Deserts." *Rural Realities* 1(4).

Murnane, R.J. 1994. "Education and the Well-Being of the Next Generation." Chapter 11 in S.H. Danziger et al., *Confronting Poverty: Prescriptions for Change*. Cambridge, MA: Harvard University Press.

Neckerman, Kathryn M. and Florencia Torche. 2007. "Inequality: Causes and Consequences." *Annual Review of Sociology* 33: 335-357.

Nelson, Peter. 1997. "Migration, Sources of Income, and Community Change in the Nonmetropolitan Northwest." *Professional Geographer* 49(4): 418-430.

_____. 1999. "Quality of Life, Nontraditional Income, and Economic Growth: New Development Opportunities for the Rural West." *Rural Development Perspectives* 14 (2): 32-37.

Nelson, Peter and W.B. Beyers. 1998. "Using Economic Base Models to Explain New Trends in Rural Income." *Growth and Change* 29(Summer): 295-318.

Nelson, Peter, Ahn Wei Lee, and Lise Nelson. 2009. "Linking Baby Boomer and Hispanic Migration Streams into Rural America—A Multi-scaled Approach." *Population, Space and Place* 15: 277-293.

Nie, Martin. 2003. *Beyond Wolves: The Politics of Wolf Recovery and Management.* Minneapolis: University of Minnesota Press.

_____. 2008. *The Governance of Western Public Lands.* Lawrence: University of Kansas Press.

Nock, S.L. 1998. *Marriage in Men's Lives.* Cambridge: Oxford University Press.

Nord, M. and J.B. Cromartie. 1997. "Migration: The Increasing Importance of Rural Natural Amenities." *Choices* 3: 31-32.

Otterstrom, Samuel M. and J. Matthew Shumway. 2003. "Deserts and Oases: The Continuing Concentration of Population in the American Mountain West." *Journal of Rural Studies* 19(4): 445-462.

Paarlberg, Don. 1980. *Farm and Food Policy: Issues of the 1980s.* Lincoln: University of Nebraska Press.

Partridge, Mark D. and Dan S. Rickman. 2006. *The Geography of American Poverty: Is There a Need for Place-Based Policies?"* Kalamazoo, MI: W.E. Upjohn Institute for Employment Research.

Pearce, Fred. 2006. *When the Rivers Run Dry.* Boston: Beacon Press.

Pellant, Mike. 1996. *Cheatgrass: The Invader that Won the West.* Boise, ID: Bureau of Land Management, Idaho State Office.

Peters, H. Elizabeth and Natalie C. Mullis. 1997. "The Role of Family Income and Sources of Income in Adolescent Achievement." Chapter 12 in Greg J. Duncan and Jeanne Brooks-Gunn (eds.), *Consequences of Growing Up Poor.* New York: Russell Sage Foundation.

Pisani, Donald J. 2002. *Water and American Government: The Reclamation Bureau, National Water Policy and the West 1902-1935.* Berkeley: University of California Press.

Pollan, Michael. 2006. *The Omnivore's Dilemma.* New York: Penguin Books.

_____. 2009. *In Defense of Food.* New York: Penguin Books.

Popenoe, D. 1996. *Life Without Father.* New York: Martin Kessler Books.

Porter, M.E. 2000. "Location, Competition, and Economic Development: Local Clusters in a Global Economy." *Economic Development Quarterly* 14(1): 15-34.

Powell, James Lawrence. 2008. *Dead Pool*. Berkeley: University of California Press.

_____. 2010. "River of Empire." *Rural Connections* 4(2): 5-8.

Power, T. 1996. *Lost Landscapes, Failed Economies*. Washington, DC: Island Press.

Power, T. and R. Barrett. 2001. *Post-Cowboy Economics*. Washington, DC: Island Press.

Pruitt, Lisa R. 2009. "The Forgotten Fifth: Rural Youth and Substance Abuse." *Stanford Law & Policy Review* 20(2): 359-404.

Rank, Mark R., Hong-Sik Yoon, and Thomas A. Hirschl. 2003. "American Poverty as a Structural Failing: Evidence and Arguments." *Journal of Sociology and Social Welfare* 30(4): 3.

Reilly, T.E., K.F. Dennely, W.M. Alley, and W.L. Cunningham. 2008. *Groundwater Availability in the United States*." Reston, VA: U.S. Geological Survey.

Reisner, Marc. 1993. *Cadillac Desert*. New York: Penguin Books.

Robbins, William G. 1997. *Landscapes of Promise: The Oregon Story, 1800-1940*. Seattle: University of Washington Press.

_____. 2004. *Landscapes of Conflict: The Oregon Story, 1940-2000*. Seattle: University of Washington Press.

Roberts, Paul. 2008. *The End of Food*. Boston: Houghton Mifflin.

Robinson, Glen O. 1975. *The Forest Service: A Study in Public Land Management*. Washington, DC: Resources for the Future.

Rogers, D.L. 1982. "Community Services." Pp. 146-155 in D.A. Dillman and D.J. Hobbs (eds.), *Rural Society in the U.S.: Issues for the 1980s*. Boulder, CO: Westview.

Rohe, Randall. 1985. "Hydraulicking in the American West." *Montana: The Magazine of Western History* 35(2): 18-29.

Ropers, Richard H. 1991. *Persistent Poverty: The American Dream Turned Nightmare*. New York: Plenum.

Roscigno, Vincent J. and James W. Ainsworth-Darnell. 1999. "Race, Cultural Capital, and Educational Resources: Persistent Inequalities and Achievement Returns." *Sociology of Education* 72(July): 158-178.

Rosenfeld, Stuart. 2009a. *A Compendium of Clusters in Less Populated Places*. Carrboro, North Carolina: Regional Technology Strategies, Inc.

_____. 2009b. *Generating Local Wealth, Opportunity, and Sustainability through Rural Clusters*. Carrboro, NC: Regional Technology Strategies, Inc.

Rosenthal, S. and W. Strange. 2003. "Geography, Industrial Organization, and Agglomeration." *Review of Economics and Statistics* 85: 377-393.

Rothstein, Richard. 2004. *Class and Schools*. Washington, DC: Economic Policy Institute.

Rudel, Thomas K. 2002. "Paths of Destruction and Regeneration: Globalization and Forests in the Tropics." *Rural Sociology* 67(4): 622-36.

Rudzitis, Gundars. 1999. "Amenities Increasingly Draw People to the Rural West." *Rural Development Perspectives* 14: 23-28.

Ryan, William. 1971. *Blaming the Victim*. New York: Random House.

Saint Onge, J.M., L.M. Hunter, and J.D. Boardman. 2007. "Population Growth in High Amenity Rural Areas." *Social Science Quarterly* 88(2): 366-381.

Sapp, Stephen G., Charlie Arnot, James Fallon, Terry Fleck, David Soorholtz, Matt Sutton-Vermeulen, and Jannette J.H. Wilson. 2009. "Consumer Trust in the U.S. Food System: An Examination of the Recreancy Theorem." *Rural Sociology* 74(4): 525-545.

Sassen, S. 1990. "Economic Restructuring and the American City." *Annual Review of Sociology* 16: 465-490.

Schullery, Paul. 1996. *The Yellowstone Wolf.* Norman: University of Oklahoma Press.

Schulte, Steven C. 2002. *Wayne Aspinall and the Shaping of the American West.* Boulder: University of Colorado Press.

Sewell, William H. and Vimal P. Shah. 1968. "Parents' Education and Children's Educational Aspirations and Achievements." *American Sociological Review* 33(2): 191-209.

Shepherd, Harold S. 2007. *Compromising Democracy.* New York: iUniverse, Inc.

Sherman, Jennifer. 2005. *Men Without Sawmills: Masculinity, Rural Poverty, and Family Stability.* Rural Poverty Research Center Working Paper No. 05-03. Corvallis, OR: RUPRI.

_____. 2006. "Coping with Rural Poverty: Economic Survival and Moral Capital in Rural America." *Social Forces* 85(2): 891-913.

_____. 2009. *Those Who Work, Those Who Don't: Poverty, Morality, and Family in Rural America.* Minneapolis: University of Minnesota Press.

Shields, Martin, David Barkley, and Mary Emery. 2009. "Industry Clusters and Industry Targeting." Chapter 3 in S.J. Goetz, S.C. Deller and T.R. Harris, *Targeting Regional Economic Development.* New York: Routledge.

Shulman, S. 1990. "The Causes of Black Poverty: Evidence and Interpretation." *Journal of Economic Issues* 24: 995-1016.

Shumway, J. Matthew. 1997. "Hot, Medium, and Cold: The Geography of Nonmetropolitan Population Growth and Change in the Mountain West." *Small Town* 28: 16-23.

Shumway, J. Matthew and James A. Davis. 1996. "Nonmetropolitan Population Change in the Mountain West: 1970-1995." *Rural Sociology* 61(3): 513-529.

Shumway, J. Matthew and Samuel M. Otterstrom. 2001. "Spatial Patterns of Migration in Income Change in the Mountain West: The Dominance of Service-Based, Amenity-Rich Counties." *The Professional Geographer* 53: 492-502.

Smith, Diane. 2013. "Yellowstone National Park and Summer of Fire." *Rural Connections* 7(1): 31-34.

Smith, W. Brad, Patrick D. Miles, John S. Vissage, and Scott A. Pugh. 2004. *Forest Resources of the United States, 2002.* Washington, DC: USDA Forest Service.

Smith, Michael D. and Richard S. Krannich. 2000. "'Culture Clash' Revisited: Newcomers and Longer-Term Residents' Attitudes toward Land Use, Development, and

Environmental Issues in Rural Communities in the Rocky Mountain West." *Rural Sociology* 65(3): 396-421.

Snyder, Anastasia R. and Diane K. McLaughlin. 2004. "Female-Headed Families and Poverty in Rural America." *Rural Sociology* 69(1): 127-149.

Sowell, Thomas. 1994. *Race and Culture: A World View.* New York: Basic Books.

Speth, James Gustave. 2004. *Red Sky at Morning.* New Haven, CT: Yale University Press.

_____. 2008. *The Bridge at the Edge of the World.* New Haven, CT: Yale University Press.

Stegner, Wallace. 1992. *Where the Bluebird Sings to the Lemonade Springs.* New York: The Modern Library.

Stern, Nicholas. 2007. *The Economics of Climate Change.* New York: Cambridge University Press.

Steward, Julian H., R.M. Adams, D. Collier, A. Palerm, K.A. Wittfogel, and R.L. Beals. 1955. *Irrigation Civilizations: A Comparative Study.* Washington, DC: Pan American Union.

Stiller, David. 2000. *Wounding the West.* Lincoln: University of Nebraska Press.

Struthers, C.B. and J.L. Bokemeier. 2000. "Myths and Realities of Raising Children and Creating Family Life in a Rural Community." *Journal of Family Issues* 21(1): 17-46.

Summers, Gene F. 1995. "Persistent Rural Poverty." Pp. 213-228 in E.M. Castle (ed.), *The Changing American Countryside: Rural People and Places.* Manhattan: University Press of Kansas.

Taylor, Joseph E. III. 1999. *Making Salmon: An Environmental History of the Northwest Fisheries Crisis.* Seattle: University of Washington Press.

Tharp, Francisco. 2009. "Death in the Delta." Pp. 293-294 in Char Miller (ed.), *Water in the 21st Century West.* Corvallis: Oregon State University Press.

Theodori, Gene. 2009. *Preparing for the Future: A Guide to Community-Based Planning.* Mississippi: Southern Rural Development Center.

Tigges, L.M. and D.M. Tootle. 1990. "Labor Supply, Labor Demand, and Men's Underemployment in Rural and Urban Labor Markets." *Rural Sociology* 55: 328-356.

Tomaskovic-Devey, Donald. 1987. "Labor Markets, Industrial Structure, and Poverty: A Theoretical Discussion and Empirical Example." *Rural Sociology* 52: 56-74.

Travis, William R. 2007. *New Geographies of the American West.* Washington, DC: Island Press.

Tyson, Karolyn. 2003. "Notes from the Back of the Room: Problems and Paradoxes in the Schooling of Young Black Students." *Sociology of Education* 76(4): 326-343.

Udall, Stewart L. 1963. *The Quiet Crisis.* New York: Holt, Rinehart and Winston.

United States Census Bureau. 2009. Current Population Survey. Washington, DC.

United States Department of Energy.

Venables, A. 2003. "Spatial Disparities in Developing Countries: Cities, Regions and International Trade." Working Paper: London School of Economics.

Vidich, Arthur J. and Joseph Bensman. 1958. *Small Town in Mass Society*. Princeton, NJ: Princeton University Press.

Von Reichert, Christiane, John B. Cromartie, and Ryan O. Arthun. 2011. "Returning Home and Making a Living: Employment Strategies of Returning Migrants to Rural U.S. Communities." *Journal of Rural and Community Development* 6(2): 35-52.

Wagner, Frederic H. 2003. *Preparing for a Changing Climate*. A Report of the Rocky Mountain/Great Basin Regional Assessment Team. Logan: Utah State University.

_____. 2007. "Global Warming Effects of Climactically-Imposed Ecological Gradients in the West." *Journal of Land, Resources and Environmental Law* 27(1): 109-121.

Waite, L.J. 1995. "Does Marriage Matter?" *Demography* 32: 483-507.

Walsh, et al. 2008. "Global Climate Model Performance over Alaska and Greenland." *Journal of Climate* 21: 6156-6174.

Wells, L.E. and J.H. Rankin. 1991. "Families and Delinquency: A Meta-Analysis of the Impact of Broken Homes." *Social Problems* 38: 71-93.

White, Richard. 1995. *The Organic Machine: The Remaking of the Columbia River*. New York: Hill and Wang.

Wilkinson, Charles F. 1992. *Crossing the Next Meridian*. Washington, DC: Island Press.

Wilshire, Howard G., Jane E. Nielson, and Richard W. Hazlett. 2008. "The American West at Risk." New York: Oxford University Press.

Wilson, Franklin D. 1987. "Metropolitan and Nonmetropolitan Migration Streams: 1935-1980." *Demography* 24: 211-228.

Wilson, W.J. 1987. *The Truly Disadvantaged*. Chicago: University of Chicago Press.

_____. 1996. *When Work Disappears*. New York: Knopf.

Wilson, William J. and Robert Aponte. 1985. "Urban Poverty." *Annual Review of Sociology* 11: 231-258.

Wirth, Louis. 1938. "Urbanism as a Way of Life." *American Journal of Sociology* 44: 1-24.

Wittfogel, Karl. 1957. *Oriental Despotism: A Comparative Study of Total Power*. New Haven, CT: Yale University Press.

Wolf, Martin. 2004. *Why Globalization Works*. New Haven, CT: Yale University Press.

Wolfe, Barbara L. 1994. "Reform of Health Care for the Nonelderly Poor." Chapter 10 in S.H. Danziger et al., *Confronting Poverty: Prescriptions for Change*. Cambridge, MA: Harvard University Press.

Woodward, Douglas and Paulo Guimaraes. 2009. "Porter's Cluster Strategy and Industrial Targeting." Chapter 5 in S.J. Goetz, S.C. Deller, and T.R. Harris, *Targeting Regional Economic Development*. New York: Routledge.

Worster, Donald. 1985. *Rivers of Empire: Water, Aridity and the Growth of the American West*. New York: Oxford University Press.

_____. 1993. *The Wealth of Nature*. New York: Oxford University Press.

Wright, Susan E. 1993. "Blaming the Victim, Blaming Society or Blaming the Discipline: Fixing Responsibility for Poverty and Homelessness." *The Sociological Quarterly* 34: 1-16.

Wu, L.L. and Barbara Wolfe. 2001. *Out of Wedlock*. New York: Russell Sage Foundation.

Yergin, Daniel. 2011. *The Quest*. New York: The Penguin Press.

Zakin, Susan. 2009. "Delta Blues." Pp. 279-293 in Char Miller (ed.), *Water in the 21st Century West*. Corvallis: Oregon State University Press.

Zuiches, James J. and David L. Brown. 1978. "The Changing Character of the Non-metropolitan Population, 1950-75." Pp. 55-72 in T.R. Ford (ed.), *Rural U.S.A.: Persistence and Change*. Ames: Iowa State University Press.

Index

Page numbers in italics refer to illustrations and photographs.
Page numbers followed by a "t" refer to tables.

217